Biz's Journey Home

Jean MacDougall-Tattan

ALL THINGS THAT MATTER PRESS

Biz's Journey Home

Copyright © 2023 by Jean MacDougall-Tattan

All rights reserved. No part of this book may be reproduced or transmitted in any form or by any means without written permission of the author and publisher.

This is a fictional work of true events. Any resemblance to actual persons, living or dead, is purely coincidental.

ISBN: 9798988335320

Library of Congress Control Number: 2023944634

Cover Design by All Things that Matter Press

Cover photo: Jean MacDougall-Tattan

Published in 2023 by All Things that Matter Press

For Phoebe Kwass, whose insight and guidance made all things possible in life. The world was a better place with you in it.

For my sister, Ruth Ann MacDougall, whose interest in horses ignited mine all those years ago when we were young. I miss you every day.

For Dagney Collins, whose beautiful smile and impish spirit graced the earth for far too short a time. You are missed.

Acknowledgments

An abundance of love and thanks to my husband, Greg, and my children, Jillian and Jason, for their encouragement and patience, even when my writing robbed them of family time. And for my granddaughter, Amelia, may my love of writing spark a desire in you to read and write.

Love and gratitude to my parents for giving me life and raising me right.

Heartfelt thanks to writing coach and author Kathie Giorgio, owner of AllWriters' Workplace and Workshop, who helped transform me from a journalist to a fiction writer, which in the beginning, was no easy task. And a big thank you to author Byron Brumbaugh, for introducing me to her.

To my friends and acquaintances who helped critique *Biz's Journey Home* after the first draft was finished. Your encouragement, suggestions, and constructive criticism helped the novel grow into something bigger and better. Sincere thanks to Natalie Eve Marquis, Cindy Collins Graham, Sarah Robinson, Ellen Coburn, Deb Gerety Hoadley, Rachel Fowler, Susan Chapman Kneeland, Barbara Frake, and Joyce Hurd.

Profound appreciation to Helen Orcutt Noble, DVM and SRH Veterinary Services, who took care of our horses from the day of their pre-purchase exams until they had to leave us for the ultimate greener pasture, always taking time to explain everything so we learned the right way to care for our horses.

An abundance of gratitude to friend and farrier Edward Gerald Vocell, who never seemed to tire of our myriad questions as we learned about proper shoeing and hoof care.

We were blessed to find riding instructor/trainer Sarah Keefe Doyle, who helped us get our horses back into shape safely, and somehow along the way, make us good enough equestrians to deserve to ride on their backs.

Deepest appreciation to Publishers Deb and Phil Harris/All Things That Matter Press, for understanding the message and recognizing the potential of *Biz's Journey Home*.

~1~

How comforting to be able to believe, that when loved ones pass, they don't go far; they remain close by, guiding us.

"Carol. Look! Can you see him out there? He sure is a beauty. A tall chestnut with a long white blaze and two white socks. And he's all ours."

Carol woke from a sound sleep, sat up in bed, rubbed her face with the palms of her hands, and then got out of bed and walked to the window to look outside. With sleepy eyes, she peered down into the backyard and thought she saw the silhouette of a man in the barn window. She rubbed her eyes and looked again, but the silhouette was gone.

As she dragged herself back to bed, she began to cry. The voice from her dream was comforting, yet heartbreaking, because it sounded like her husband, Logan, who passed away suddenly from a heart condition two years before. Their daughter Jill was just ten years old. The words she heard in her dream were the very ones he said as he built their barn and pretended to see the horse he wanted to buy for Jill standing in the paddock.

Carol lay in bed, thinking about Logan and the wonderful life they had together. She missed him terribly and would give anything to see him and talk with him again. She loved to talk with him. About anything. It felt infantile, but she swaddled herself in her comforter and eventually faded back to sleep. When her alarm went off, she got up with a heavy heart, dressed, and went downstairs to make breakfast before she took Jill to Willow Bend Farm where a day of hard work and fun was ahead of her. Carol didn't think they could afford a horse anymore, so on weekends, Jill cleaned stalls and helped exercise horses in exchange for riding lessons.

Jill finished her apple pancakes and shouted, "I'm ready to go, Mom. Hurry up. I don't want to be late."

"Okay, honey. Go ahead and get in the car. I'll be out in two seconds," she replied. Carol emerged from the house with her pocketbook and keys in hand, trying to make sure her smile was large and bright so Jill wouldn't see the pain in her heart.

"What are you so happy about?" asked Jill.

"I'm happy because I know how much you love horses and look forward to being *surrounded* by them on weekends."

Carol put the keys in the ignition as Caleb, their next-door neighbor, came out of his house. They waved and he waved back. "Have a good day," he said as they started to pull away." Thanks, Caleb. You, too," said Carol.

"I'll see you later, Caleb," said Jill.

"You betcha, sweetheart. I want to hear all about the horses when you get back."

Carol loved Caleb. They lived next door to him since before Jill was born. They weren't related, but he felt like a father to her, and she knew Jill loved him like a grandfather. Caleb filled a void for both of them because Carol's dad passed away, and Logan, an only child, lost both of his parents in a car accident when he was in his mid-twenties, so Jill didn't have a grandfather. Carol felt blessed to have Caleb close by.

Before she pulled onto the main road Carol looked at Jill and pinched her cheek. Jill's smile was infectious. She kept her smile all the way to the barn, which was close enough to their house that they could see it in the distance from their yard. Jill told Carol time and again that she could easily walk to the farm, but it was a busy road with no sidewalks, so Carol insisted on driving. When they pulled up to the main barn, Jill eagerly jumped out. "Bye, Mom. I'll give you a call when I'm ready to come home."

Carol put down her window. "Are you forgetting something, young lady?"

Jill looked around before she shuffled back to the car for a hug and a kiss on the cheek. Carol laughed. "What's the matter? You don't want anyone to see that your mother still gives you a hug and a kiss goodbye?"

"Mom. I'm twelve. Almost a *teenager*. I don't want to be teased."

"Okay. I'll try to do it when nobody's around. Have a wonderful day, honey. I'll see you later." As Jill walked away, Carol wondered which lesson horse she'd ride after she finished her assigned chores. She hoped it was Jayden. Jill described him as a handsome black and white paint. His ears and forehead were solid black and an upside-down triangle of black dipped right between his eyes. The rest of his face was white, and he had two bright blue eyes. Exotic-looking. And very well-behaved. Carol hoped to meet him sometime soon.

After she dropped Jill off, Carol ran an errand and then went back home to have a hot cup of tea and do some long overdue housework. She needed to stay busy because if she didn't, grief consumed her. She didn't sleep well because her head was filled with thoughts of Logan. And then she felt hurt, even a tad rejected, when Jill didn't want to hug or kiss her goodbye. She understood that she had to face the fact that Jill was growing up, but she couldn't bear the thought of losing her. It was hard enough living without Logan. He was a wonderful husband. So kind. Considerate. Caring. They were so in love, and he was an amazing father to Jill. Carol had so many marvelous memories of their life together.

At lunchtime, she put on her jacket and went out to the barn. She felt Logan's presence the most there. One of her favorite things was to sit quietly by herself and remember how he built the barn. She recalled so many details that when she closed her eyes, it played like a movie in her mind.

Her eyes were closed when Caleb walked in. "The barn door was open, so I figured you were out here," he said.

Carol jumped. "Oh, Caleb. You startled me."

"I can see that. Sorry. Are you okay?"

Carol sighed. "Memories of Logan are tugging at my heart today, Caleb. This barn was his special project. When I want to feel closer to him, I come out here."

Caleb's gaze dropped to the floor. "He's been on my mind an awful lot too, and I'm not sure why. But I miss him somethin' awful."

Caleb's voice cracked when he spoke, and Carol's eyes welled when she saw a tear roll down his cheek. She walked to Caleb and hugged him. "Does grieving ever end, Caleb? I'm beginning to think it doesn't ... but we have to be strong, especially for Jill."

Caleb nodded. "I can tell you from experience that grief doesn't end, but it does get better, Carol. It just takes time."

Carol stepped back, put her hands on her hips, looked up at the barn loft, and inhaled. "Time heals all wounds. That's what everyone tells me, Caleb. But it's been two years and I miss Logan just as much now as I ever did."

Caleb stood beside Carol, put his arm around her shoulder, and squeezed. "It'll get better. I promise."

Carol figured that Caleb was right, but she still wondered if their hearts would ever mend. Especially Jill's. Her father meant the world to her. Daddy's little girl. In her heart, Carol knew Jill was the one who struggled the most.

Throughout the day, Carol was preoccupied. No matter how hard she worked, her mind was on her dream. She heard the voice and the words over and over again. And the silhouette looked exactly like Logan. The dream made her feel sad, but at the same time, loved and protected. She dreamt about Logan in the past, but those dreams weren't as vivid. This one felt real. Like it actually happened, and Carol couldn't shake the feeling that the dream meant something more.

Susan Robinson, the barn manager at Willow Bend, knew the farm and its horses like the back of her hand. She was a whiz at operations, workflow, and efficiency. She had one stall open, and it was about to be filled with a new horse named Official Business—Biz for short. Barn workers were readying the stall for him while she figured out how to best incorporate him into the herd. At Willow Bend, new horses were eventually paired up with a buddy. Susan planned to turn him out with Jonas because he was a gentle and kind soul, and she knew Biz would be safe with him. Initially, Biz's owner, Raymond Ellington, wanted Biz turned out alone so he wouldn't get kicked or injured and lose his value. Susan had to convince him that Biz would be safe with Jonas.

Jonas was big. Susan noticed that other horses never challenged him. He never challenged them, either. He was quiet and mostly kept to himself. Everything about Jonas told Susan that he felt no need to compete with the show horses. It was obvious that he was confident. She hoped he would be a stabilizing factor and comforting to Biz because he was as solid as they come, physically and psychologically.

Susan loved Willow Bend Farm. It was the perfect place to live and work. A couple of years ago, she answered an advertisement for a barn manager position because it included a salary, a free apartment on the farm, and a discounted rate for stalls. When Noah, the barn owner, interviewed her, he told her he was impressed that she had a bachelor's degree in equine studies, was a certified riding instructor with years of experience, and had an excellent reputation. A few days after her interview, Noah called and offered her the job. He said that he called her references and was so pleased that he was willing to give her free stalls for up to four of her lesson horses, as long as she taught exclusively at Willow Bend. Students without horses of their own were able to come to Willow Bend and take lessons on Susan's horses. Students with horses had to board their horses at Willow Bend to take lessons. Noah said he was sure that riders would seek Susan out as an instructor, and therefore, his stalls would always be filled.

Susan accepted the position and was very happy with their arrangement. The apartment was above one of the smaller barns at the back of the property and even had skylights. The living room had a sliding glass door and a small balcony, so she had a beautiful view of the pastures, paddocks, barn, and outdoor riding arenas. Horses were her life, and her lesson horses were chosen with great care. They had to be extremely well-behaved because her students needed to be safe. She had to be safe, too, because she couldn't afford to be out of commission. Each day, when she made her rounds on the farm, she brought her horses a carrot and spent a few minutes with them. She was particularly pleased with her newest lesson horse, Jayden. He was talented enough to challenge riders to the next level and he had a very sweet temperament. She wished she had more time to ride him, but more often than not, something interfered. She continually promised herself that she'd make time, but it hardly ever happened.

Susan was pleased that Jill was riding Jayden. Jill was young, but she had a lot of riding experience, and she was an excellent horse handler. She applied to Willow Bend about a year and a half ago, but at that time, Susan didn't have anything for her. Periodically, Jill and her mother stopped by to see if there were any openings. Susan liked the fact that Jill was persistent. A month ago, a position opened, so Susan called, and she was happy she did. Jill was mature for her age, and she had an excellent work ethic.

***

Jill looked forward to weekends because horses made her feel alive. She had her first pony ride at a local fair when she was four and was hooked ever since. She started beginner horseback riding lessons at a very small and inexpensive riding facility across town when she was in first grade. Her lesson was the highlight of her week, but it wasn't just the lesson that she looked forward to. She just wanted to be around horses. When she became tall enough, her lesson included grooming and tacking up the horse and she loved it. She wanted to take care of the horses because they made her feel good inside. She felt at peace around them. Happy. Her weekly lessons continued until her father died. After that, money was tight.

The town that Jill and her family lived in was small, so everyone knew one another. When word got out that Jill wasn't riding, an elderly woman who owned a two-stall barn asked Jill if she would help take care of her horses in exchange for riding time. It was good for both of them. Jill was exceptional at grooming and cleaning stalls. Meticulous. If she walked by a stall and saw manure on the floor, she had to clean it. The thought of horses stepping in poop made her crazy. Her mother sometimes joked that she wished Jill cleaned her bedroom as well as a stall, and Jill light-heartedly replied that if her mother allowed her to keep a horse in her room, she would.

Jill enjoyed working at that barn and she was extremely grateful for the riding time, but after a while, she realized that she missed riding instruction. She knew Willow Bend let kids work in exchange for lessons, so she periodically checked in, and was thrilled when Susan finally called.

At Willow Bend, Jill groomed the horses with great care. Particles of sand and dirt under a saddle could irritate the horse's back and cause sores, so she brushed her horse thoroughly before each lesson. After lessons, she brushed them again and then lightly rinsed their backs with a wet sponge to remove sweat marks. She picked out hooves before and after lessons to make sure they were clean and free of rocks, and if she had time, she braided their manes and tails to add a finishing touch. She was so happy at the barn that she didn't mind that it interfered with her social life. On Saturday and Sunday, friends took a back seat to horses. She made time for friends at school during the week.

~3~

Winter was about to lose its grip on Northeastern Massachusetts. Days were warmer, but the nights were cool, and the crisp morning air made the horses eager to romp in the pasture and work off some steam. Excitement was in the air because a new horse named Official Business was supposed to arrive in the afternoon. He wasn't coming for a visit. He was going to live there, and members of the herd were curious.

From his stall, Jonas, a mature and muscular black Percheron draft horse originally from Virginia, listened as the horses ate breakfast, and talked. He paid particular attention to comments made by the stallions and geldings, who seemed worried because Official Business was supposed to be handsome and quite an athlete. It was apparent that they feared the mares would be more interested in him than them. Jonas remembered his younger days when that was important to him too.

"I wonder how he looks," said Günter, a tall dappled light gray Hanoverian stallion.

"He's a tall chestnut with a long white blaze and two white socks," said Jonas, whose deep commanding voice resonated from the back of the barn.

Günter turned his head and looked down his nose at Jonas. *"You've seen him, Jonas?"*

Jonas ignored Günter's tone. "Yes, sir. Years ago, he competed at a farm in Virginia where I lived. His nickname was Biz, and he earned quite a name for himself in the show ring. People said he could jump the moon because he jumped the tallest fences with ease." Jonas immediately noticed a scowl on Günter's face.

Luis, a liver chestnut Lusitano from Portugal, snapped his head back. "He earned quite a name for himself? How so? Has he ever earned any *titles*?" Luis competed in dressage—graceful and delicate moves as if dancing with a rider on his back. Jonas was aware that Luis aspired to be an upper level dressage horse, but he wished he wasn't so full of himself.

Jonas looked Luis in the eyes. "He was Virginia Hunter-Jumper Champion at one time." Luis lifted his eyebrows and glanced at Günter because the hunter-jumper circuit was his territory. Jonas chuckled when Günter glared back at Luis.

"Well, he sure sounds interesting to me," squealed Opal. "I can't wait to get a peek at him. I bet he's *gorgeous*."

Jonas thought Opal was beautiful. She was a palomino quarter horse with a lovely light golden coat, and a mane and tail the color of fresh cream. Her wavy mane was so long that it draped over her shoulder. Her tail was thick and lengthy enough that it dragged on the ground behind her. When Opal wasn't at a show, her tail was braided and folded into a protective covering to keep it off the ground. Opal's registered name was CHP Pure Opulence, and it fit her because she was shown in-hand, which meant she was led into the ring without a rider on her back and judged simply on her conformation and beauty.

"Yes, I bet he's *really* gorgeous," quipped Luis, as he turned his butt to everyone.

Aiyana, a red dun mustang in the stall beside Opal, whispered, "He does sound interesting. He certainly has their reins in a twist."

Abdul, the youngest horse, a three-year old bay Arabian gelding, stood quietly with his ears up and listened.

Jonas was owned by Noah, but he didn't compete at fancy horse shows. His type of showing was getting gussied up to pull Noah's fancy wagons at fairs, parades, social events, weddings, and funerals. Jonas was powerful. He could pull thousands of pounds without breaking a sweat, but none of the show horses at Willow Bend thought that was something to brag about. It amused Jonas that the show horses regarded him as a simple workhorse who was *lucky* to live with them at a show barn like Willow Bend. But Jonas didn't care what they thought. He understood that he was more than a workhorse. Much more.

After breakfast, when they were all turned out in their paddocks, Jonas noticed that the horses paid particular attention each time a truck entered the driveway. Finally, at the end of the day, about an hour before suppertime, a big white truck with a silver and white trailer pulled in.

"I bet that's him," whinnied Opal. "I can't wait to see what he looks like."

The driver parked, got out, and opened the side door of the trailer. While he attended to business in Willow Bend's office, every horse in the pasture had their eyes on the trailer, hoping to catch a glimpse of the hunter-jumper champion. When Biz finally stuck his head out, Jonas immediately recognized him. His head was large with well-defined cheekbones. His long white blaze extended from his forehead down past his nostrils, which made him look distinguished. But Jonas thought it was odd that Biz looked around with no expression and didn't make a sound.

"He doesn't seem excited to be here," said young Abdul. "What kind of horse is he?"

"I believe he's an Anglo-Trakehner," Jonas said.

"What's that?" asked Opal, without taking her eyes off of Biz.

Günter lifted his nose in the air. "What is it? It's a *half-breed*. Half-thoroughbred and half-Trakehner. Half-racehorse and half-European warmblood. An interesting combination, but he's not a *purebred* like me."

About fifteen minutes later, the driver came out of the office and went to the back of the trailer. When the ramp touched the ground, Biz slowly backed out and stood in the middle of the driveway. The driver took hold of the lead rope and walked him into the barn. As Biz passed by the paddock fence, Jonas saw him look up, and then quickly look down, probably because all the horses were staring at him. As Biz walked toward the barn, Jonas noticed how skinny he was. His ribs were showing, even under his long winter coat.

"He doesn't look good," said Luis. "Jonas, I thought you said he was a champ."

Jonas felt a knot form in his stomach. Biz was about the same age as Jonas, but he looked so much older. Biz was no longer the horse Jonas remembered and he wanted to know why.

Muscles in Günter's face bulged as he clenched his jaw. "What *happened* to him?"

Jonas was perplexed by the level of concern Günter displayed for a horse he never met.

For the first hour after he arrived, Biz was alone in the barn. When it was time for the horses to go in, Jonas was first in line. The sound of his hooves on the barn floor was the first to interrupt the silence as members of the herd made their way to their stalls. Biz was in the stall at the back of the barn next to Jonas. As Jonas ate, he occasionally looked up at Biz, who mostly chewed his grain and looked at the floor. Their eyes met once, but Biz turned away, making it clear that he wasn't interested in any conversation.

***

The next morning, Susan put Biz out in the big pasture by himself. Jonas noted that he grazed way back in the corner and wondered if he wanted to be alone, or just didn't want to see all the horses staring at him. He figured that Biz knew they were talking about him. Jonas wandered around his paddock, keeping a watchful eye on the farm, while he pondered about Biz. During his rounds, he saw Jill's mother dropping her off for the day. Then a big hay truck pulled in. Must be a new driver, thought Jonas, as Susan pointed to the hay barn, and then motioned for Jill to show the driver where the hay needed to be stacked. Jill was a nice kid. She had a nice way about her. Over the years, Jonas saw barn workers come and go. He had instincts about who was special, and he thought Jill was very special. His thoughts were interrupted by Günter, who meandered to the paddock fence to talk.

"Jonas, has Biz said anything yet?"

Jonas shook his head. "No. That boy is carrying a lot of pain and he isn't talking about it." Jonas wondered if he ever would.

~4~

Jonas developed a soft spot in his heart for Biz. Physically, he didn't look well, and psychologically, he seemed to be suffering. He was reclusive, but not rude. Somehow, his kindness radiated through his pain. Jonas wanted Biz to know that he was a friend, but he was keenly aware that he had to approach Biz slowly.

At first, Jonas and Biz stayed at opposite ends of their paddock, but each day, Jonas grazed just a few steps closer. Biz didn't appear to mind, so Jonas worked his way close enough to talk. "Nice day today," said Jonas as he looked up at the sky.

"Yes. Real nice," said Biz, keeping his head close to the ground as he munched on grass. Biz didn't make eye contact with Jonas, but Jonas was still hopeful because Biz answered and didn't turn away.

The next day, Jonas said, "Looks like rain."

Biz replied, "Yes. The pasture could use it. The grass is starting to turn brown."

Jonas looked at Biz with kindness in his eyes. He was pleased that Biz's eyes softened when he looked back, but disappointed when Biz turned and walked away. *Baby steps,* thought Jonas.

The nights were still chilly, so the horses sometimes got a hot bran mash for supper. Each horse got a quart of table bran mixed with hot water, molasses, chopped carrots, and apples.

"This tastes good," said Biz. "One of my owners used to give me bran mashes. She put peppermints in too."

Jonas was pleasantly surprised that Biz initiated the conversation, so he quickly replied, "We sometimes get a bran mash on Fridays if it's cold out. I love them too."

Jonas wondered who Biz's owner was. He was at the farm for over a month, and no one came to see him. Nobody brushed him except Susan. Nobody rode him or even came to talk to him. Jonas began to understand why Biz seemed so distant and sad.

As Jonas befriended Biz, the other horses watched attentively from their paddocks. They told Jonas that they needed to know how an accomplished competition horse went from being a champion to a skinny horse with no owner and no career. It seemed to especially trouble young Abdul.

"Günter, have you noticed that nobody's come to see Biz?" asked Abdul with pursed lips. "Not even one person has come to check on him."

Günter pumped up his chest and lifted his head in the air. "Of course, I've noticed. Evidently, he wasn't as good a show horse as we heard, or he'd still be bringing home the ribbons."

Jonas understood why Günter was relieved that Biz was not the handsome athlete he expected, but he was deeply annoyed by Günter's selfish concern. Jonas knew that Günter wanted to know how a champion could end up disheveled because if it happened to Biz, it could happen to him.

"Look at him," said Opal. "You can tell that he was once *really* something."

"There's the keyword ... *once*, as in the past," said Luis as he stared down his nose at Opal. "As for now? Well, he looks like a *loooser* to me."

"That's mean," said Aiyana. "Just because he's not a show horse anymore doesn't mean he's a loser. A loser doesn't have kind eyes. I like him."

"Ohhhhh, she *likes* him!" mocked Luis, and then he and Günter locked eyes and walked away.

Opal sighed. "I wish he was in a little bit better shape. Then maybe I could learn to like him."

Jonas shook his head.

~5~

During his first month at Willow Bend, Biz watched owners arrive at the farm, get their horses, and spend time with them. He felt sad and empty inside when he saw the horses getting brushed and groomed. They had shiny coats, their manes and tails were braided, and their hooves were polished. It made him remember the days when Maggie owned him, and they got ready for shows together.

Biz and Maggie were a team and he loved her very much. During the four years they were together, they performed so well that they won just about every show class they entered. When he won the title of Virginia Hunter-Jumper Champion, he knew how proud Maggie was of him. He heard it in her voice and saw it on her face. Her chocolate brown eyes twinkled with joy, and her bright white teeth sparkled through her wide smile. He was proud to have Maggie as his owner. Life was good, and then came the worst time of his life.

Maggie was offered a lot of money for him. A stockbroker from Massachusetts saw him at a show and wanted him for his daughter. At first, Maggie said no, but he kept offering more and more money. Finally, he made an offer Maggie didn't refuse. A short time later, with a broken heart, Biz was on a trailer headed from Virginia to a new stable in Massachusetts. He hoped it was a bad dream and he would wake up and see Maggie, but that never happened. When he arrived in Massachusetts, he was frightened. He was never in that part of the country before and didn't know anyone.

Within a day or so of his arrival, he learned that his new owner was a young girl named Ashley Ellington. Over time, Biz learned that when Ashley was a little girl, she had a pony named Snuggles. As Snuggles grew older, Ashley became too big and heavy for her, so she needed a bigger horse. When her father heard about Official Business, the hunter-jumper champion, he was determined to buy him for his daughter, no matter what the cost. And he did.

Biz's relationship with Ashley was strained from the beginning. She was used to riding an older well-behaved pony that took exceptional care of her. She was always able to just hop on and go for a ride without worrying about safety. When she tried to do that with Biz, he was too young and full of energy. Eventually, Ashley fell off and was badly hurt. At first, her concussion, broken ribs, and dislocated shoulder kept her from riding, but eventually, it was her fear, so Biz wasn't ridden for years. He wondered why they didn't sell him.

Just before Biz was moved from that barn to Willow Bend, he learned from conversations between the barn workers that the Ellingtons were moving him to save money on monthly board. When he was a champion, winning ribbons, there was no limit to what Mr. Ellington was willing to pay. The news that they were moving him to save money made Biz feel worthless.

~6~

The weather was getting warmer at Willow Bend and the horses knew they would soon be asked to go out on the trails, which were muddy from the spring thaw. In some places, thawing caused the ground to become unstable and it collapsed when the horses walked on it. It made some of them frightened to take a step.

From a distance, Abdul noticed Aiyana walking cautiously in her paddock. He remembered that when the ground collapsed, it reminded her of a terrifying experience at another farm. She told Abdul that it snowed during the night, so when the horses were let out in the morning, they romped and played and forgot about the pond buried under the snow as they galloped back and forth. While galloping, Aiyana stepped down hard, heard a crack, and felt the ground collapse underneath her. She fell through the ice into the cold water, and it took farmworkers and emergency responders hours to get her out. She wasn't badly hurt, but she was very cold and had cuts on her legs and belly from the jagged edges of the ice. She never forgot how afraid she was, or how long it took for her to stop shivering, no matter how many blankets and heat lamps they put around her. Abdul shook with fear as she told the story. She said that memory never left her, and when the ground collapsed during the spring thaw, it almost felt the same.

Abdul shifted his gaze toward the rays of the sun. He relaxed and enjoyed the warmth for a few moments before he trotted around and watched the barn helpers clean the paddocks. Scraping manure off the ground at that time of year was hard work. Manure was wet and heavy in muddy sections and still frozen to the ground in shady areas. Movement off in the distance caught his eye. Jill finished her riding lesson with Susan in the outdoor arena and walked Jayden back to the barn. Abdul didn't know Jayden well because Susan's horses were in the stalls closest to the riding arenas, at the other end of the barn. Occasionally, Abdul passed by Jayden in the main aisle. He was fascinated by Jayden's two blue eyes. They were pretty ... and spooky.

As Abdul absent-mindedly watched Jill and Jayden, he heard someone call his name. He stopped, and let his ears follow the voice until he saw his owner, Melissa, standing near the back entrance of the barn. She called him again, but he didn't move. He didn't know why, but he felt uneasy. Something was different. When he didn't come, Melissa got his halter and lead rope by the gate and walked out to get him.

"Hey, you. Why didn't you come when I called? Come on. I have a special adventure planned for you," said Melissa as she put on his halter and attached the lead. As they walked toward the gate, Abdul thought about the word adventure, stopped, and looked deeply into Melissa's eyes. Melissa laughed. "Come on, silly, we're going on a trail ride and we're going to have fun."

In the barn, Melissa put Abdul in the cross ties, brushed him, cleaned his hooves, and then went to the tack room to get his saddle and bridle. Abdul was nervous. He wasn't ridden much, and Melissa planned to take him into the woods. He was never out on the trails, and he vividly remembered Aiyana's story. He didn't think he was ready.

Melissa put Abdul's saddle and bridle on, and then led him outside. With each step, Abdul felt his eyes grow larger. Melissa led him to the outdoor mounting block and asked him to stand beside it while she climbed the steps and then eased herself into the saddle. Once on his back, she asked Abdul to walk toward the woods. Abdul started to, but a short distance beyond the paddocks, his fear overcame him, and he couldn't move. Off in the distance, Abdul saw Jonas and Biz watching. They whinnied to him, but Abdul couldn't answer.

"Walk, Abdul," said Melissa, but Abdul planted his feet firmly.
"Walk, Abdul," commanded Melissa as she kicked his sides. Melissa's loud voice drew the attention of people at the farm. When they looked in Abdul's direction, he saw concern in their eyes. He hoped they would intercede, but they appeared hesitant. *Why won't they help?* he asked himself.

Melissa, an inexperienced rider, even though she was nineteen, must have become aware that people were watching because Abdul felt her body tense, and then she screeched. It startled him. He took a step forward, stopped, and then started to walk backward toward the barn. Melissa lost her temper and hit him repeatedly with the whip. "Walk forward," she screamed.

Abdul took another step backward and then he stepped sideways and his foot broke through the ground. He panicked. He was afraid to go forward, backward, or sideways. Not knowing what to do, he stood still, and Melissa whipped him until he couldn't take it anymore. He reared up on his hind legs, lost his balance, and fell over backward on top of Melissa.

When Abdul managed to get up, he looked down at Melissa and realized that she wasn't moving. Frightened, he galloped back to the barn, and barn workers ran to help Melissa.

* * *

Susan was in her office, putting together a spreadsheet of monthly expenses when she heard yelling outside. Normally, she didn't pay too much attention to loud voices, because barn workers and horse owners often shouted to each other across the large paddocks. But there was something urgent about the tone and it alarmed her. She immediately sat up in her chair, cocked her ear, and knew it was an emergency. She bolted out of her office and ran down the main aisle of the barn as her heart pounded and her palms began to sweat. When she got outside, she saw Melissa on the ground, dialed 911 on her cell phone, and cautioned those around Melissa not to move her. "Don't touch her. If she has a spinal injury, it could make things worse. The ambulance is on its way." She was relieved that Melissa was conscious and asked one of the workers to bring ice water and a cloth.

"Can you wiggle your toes, Melissa?"

Melissa nodded and started to cry.

"Thank goodness. Can you tell me what hurts?" asked Susan.

Melissa said she had a pounding headache and excruciating pain in her hips. When the ice arrived, Susan put a cold compress on Melissa's forehead and held her hand until the ambulance pulled in.

"Do you remember what happened?" asked Susan.

"He reared up, I fell off, and then he fell on top of me," said Melissa.

Melissa didn't look her in the eye, so Susan knew there was something she wasn't telling her. An EMT and a paramedic were in the ambulance when it finally arrived. As the paramedic performed her assessment, Susan saw fear in Melissa's eyes.

"I'm scared, Susan," said Melissa with tears rolling down her cheeks.

"I know you are, but you're in very good hands now. Do you want one of us to go to the hospital with you?" asked Susan as they gingerly placed Melissa on the backboard and started to load her into the ambulance.

Melissa shook her head.

"Are you sure?"

Melissa nodded. "I'm sure, but please call my mother."

"I'll call her right now. Is there anyone else you want me to call?" asked Susan.

"Nobody else. Please ask her to hurry."

Susan promised she would. As the back doors to the ambulance closed, Susan wrung her hands. Melissa was nineteen and able to make health care decisions for herself, but she was so immature that Susan tended to regard her as a child. She was worried about her.

Susan knew most of the emergency responders in the area, so she looked intently at the paramedic for a sign that Melissa was going to be okay. When the paramedic gave Susan a quick nod, she felt a weight lift off of her shoulders. Melissa sustained injuries, but she was not in grave danger.

After Susan called Melissa's mother, she spoke quickly with the barn workers who saw the accident, and then went into the barn to check on Abdul.

***

Carol showed up early to pick Jill up from Willow Bend because she wanted to walk around and look at the horses. She meandered around, looking for her, and found her cleaning stalls at the back of the barn.

"You're early," said Jill. "I'm not ready and I still have a lesson."

"I know I'm early. I need some horse smells, and I'd like to watch your lesson, if you don't mind."

Before Jill answered, they heard a commotion outside and went to the barn door to see what it was about. Carol gasped as she watched a young woman hit her horse until he reared and fell on her. When the horse got up, he glanced down and then ran toward the barn. They were standing just inside the back entrance when he came in. His breathing was rapid, he was visibly shaking, and the veins in his neck were popping out. Carol watched in awe as her daughter calmly walked toward him, speaking in a soft voice.

"It's okay, Abdul. You're safe now." Appearing completely fearless, Jill gently took his reins in her hands, and with great care, walked alongside him to his stall. Carol followed, but she couldn't help but feel worried about Jill because the horse, though small, was wound up like a top. In his stall, Jill stood at his side, gently rubbed his neck, and looked kindly into his eyes. He took a deep breath and snorted when he blew it out. Carol felt herself relax. "If it's okay with you, Abdul, I'd like to take off your saddle and bridle and brush the mud off of you. You're okay now. Take another deep breath," said Jill.

Jill spoke softly as she brushed Abdul, and then put on his blanket. "I hope this warms him enough to help stop the shaking," said Jill. They stayed with him until the trembling stopped, and then Jill gave him a little bit of hay to eat while they went back to the barn entrance. "I hope Melissa's okay," said Jill.

As Jill watched the paramedics, Carol saw her gaze drift to the far pasture, and then she stood at attention. "What is it, honey?" asked Carol.

Jill pointed. "Mom, I see the horses at Willow Bend just about every weekend. Why did I never see *him* before?"

Carol looked and saw a tall chestnut with a white blaze.

"I wonder where he came from and how long he's been here," said Jill, seemingly mesmerized. As Jill stared, Carol heard the words from her dream come rushing back. *"Carol! Look! Can you see him out there? He sure is a beauty. A tall chestnut with a long white blaze and two white socks. And he's all ours."*

Carol's thoughts were interrupted when Susan rushed into the barn. "Where's Abdul? Is he all right?" she asked.

Jill turned to face her. "He ran in here after the accident. I managed to calm him and put him in his stall."

Susan went over to the stall. "You were able to take his saddle and bridle off?"

"Yes," said Jill. "He was a nervous wreck, but he didn't do anything that made me feel afraid. He was a good boy, but he was shaking so much that I put his blanket on, hoping it might warm him enough to make it stop."

Susan looked at Jill with admiration. "Great job, Jill."

Susan glanced at Carol. "That's a heck of a kid, you've got there. I'm lucky to have her."

"Thank you, Susan. That makes two of us," said Carol.

"Well, since you have everything under control in here, Jill, I'll go to my office and make some calls."

Susan left, and Jill's gaze immediately shifted back to the chestnut horse. "Did I not notice him because he grazes so far back in the pasture?"

Carol knew Jill was thinking about her father. He *loved* chestnut horses. Especially when they had long white blazes and white socks. Carol hugged Jill and she didn't seem to care if anyone was watching. "I miss Dad," whispered Jill.

"I miss him too," said Carol.

"I feel so lost without him, Mom."

"I know you do, honey."

Carol tried to keep her emotions in check around Jill because she didn't want her to worry. She wanted Jill to feel safe. Protected. Carefree. If she revealed the depth of her pain and let her emotions flow would that help her? Carol didn't think so.

***

During the rest of the afternoon, Susan asked barn workers what happened, and they all said it was Melissa's fault because she was so heavy-handed with her whip. It troubled Susan, but she promised herself that she wouldn't bring it up to Melissa's mother when she called to check on her condition. Melissa was an adult, so Susan had to address the matter directly with her, not her mother. Later that night, Susan called Melissa's mother for an update and was told that she had a serious concussion and a broken pelvis, but no spinal injuries, and she was expected to make a full recovery. Susan was relieved that Melissa was okay. She knew she had to address the way Melissa used her whip, but she had time to figure out how to bring it up because it was going to be a long time before Melissa was back at the barn.

Susan's rules about whips were firm because they were for the safety of everyone. Students were able to carry a whip, but it was supposed to be used as a gentle tool, not brute force, because that caused horses to panic and hurt themselves, riders, or innocent bystanders. Melissa had no patience and minimal riding experience, so she was over her head with a young horse like Abdul. A whip was the last thing Melissa should have used. Susan had to be diplomatic in her approach with Melissa because she was sure that the accident destroyed what little confidence she had.

* * *

Knowing the herd as he did, Jonas expected a nasty gossip session following Abdul's accident and he wasn't disappointed.

"Melissa deserved everything she got. She has *no* idea what she's doing. If she wanted to take Abdul on a trail ride, she should have waited until the ground was dry. He's never been out there before. His eyes were so big. Doesn't she know what that means?" asked Aiyana.

"I can't believe how *hard* she hit him with that whip," whimpered Opal.

"Oh, come on. You've been in the show circuit for years. You know about whips," snarled Günter.

Luis stomped his foot and rolled his eyes. "It wasn't all Melissa's fault. Abdul acted like a little *twit*."

Aiyana gasped. "Don't be mean. He's just a baby. He needs someone with a soft voice and kind hands."

Opal sighed. "Speaking of soft voices and kind hands, have you met that new girl who works here?"

"You mean Jill?" asked Aiyana.

"Jill? Ooooh yes. The *poor* girl," said Günter. "She can't afford a horse, so she cleans stalls in exchange for riding lessons."

Jonas felt his eyes roll in his head. During their time together at Willow Bend, Jonas heard Günter say a lot of mean things, but that was a new low, even for him.

Aiyana clenched her jaw and stared at Günter. "I don't care how much money she has, or doesn't have, for that matter. She's nice to us. That's all I care about. I like her. And I bet she'd never use a whip. She doesn't have to. She seems to understand us."

Günter and Luis stared at Aiyana, and then looked at each other and chuckled. "Impossible," said Luis.

"People never take the time to understand us. They don't know how," Günter said.

Jonas had to agree with them. Far too few owners took the time to truly understand their horses. Noah, his owner, wasn't like that, but over the years, Jonas learned that Noah was the exception, not the rule.

~7~

Days later, as Jill cleaned stalls, she kept wondering about the tall chestnut, so when she finished her barn work, she went to Susan's office to ask about him. She knocked on the office door and Susan told her to come in.

"Hi, Susan. I hope you're having a good day," said Jill.

"I am. Thanks for asking. What's up?"

"I was wondering about Melissa. Is she going to be okay?"

"Eventually, yes. Her injuries are serious, but they expect a full recovery."

Jill sighed. "That's good news. I saw the accident and it was pretty scary."

"What did you see?"

Jill explained in detail, and the expression on Susan's face was a mixture of concern, anger, and sadness. "Thank you. That's what everyone else said too and it's troubling. I don't allow *anyone* to use a whip in that manner. It's just plain wrong and someone always gets hurt. I'm going to have to talk to her about it."

Jill nodded. "Susan, as I watched the paramedics, I saw a new horse in the pasture with Jonas. Who is he?"

"That's Biz. He's in rough shape, but he's a really sweet boy. He was pretty skinny when he got here, and he hasn't been worked in a long time, so he has very little muscle."

Jill felt her heart sink. "Why?"

Susan leaned back in her chair. "I'm still trying to piece that together. He's only been here a little while."

"He looked so handsome, standing beside Jonas in the pasture. I don't know why I never saw him before."

"Well, that's probably because you're only here on weekends, and Biz's stall is in the wing where you don't usually clean stalls. He's over by Jonas."

That made sense to Jill. Willow Bend was a big place. There were four large barns arranged like a plus sign. At the center, where they all came together, was an indoor riding area big enough for two regulation-size riding rings. "I think he's beautiful ... How old is he?"

"I was told he just turned fifteen. Why?"

"I don't know. I guess I'm just curious. Well, I'm glad Melissa's going to be okay. Sorry to bother you, Susan. You look busy."

"You are *never* a bother, Jill. Have a good day and tell your mother I said hello."

"I will." Jill's mind filled with questions about Biz. She felt drawn to him and decided it was time to meet him.

***

Barn workers were outside by the paddock, talking about Melissa, and Abdul heard them. They said that when he reared and Melissa fell off, she hit her head and suffered a concussion. When he fell on top of her, her pelvis broke. No one was sure when she'd be back at the barn, but they knew she wouldn't be riding anytime soon.

Abdul felt ashamed that he lost control of himself, but he didn't understand why she hit him relentlessly. He wasn't being naughty. He was frightened. "Sorry, Melissa. I didn't mean to hurt you," he said.

Later that morning, feeling overwhelmed, Abdul stood with his butt to the fence that separated him from Biz's paddock.

"How are you doing, little buddy?" asked Biz.

Abdul jumped. He wasn't expecting Biz to talk to him. Jonas was away from the farm, working with Noah, and Biz hadn't said a word to anyone except Jonas since he arrived.

"Not so good," answered Abdul.

Biz looked down. "I thought that might be the case, so I wanted to let you know that I understand."

"You do?"

"More than you know."

Abdul sensed that what Biz was about to say was important, so he listened intently.

"I had an experienced owner named Maggie. She owned me when I won all of my titles, and then I was sold and my new owner, Ashley, wasn't a good rider. One day, I started to canter out on the trails. She squeezed with her legs, so I thought she wanted me to go faster, but she also pulled back on the reins like she wanted me to stop. I felt confused and started to sense that Ashley was scared. I didn't understand why so I kept running. Ashley lost her balance and fell to the ground. I heard her cry, but I couldn't get myself to stop and left her alone in the woods." Biz gently shook his head as if trying to shake the memory from his mind. "Ashley had a concussion, broken ribs, and a dislocated shoulder."

Abdul couldn't believe his ears. He felt sorry for Biz, but he was thankful that he shared his story because he didn't feel so alone. With gratitude, Abdul walked closer to the fence, reached his head over, and gently touched his nose to Biz's shoulder. When Biz looked at him, his eyes were moist.

"Was she mad at you? How long did it take until she forgave you?" asked Abdul.

Biz looked off in the distance. "She came to the barn a few times, but said she was too afraid to ride. I don't know if she ever forgave me."

"Is that why no one comes to brush you?" Abdul suddenly realized that his question might have hurt Biz's feelings. He felt terrible when Biz looked at him and his eyes welled.

Biz swallowed. "Our accident happened during our first year together. I haven't seen her in at least five years." Biz turned and slowly walked away.

"I'm sorry, Biz. I didn't mean to make you sad," said Abdul.

"It's okay. I know you didn't. I just wanted you to know that you're not alone."

Abdul understood that Biz shared his story to make him feel better, but it made him wonder if the same thing could happen to him. What if Melissa never forgave him? Would he be alone for years, too?

***

Biz was quiet as he ate supper that night.

"You okay, brother?" asked Jonas. "You've been awful quiet."

Biz didn't say anything until the silence became overwhelming. "I did the same thing as Abdul. That's why I don't have anybody."

Jonas stopped chewing and looked at Biz. "What happened?"

Biz told Jonas the story.

"Why did her father buy you? Didn't she ride you first?"

"No. I didn't meet Ashley until I came to Massachusetts."

"He bought his daughter a new horse without knowing if you were right for each other?"

"Yes."

Jonas snorted in frustration. "Man! Why don't people understand that you have to match the rider to the horse?" Jonas stepped closer to Biz, and with compassion in his voice, he asked. "Do you miss her, son?"

Without hesitation, Biz answered, "No, but I do miss Maggie."

Jonas tipped his head. "Who's Maggie?"

"Maggie owned me before Ashley's father, Raymond Ellington, bought me." Biz felt his heart ache at the mere mention of Maggie's name. His emotional pain was so intense that he turned and faced the wall, signaling that the conversation was over.

Before he went to sleep that night, Biz tried to remember everything he could about Maggie. He loved her so much. It was over six years since he saw her. With his eyes closed, he pictured her face. He remembered the scent of her perfume, how it felt when she brushed him, the sound of the kisses she planted on his wet nose, and the taste of the peppermints she put in his bran mash.

"Why, Maggie. Why?" whimpered Biz. He wondered how she could have ever sold him.

***

During the days that followed Melissa's accident, at bedtime, Carol lay in bed, thinking about Logan and the empty barn in their backyard. Some nights, she drifted off to sleep, only to be awakened in the early hours of the morning to, *"Carol! You finally saw him out there. Isn't he a beauty?"*

When Carol rolled over and looked at the clock, it was always too early to get up, so she lay there, half-asleep, wondering why, over the past couple of months, she kept hearing Logan's voice and his words. On some of those mornings, she got out of bed to look at the barn and was always disappointed when she didn't see the silhouette. A few times, as she got back in bed and curled up with the warm blankets, she felt a slight breeze, and for an instant, smelled a faint scent of Old Spice, the aftershave he always wore. Carol was beginning to feel Logan around her all the time. She wondered if Jill felt it, too. She hoped so because it was a nice feeling that made her feel protected. Warm inside. She wanted to ask Jill, but she was afraid to stir up emotions and make her sad.

~8~

It was a nice day, so as usual, right after breakfast, the horses were turned out in their paddocks. Biz felt lucky because he and Jonas were going to spend the day in the big pasture. Susan rotated the horses from their paddocks to the pasture on different days of the week because it had more grass. It was their turn, and the grass was delectable. Biz was deep in thought as he grazed, but when Jonas moseyed over beside him, he was eager to talk.

"Jonas? How come people think it's okay to just buy and sell us?"

Jonas shook his head. "I don't know."

"They buy us, we get attached to them, and then next thing you know, we've been sold. New owner. New home. No one even tells us why. Do they ever think about what we need?"

Jonas took a deep breath and let it out before he spoke. "Some do, but I'm afraid those owners can be few 'n' far between."

"But why, Jonas? Why does it have to be that way?"

"Because for people, some of them anyway, it's about money and feeling important. They want a horse that wins because it makes them look good. The more a horse wins, the more it's worth, so they sell it, make some money, and buy a new one."

Biz knew Jonas was right because he saw it happen time and again. But he didn't think Maggie was like that. As he thought about Maggie, he felt his body become heavy and his chest grew tight. He tried not to think about her because it always made him feel that way. She broke his heart.

"We were a team," said Biz. "I loved her, and I thought she loved me. Maggie never yelled and she never whipped me. I was happy, Jonas. The worst part was that she never even said goodbye." Biz saw the concern on Jonas's face as he continued to explain his history with Maggie. She bought him from a trainer named Shannon when he was four. He would never miss Shannon because she was mean. She whipped him; sometimes so hard that the whip left marks on his skin. Like Melissa, Shannon didn't have patience. And she was a horrible trainer. Half the time, Biz didn't understand what she wanted.

Then Maggie came to the barn. She wanted to meet Biz after she heard Shannon brag about him. When she arrived, Shannon was jumping Biz in the indoor arena. One fence was very high, and the approach Shannon took didn't feel safe, so he stopped, and Shannon flew over his head. When she got up, her face was red, and her teeth were clenched. Biz saw her head jerk when she realized that Maggie probably saw the whole thing. Biz assumed that Shannon felt embarrassed because she yelled and then she whipped him. Maggie seemed outraged and told Shannon that the problem wasn't Biz, it was her, and the first thing she needed to do was throw away the whip.

"If you know so much, *you* get on him. Let's see what *you* can do," yelled Shannon.

While they argued, Biz ran to the end of the arena to get as far away from Shannon as possible. When Maggie walked away from Shannon and approached him, she moved cautiously and spoke quietly. She gently stroked his neck and looked deeply into his eyes, as if asking permission to get in the saddle. Biz immediately trusted her and positioned himself in a manner that let her know it was okay. She gently got on and they just walked around the arena until they were comfortable with each other. When Maggie asked Biz to trot, he did so willingly, and then she asked him to canter. Her instructions were clear. Biz felt himself relax and when Maggie asked him to jump a fence, he did it without hesitation. When she asked him to jump the tall fence that he refused to jump for Shannon, the approach she asked him to take felt right, so he jumped it. Beautifully. Not too long after that, Maggie bought Biz and he was in a trailer headed to her barn for the best five years of his life.

"Is that how you became a show jumper?" asked Jonas.

"Yes. We trained hard and won just about every class. Work was fun with Maggie. I became a champion because of her. She understood me and I trusted her. I knew she'd never do anything to hurt me."

"Do you know why she sold you, son?"

Biz sighed. "All I know is that after I won my big title, Ashley's father kept offering money. I didn't think anything would ever come between me and Maggie, but maybe everything does come down to money, Jonas."

Jonas asked, "Is it possible that Maggie needed money?"

Biz never thought about that. "I think we both had all that we needed."

Jonas shook his head. "Maybe there were things you didn't know. Maybe she never said goodbye because she couldn't. Maybe she thought she let *you* down. Could her heart have been broken, just like yours?"

Biz didn't know what to say. Was it possible that Maggie never wanted to sell him? Was her heart just as broken? Was that why she never said goodbye? Deep inside, Biz knew Jonas was right. The more he thought about it, the lighter he felt. Biz was grateful to have a friend like Jonas. Their talk made him feel better.

~9~

The weekend arrived with rainy, chilly weather and high winds, so Susan asked the help to keep the horses in the barn. As Jill made her morning rounds, she checked to make sure the horses had their morning ration of grain, plenty of water, extra hay, and that their stalls were clean. Late in the morning, when her work was done, she had time to visit Biz in his stall. When she got there, she stood and just looked at him for the longest time. He wasn't in the best shape, but he was still incredibly handsome. Something about him felt regal. When she saw mud on his right side, she decided to clean him up, but when she touched him, he flinched and moved away. "It's okay. I'm just going to clean the mud off of you," said Jill as she looked into his eyes.

She left him to get some brushes and came back a few minutes later with a curry, a hard brush, a medium brush, a soft brush, and some hay cubes. She gave Biz a hay cube to chew on as she gingerly curried the heavy mud from his coat. She curried carefully, just in case he flinched because he was sore, but she soon realized that she must have approached him too quickly. "Have you been rolling in the mud, Biz? I hope you had fun. You sure are dirty," laughed Jill.

By the time she was done, Biz munched on quite a few hay cubes, and his coat had a little bit of a shine. Jill was enjoying herself. "Maybe I could brush you more often, Biz. Would you like that?" she asked as she rubbed his ears. Before she left his stall, she gave him a little kiss on his nose. After she locked the stall door behind her, she gazed at him again. He had a beautiful face and the kindest eyes. From the day she first saw him, she yearned to be around him and was completely at home in his presence.

***

Abdul was moved from his stall to one closer to Biz. He heard that one of the boarders insisted that her horse be closer to the big barn doors where there was plenty of fresh air. She offered extra money, so Noah asked Susan to move Abdul. He loved the idea of being closer to his friend. In his new stall, he let out a sigh.

"What's wrong, little buddy?" asked Biz.

Abdul looked at the floor and sighed again as he told Biz how tired he was of just standing around. The accident was weeks ago, and Melissa still didn't come to see him. "I wonder if she's even called to ask how I am," said Abdul. "I didn't mean to hurt her, Biz. I really didn't."

"I know you didn't. I didn't mean to hurt Ashley either. It's been so long since I've seen her, that I probably wouldn't recognize her if she walked through the door."

"Really? Do you ever miss her?"

It took a few seconds for Biz to answer. "At first, I felt sad, but after a while, I got used to being alone. Then, the more I watched how some people treated their horses, the more I liked being by myself. Pretty soon, I didn't care anymore."

Abdul felt his eyes moisten. "That makes me sad, Biz. Are *you* sad?"

"Maybe I am. Maybe I am."

Abdul didn't know what else to say. If he had a hard time being alone for weeks, he couldn't imagine how it felt to be alone for years. Abdul thought about how he came to be alone. When he looked up, Biz was looking at him with his head tipped to one side and an affectionate twinkle in his eyes. "I don't know if Melissa called to check on you, but I'm sure you haven't seen her because she's still recovering."

Abdul blinked. "Biz, why didn't Melissa know that I was scared? You and Jonas knew, and you were way out in the pasture. You even whinnied to let me know you were there."

Furrows formed in Biz's forehead. "People think they should only have to ask us to do something once. How we feel doesn't matter. We aren't supposed to have feelings, Abdul. We're just here to serve them."

Abdul gasped. "But we *do* have feelings and we do matter. Why didn't anyone help me?"

With a pained look, Biz replied, "It looked like they wanted to, but you seemed frantic. Maybe they were afraid of getting hurt themselves. Or maybe they feared that if they intervened, it would make Melissa even angrier, and that could have made things worse for you."

Abdul understood why they might have been unwilling to put themselves in harm's way or cause problems, but he thought it made more sense to take a risk when someone needed help.

~10~

The following Saturday, Jill had to get to the barn early because it was her turn to feed breakfast to the horses. On that particular day, by choice, she was taking care of the wing where Biz was stabled. As she made her way from stall to stall, she gave them their grain, topped off water buckets, and threw hay in their stalls. Finally, she made it to the back of the barn and fed Jonas, Abdul, and Biz. After Jill gave Biz his grain, she took time to simply be with him because in no time at all, she would have to help the rest of the barn crew turn out the horses and clean stalls. She loved looking at him. Being with him.

Jill always earned a riding lesson on the days when she cleaned stalls. On that particular day, Susan promised her a lesson on the horse of her choice. Since nobody ever rode Biz, she wondered if she could ride him instead of Jayden. Just the thought of riding Biz put a bounce in her step. After she locked his stall door behind her, she looked deeply into his eyes and said, "I would love to ride you, Biz. Would you like that?"

Biz's ears went up and he tipped his head slightly. When he looked at her, there was a slight twinkle in his chocolate brown eyes and it touched her heart. After Jill finished her chores, she found Susan to ask if she could ride Biz that day. She was disappointed when Susan said it wasn't possible because they needed permission from his owner. "That's too bad," sighed Jill. "He could use some exercise, and he seems lonely."

On her way to the tack room to get Jayden's saddle and bridle, Jill wondered if she would ever get to ride Biz. Logically, it seemed that the answer was no, but *something* told her to keep trying because the answer was supposed to be yes.

***

Susan agreed that it would be good for Biz to get some exercise, so she promised herself that, later in the afternoon, she'd call Mr. Ellington. When she did, he said he didn't want Biz exercised or used as a lesson horse because he didn't want him to get hurt. "We paid a lot of money for that horse, and we don't want to ruin our investment."

Susan was flabbergasted. Before she said anything, she took a deep breath because she knew she needed to respond to Mr. Ellington's comment, not react to it. "Mr. Ellington, do you understand that you've already hurt your investment? It doesn't matter how much you paid for Biz. If he's not in good condition, his value drops. Biz is underweight and out of shape."

Susan heard him clear his throat. "How can he possibly need more food? He gets plenty of hay and the same amount of grain he's always been given. If he's not exercised, he's not burning enough calories to warrant extra food. You're just trying to scam money out of me."

Susan felt her mouth go dry. She wanted to scream, and maybe even swear at Mr. Ellington, but she knew that wouldn't benefit anyone, so she kept her cool. "Mr. Ellington, why would you think that? Nobody's trying to scam you. I'm just trying to provide the best possible care for your horse."

"No extra food and no exercise. Period," said Mr. Ellington.

Susan knew from his tone that it wasn't the right time to pursue the matter: He wasn't going to listen to a word she said. She politely ended the call, but promised herself that she would bring the subject up again. Soon. She thought it was best to let her words marinate in his head for a while. *Does he think he's protecting his investment by letting Biz stand around and do nothing all day? He's skinny, out of shape, and depressed*, thought Susan. She knew Biz needed extra food to put on weight, exercise to build muscle, and someone who cared about him. She wasn't worried about Mr. Ellington's accusation because it had no merit. She decided that if she couldn't get Mr. Ellington to change his mind, she would get Noah onboard, as well as a veterinarian, to persuade him.

At the end of Jill's riding lesson with Jayden that afternoon, Susan told her she called Mr. Ellington, but he said no. Susan saw how quickly Jill's smile faded and realized that she unrealistically hoped she would be able to ride Biz. Then, after a minute, Jill sat up in the saddle and looked at Susan with determination. "Susan, can I just groom him? There's no way it could hurt him or their investment, right? It would be good for him. He just seems so sad. Please?"

Most boarders groomed their horses, but a few paid extra specifically for grooming. When that happened, Susan normally delegated it to one of the stable hands. Mr. Ellington only included enough extra money for Biz to be groomed once a week. Biz was in such rough shape that Susan decided to take care of him herself, but she knew Biz would be in good hands with Jill and some additional grooming would be good for him.

"He's a big horse and you're a small girl, so be careful," said Susan.

Jill's smile grew so wide that a small tear flowed gently from the outside corner of her eye. *This clearly means the world to her*, thought Susan.

At the end of her lesson, Jill rushed out of the arena with Jayden in tow. "Don't move too fast. That's how accidents happen," yelled Susan. "If you're going to groom Biz tonight, please call your mother and let her know, just in case she has other plans for you. I don't want Carol to be upset with me because you didn't get your homework finished."

"I will," shouted Jill. "Can I use the office phone?"

"Of course."

Susan reminded Jill to call Carol because she knew that, as soon as Jill finished brushing Jayden, she was going straight to Biz's stall. The thought made her chuckle. Jill had a long day of cleaning stalls and tending to horses. Then, at the end of her shift, she got Jayden ready for their lesson, took the lesson, and was about to brush him and put him in his stall for the night. How she had enough energy to tend to Biz was a mystery.

When she passed by her office door a short while later, Susan heard Jill on the phone.

"Mom? You're never going to believe it. Susan is letting me groom Biz from now on. She told me to call and let you know that I'll likely be running late. Yes. I'm starting today. Right now. I'm so excited. I'll call you when I'm finished. Thanks, Mom."

Susan asked herself why Jill was so drawn to Biz. During the short time that Jill worked at Willow Bend, she was polite and kind to everyone, but she almost seemed more at home with horses than people. Susan wondered if Jill was drawn to Biz because she also felt alone and sad.

***

A couple of hours before suppertime, Biz heard someone approaching. He looked up and saw Jill walking toward his paddock. "Hey, Biz," she whispered. "Your owner won't let me ride you, but Susan said I can groom you. I'm going to bring you inside and get your brushes."

As Jill walked Biz toward the barn, his front right foot felt a little bit sore. Once in the barn, Jill put him in his stall and went to get his grooming supplies. Biz watched her walk down the center aisle to the tack room. He felt disappointed when Jill said she wouldn't be able to ride him, and it caught him off-guard. *Would it be fun to be ridden again? How well could Jill ride? I don't want her to get hurt,* he thought. But the grooming sounded good. When Jill brushed him that one time, he enjoyed it and he *loved* the hay cubes. For a very long time, nobody paid any attention to him. Did he want to get attached to another person? Could he trust someone again?

After a few minutes, Biz stuck his head over the stall door to check on Jill. He was happy to see that she was on her way back. She put his grooming box on the shelf beside his stall in the barn aisle and then opened the stall door. She stood on her tiptoes to remove his regular halter and then slid the top of his grooming halter, which allowed better access to his face, over his ears. Once the halter was fastened, she clipped on the lead rope and walked him into the aisle to put him in the cross ties.

First, Jill used the rubber curry to loosen dirt from deep within his coat. It felt so good that it tickled in spots. When he wiggled, Jill giggled. One tickle spot was at the top of his neck. Jill seemed to have a little bit of trouble reaching it, so Biz lowered his head to make it easier. When she curried his belly, he could feel his lips quiver uncontrollably. She curried that same spot over and over and Biz wondered if she did it just to watch his lips. He liked the sound of Jill's giggle. It was warm and genuine. She gave Biz a hay cube before she changed to the hard brush, and it tasted so good that Biz closed his eyes and sighed.

Next, Jill used the hard brush to loosen dirt deep in his coat, right down to his skin. He enjoyed another hay cube before she switched to the medium brush to clean out the finer particles of dirt under the surface of his coat. Another hay cube was savored before she finished with the soft brush, to eliminate dirt from his coat's surface. When she finished brushing him, she sprayed detangler and conditioner on his mane and tail. Biz felt her tug lightly as she untangled snarls, but it was worth it, because when she finished, the comb slid right through, just like during his show days. He felt good and wanted to see how he looked, so he bent his neck to see his back and side. His coat glistened. Wow. I haven't looked like this in a long, long time, he thought.

Jill left to put his brushes back in the tack room. When she returned, she reached deep into her pocket and pulled out a peppermint. Biz smelled it through the wrapper and felt excitement course through him. He felt himself stand taller. He wanted the peppermint so much that he reached his head forward and used his lips to forcefully, but gently, pry the mint from Jill's closed hand. She laughed out loud and didn't appear to care that he left slobber all over her fingers.

After Jill gave him the mint, she kissed him on the nose—twice. A wave of emotion overcame him as he remembered when Maggie gave him peppermints and kissed his nose. His affection for Jill surprised him. For the first time in years, he felt happy. Like he was home again.

Jill released the cross ties to lead him back to his stall, but when he pivoted on that front right foot to turn, the level of discomfort caused him to limp. He felt loved when Jill took the time to put him back in the cross ties to see what was wrong. When she lifted the hoof and pressed the heel, it hurt so much that he tried to pull his foot away. Jill apologized, and then she disappeared into the tack room and returned with a hoof pick, a hoof brush, a small bucket of warm water, a rag, and medicine. When she cleaned his hooves, she found thrush. The smell of the black gooey substance in the crevices of his hooves was awful. She meticulously cleaned every crevice, then washed all four of his hooves, let them air dry, and applied medicine. When she finished, the love in her eyes touched him deeply.

Jill walked Biz into his stall, and as she unclipped the lead rope from his halter, he reached over and rubbed his face gently on her arm. Jill smiled at him. "You're welcome, Biz. I'll come by and check on you tomorrow, okay, boy?" Jill gently rubbed his cheek and kissed him on the nose again. "I was going to hunt Susan down to tell her about the thrush, but there isn't anything else she can do tonight, so I'll tell her when I come back tomorrow," said Jill as she closed his stall door. "Goodnight, handsome."

Jill finished cleaning the aisle floor just in time for the rest of the horses to come in for supper. As Jonas passed by Biz's stall, his ears went up and he sniffed in a very animated way. "Do I smell a peppermint, brother?"

Biz saw the smirk on his face and chuckled. "Yes, and it was good." Biz felt a new chapter opening in his life and it frightened him almost as much as it excited him.

~11~

The next day Susan was in the tack room, sweeping and organizing when Jill came in. Susan saw the look on her face and asked what was wrong.

Jill shook her head. "Does anybody care about Biz? Nobody comes to see him. No one comes to brush him, and nobody comes to pick out his feet. Last night, when I groomed him, he was limping on his front right foot. He had thrush up into his heel. It was so tender that he flinched when I pressed on it. After I cleaned that foot, I checked all of them. He had thrush in all four feet, Susan. Isn't that abuse?"

Susan took a deep breath and sat down on one of the large wooden tack trunks. "No, it's not abuse, but it could be neglect," said Susan. "The Ellingtons include only a small amount in the board check for grooming. I've been doing it myself on Monday afternoons when I have a short window of available time. I assure you that he didn't have thrush the last time I cleaned his hooves. Horses tend to develop thrush when they're in damp or moist environments. Standing in mud from the spring thaw or rain makes all horses susceptible."

Jill nodded, but Susan saw so much emotion on her face that she decided to stay seated and just listen until she got it all out.

"It's not fair. I want a horse so badly, but I can't afford one. Yet some people can afford anything they want, but they don't take care of it. I feel so bad for him. I just want to take him home. He's the only horse in the barn without someone who loves him."

Susan watched Jill's eyes fill with tears. She dropped her broom and hugged Jill because she knew Jill meant every word.

"Jill, when you work in this business, you have to take the good with the bad. Some people see their horses as partners, love them, and take exceptional care of them. Others dump their horses here and never come to see them. Some come every day but think the answer to every problem is corporal punishment. And some have horses just for prestige. They keep them in good health so they can win. When a horse gets old or injured and can no longer compete, they just get rid of it."

Jill nodded. "Why don't they care about Biz?"

Susan exhaled. "Mr. Ellington does care about his investment. He paid a lot of money for Biz and doesn't want his investment harmed."

Jill sat down beside Susan. She leaned forward with her elbows on her thighs. Her chin rested on her intertwined hands as she looked at the floor. "I don't understand."

Susan leaned forward too. "Well, I'm not sure how much he paid for Biz, but I understand it was plenty. When Biz first arrived here, Mr. Ellington didn't want him in the pasture with other horses because he was afraid he'd get kicked and have to be put down. After a lengthy discussion, I managed to convince him to let Biz go out with Jonas, but Mr. Ellington was adamant about not wanting anyone to ride him. He's afraid Biz will get injured, and then he won't be worth as much."

Jill looked into Susan's eyes. "But what about Biz? He isn't happy. He doesn't have anybody who cares about him and he doesn't look good."

Susan inhaled. "I know he doesn't, Jill. He's thin, but Mr. Ellington won't pay extra money to increase his food. He says Biz isn't being exercised, so the amount of food he's getting should be more than enough."

The whole situation frustrated Susan. Mr. Ellington was wrong, and Jill was right, but she felt like her hands were tied.

Jill stood up and paced. "If Mr. Ellington pays for full board, why can't you give it to Biz anyway?"

Susan stood and leaned the back of her body against the wall. "I wish I could, but horse boarding is a business and it's hard to earn a living if you don't keep expenses down. Noah, the owner of Willow Bend, keeps his head above water because he runs a tight ship. Full board includes only so much grain per day and Biz already gets the maximum amount. I'm sorry, Jill. I know it doesn't seem fair. I love my job because I get to work around horses all day. The downside is situations like this."

Jill mindlessly picked at her thumbnails. "Why isn't this considered abuse?"

Susan sighed. "Because Biz is being groomed and his hooves are trimmed regularly. He's in a nice barn with suitable shelter, and he's fed three times a day. Authorities would not consider that abuse."

"Okay, then what about neglect?"

Susan put her hand on Jill's shoulder.

"Jill, I understand why you feel that he's neglected. From an emotional standpoint, I agree wholeheartedly. Biz was underweight when he arrived at Willow Bend, but he hasn't *lost* any weight since he's been here. If he was losing weight, I'd be putting a lot more pressure on Mr. Ellington and probably be threatening to call the authorities. Give me some time. I need to figure out how to get him to listen to me. Trust me. I will figure it out." Susan knew Jill wasn't able to let it go when she started to pace back and forth again and started to cry.

"Does Mr. Ellington think he's protecting his investment by neglecting Biz? Susan, I'll pay for his extra grain and hay, and I'll groom him every day."

Susan felt her jaw drop. "I can't let you do that, Jill."

"Why? I thought it was about money."

Susan took hold of Jill's hands. "Why do you want to do this?"

"Because Biz needs somebody. He stands proud, but his body is worn. He's afraid to trust, but I think he wants to. I think he remembers when life was good. I want him to *feel* like that again."

Susan closed her eyes before she spoke. "Jill, that's going to take more than food. It's going to take exercise and Mr. Ellington doesn't want him worked."

Jill stood with her arms crossed tightly around her chest. Susan felt remorse as she watched the expression on Jill's face turn from righteous indignation to helplessness and defeat, and she hated that her words contributed to the transformation. After a while, Jill lifted her head and Susan noticed a spark in her eyes.

"Did he say that nobody can play with him? I could chase him around the paddock, you know, get him running and feed him carrots."

Susan couldn't keep from smiling. She admired this young woman's tenacity, but she didn't want her to spend her time and money on a horse she might never get to ride. And she worried that Biz might get attached to Jill, only to have her taken away.

Jill looked at Susan pleadingly. "Susan, can I *please* pay for his extra food?"

Susan shook her head. "Jill, that's a lot of money. It could be up to sixty dollars a month. You can't afford that."

"Yes, I can."

Susan saw the strength of Jill's commitment and lowered her head in defeat. "Heaven help me. I can only say yes if your mother agrees. Have her call me. If she's okay with this, we must keep it between us. Nobody can know, Jill. *Nobody*."

Jill nodded emphatically and hugged Susan. "Thank you so much, Susan. I'll tell Mom to call you, but she'll probably want to talk with you face to face."

Susan hoped she was doing the right thing and prayed Jill's mother would not be upset. If her mother agreed, Susan figured she'd probably have to tell Noah.

***

Jill's stomach was in a knot as she waited for her mother to come to the barn to pick her up. When she pulled in, the knot got tighter, and her stomach hurt when she opened the car door and lifted herself inside.

"How was your day, honey?" asked her mother.

"Fine," lied Jill.

During the short ride home, Jill was quiet. Out of the corner of her eye, she saw her mother glance at her several times. As soon as they arrived home, Jill jumped out of the car before her mother could ask questions. When her feet hit the ground, she saw Caleb tending to his gardens. He had a vegetable garden bordered with a thick row of flowers. He gave Jill and her mother free vegetables and lovely bouquets all season long.

"Afternoon, Jill. What a beautiful day. I sure hope ya had a good one."

Jill smiled. "I did, Caleb. I hope you did, too." Jill wondered if Caleb could tell that she was upset. Somehow, he always knew, and he was exceptionally talented at finding clever ways to get her to talk about it. She loved Caleb and she knew her mother did, too. Her mother didn't want her to call him Caleb. She preferred Mister Mackenzie, but Caleb said it made him feel old, so he insisted on Caleb.

Jill spent a few minutes by the garden with Caleb before she went into the house to wash up for dinner. At the table, she played with her food as she tried to come up with the perfect words to begin their conversation.

"What's on your mind, honey? You're very quiet tonight," said her mother.

"Nothing, Mom. I'm fine."

Her mother reached across the table and gently put her hand on top of Jill's. "Fine? I highly doubt that. You haven't eaten a bite and you keep putting your hand on your stomach."

Jill looked down and realized that her hand was resting on her belly. In her peripheral vision, she saw her mother lean back in her chair. She regarded her mother as a kind and generous person, but also practical. She had to convince her, just like the time she saved to buy an expensive backpack, but decided to instead give the money to a little boy in town who needed a bicycle because his was stolen and his parents couldn't afford to buy a new one.

"Mom, you remember Biz, right?"

"The new horse at the barn?"

"After I groomed him the other day, he rubbed his face on my shoulder. It felt like he was saying thank you. He's kind and gentle, and he appreciates everything I do for him."

Her mother raised one eyebrow. "And?"

"Mom, he's skinny and his owner won't pay for extra food. I asked Susan if I could pay, but she said no. Mom, I *really* want to. When I begged Susan, she asked to talk to you. Can I, Mom? *Please?*"

Her mother leaned forward, placed her elbows on the dinner table, and balanced her chin on her intertwined hands. "Honey, why would you want to pay to feed somebody else's horse?"

Jill started to cry. "Because they don't care about him. I just love him, Mom. He deserves a chance and I want to be the one to give it to him. Please let me do this. *Please!*"

Her mother frowned slightly. "What if you spend your money, and then his owner decides that he doesn't want you around Biz anymore?"

Jill felt her chest flinch. She never thought about that. What would she do if Mr. Ellington banned her from seeing Biz? "Mom, I can't imagine not being around Biz, but I wouldn't care about the money. I want to help him."

Jill saw the hesitation in her mother's eyes. She appeared to understand how much it meant to her, but she seemed troubled. Her mother took a big breath and sighed. "Look honey, I'm not saying no, but I'm not saying yes, either. I have to talk to Susan."

Jill felt her lips curl into a slight smile because her mother was at least keeping an open mind. After dinner, Jill did the dishes without being asked and then kissed her mother on the cheek. She started up the stairs to do her homework and then turned around. "Mom, promise me one thing. When you go to the farm to talk with Susan, please make time to visit Biz." Jill hoped with everything she held in her heart that when her mother saw him up close, she would understand.

Up in her room, Jill stood in front of her window, looking down at the barn, and off in the distance, she heard a barred owl. Her father loved owls and taught her how to identify the calls of each species in the area, especially his favorite, the barred owl. He said he was in awe of owls in general because they symbolized intuition, protection, wisdom, and truth. He loved barred owls in particular because they had such a presence. Tall. Upright. Broad-headed and camouflaged. They had brown instead of typical yellow eyes, and they were the most vocal of all owls. Her father thought they were spiritual. And he hoped that if there was life after death, he could come back as a barred owl, so he knew what it was like to fly. Soaring above it all, in inaudible flight. Stealthy and all-knowing. Each time he heard a barred owl, he stopped whatever he was doing and smiled. He even figured out how to do the nine-beat call: *who cooks for you? Who cooks for you nooow?* And he sometimes called back to them across the open fields.

~12~

The next morning, right after Jill left for school, Carol got dressed and drove down to Willow Bend. She wanted to know everything. When she walked into the barn, she was inundated with the smell of horses. She loved the smell so much that she stopped, closed her eyes, and inhaled. Her mind danced as she walked down the center aisle and looked at every one of the horses. She was mesmerized by their magnificence. As she passed each stall, the horse inside looked up. They were all different. All beautiful. Even as they simply ate breakfast. She loved the sound of them chewing.

The day Jill applied to work at Willow Bend, Carol went with her. They met in Susan's office and toured the facility, but the horses were all outside so Carol didn't experience what it was like to be in the barn when all the stalls were occupied. She understood why Jill cherished her time there. Following her initial visit to Willow Bend, when she dropped Jill off or picked her up, she didn't want to look like a helicopter mom, so she usually waited in the car. What a mistake! She made a mental note to go inside the barn more often, especially during breakfast or supper time, so she could see and smell the horses up close and listen to them eat. The sound was comforting and the look on their faces was calming. They seemed to savor every morsel. Carol was so enamored with the horses that she didn't hear anyone approaching.

"Can I help you?" asked one of the barn workers.

Carol quickly turned to face her. "Yes. I'm looking for Susan."

"I think she's in her office. I'll get her for you."

"Thank you very much. Please tell her it's Carol Ainsley, Jill's mother."

A few minutes later, Susan came around the corner. "Carol, it's so nice to see you!"

"I hope this is a good time. Jill said you needed to talk."

Susan smiled wryly. "Yes. It's perfect timing. Let's go to my office where we can speak privately. Have I told you how much I enjoy having Jill here? She's a great kid and a hard worker, but what I like most is that she's incredibly kind to the horses."

Carol nodded. "Thank you. It's always nice to hear. She's in love with horses, but she never took an interest in a horse the way she did with Biz. I want to know all about him."

Carol listened to every detail about Biz and his owner. She was impressed by Biz's reputation in the hunter-jumper show circuit, bewildered by his circumstances, and happy that Susan believed Jill was safe around him. She felt butterflies dance in her stomach when she asked if she could meet him.

"Yes, of course, you can. He's down back in his stall. I'll walk you there."

When Carol turned the corner and saw him up close for the first time, her heart jumped. Right away, she knew why her daughter insisted that she make the time to meet him. And why Jill was so drawn to him. Instantaneously, her mind drifted to Logan and his words echoed in her head.

Carol. Look! Can you see him out there? A tall chestnut with a white blaze and two white socks, and he's all ours. He sure is a beauty."

Biz's big, chocolate brown eyes seemed to stare right into Carol's soul. They were kind eyes; the type that made you want to touch his face.

"Oh my, I can see why she loves him. He's beautiful," said Carol. She felt her eyes fill with tears, but she couldn't stop smiling. Biz took a step closer to Carol as if asking her to touch him. She instinctively reached out and brushed his cheek. In return, he gently nudged her arm and immediately won her heart. Carol knew that one way or another, Biz would become part of their family. She just wasn't sure how.

Carol got Jill interested in horses because she loved them herself. She wanted one as a child, but her mother said they couldn't afford it. When she was old enough, she offered to get a job to pay for one, but her mother still said no. As an adult, Carol married young and never gave much thought to having a horse because she believed they were too expensive. She managed to put horse ownership out of her mind until she drove by a pasture and saw a horse running. It took her breath away and the image didn't fade from her memory for days. Carol dreamed of keeping a horse at home, but never told her secret dream to her husband. Later, when Jill was old enough to express an interest, they both wanted it for her.

"Call me crazy, but this feels like the right thing to do," said Carol. "There's just something about him. Jill cares about Biz. If it will make her happy, it's fine with me, but what about his owner?"

Susan looked around, probably to make sure nobody could overhear them, then took her by the arm and guided her back to her office and shut the door. "I have to be honest. He doesn't know anything about this, and I don't think he'd like it. He won't pay for extra food, but in his defense, he hasn't seen Biz in years, so he has no idea how he looks."

"He hasn't seen him in *years?* Does he care about him?" asked Carol.

"He sends a check every month and believes it should take care of all his needs."

"When did he last see him?"

"I really don't know. I can tell you with certainty that he hasn't seen Biz since he arrived here. And the driver who delivered Biz here said it was years since Biz had a visitor at his last barn."

"Well, somebody has to take care of him, so I guess we will. How much do you think the extra food will cost?"

Susan seemed puzzled by Carol's response. "Well, I'm not completely sure yet. I told Jill that it could cost as much as sixty dollars a month, but I have to figure it out. It definitely won't cost that much initially because we have to gradually increase his food, so he doesn't colic. Somewhere along the way, I'll be able to figure out when he starts to gain weight. So it could be that much, or it might be less. May I ask why are the two of you so taken with Biz?"

Carol sighed. "My husband, Logan, Jill's father, died suddenly two years ago when Jill was ten. Jill and her father were *extremely* close. Inseparable. Logan built a barn so Jill could get a horse and keep it at home. He envisioned a tall chestnut with a white blaze and two white socks standing in the paddock. He described the horse to Jill and always asked her to picture him standing under the big oak, waiting for her to come home from school. After he passed away, we didn't pursue it, mostly because I didn't think we could afford it. Jill even stopped riding lessons. That was when she decided to work in exchange for riding time, and I went back to work. I'm very lucky that I can work from home, doing medical coding and billing, but our barn is still empty."

"Oh, Carol. I was new to this area at that time, and I didn't hear about it. I'm so sorry," said Susan.

Carol looked down at the barn floor. "Me too. Jill loved her father so much, and Logan was crazy about her. She was everything to him. No one could make her laugh the way he did. He loved horses mostly because Jill loved them. He wanted her to have her dream. So do I."

When they finished talking, they agreed that Jill could groom Biz for one hour every day after school as long as her grades didn't suffer, and she could work late on Fridays to earn money to pay for Biz's grain, but it had to be their secret.

Before Carol left, she felt compelled to walk back to Biz's stall. He looked at her lovingly and she reached out and brushed his cheek with her fingers again. "You are such a handsome boy, Biz. I feel like I love you already. You're family now. We'll help take care of you."

Carol looked into Biz's inviting eyes and then kissed him on the nose. "I'll see you soon, Biz, and I'm sure Jill will come by to see you today, right after school."

We're not doing anything wrong, thought Carol as she walked to her car. We're doing the right thing by lending a hand to a horse in need, and it will help Jill in the process. It seems like a win-win to me, and if his owner gets upset, then so be it.

***

Susan thought about Carol and Jill for the rest of the day. She didn't have children of her own, but she understood Carol's need to help her daughter. She respected her for it, and her heart broke for Jill. When Carol described the horse Jill's father wanted to buy for her, she understood why they were enthralled with Biz. She wished she had a father like that.

Susan's father didn't die when she was young, but her parents got divorced when she was eleven and her father eventually disappeared from their lives. Susan understood how Jill felt because she experienced a similar void. Jill's father died, so when he left Jill, he didn't have a choice. Susan's father had a choice, and because of that, her feelings of abandonment were bitter.

Susan's love of animals got her through her childhood. Her mother let her have a cat and a dog, but she drew the line at a horse because they were expensive to buy and expensive to keep. Like Jill, Susan worked in exchange for time in the saddle. She didn't work in a big facility like Willow Bend. She cared for horses owned by people in and around her neighborhood and they paid her back by letting her ride. The neighbors taught Susan how to take care of horses, but she quickly learned that custodial care of horses was very different from nurturing a relationship with them. The horses taught her that. She followed their lead when it came to building trust and bonding. Susan taught herself how to ride by listening to what the horses told her. She watched their eyes and ears and listened to what they communicated through body language. She didn't have professional lessons until she was sixteen and had a part-time job to pay for them, but by then, she pretty much figured it out. She bought her first horse a year later and could hardly hold in her exuberance.

Her love for him made her want to live at home during her first two years in college. When she applied to colleges for her bachelor's degree in equine studies, she looked only at schools that had intercollegiate equestrian teams that allowed students to bring their own horses to campus. She was accepted to a school in New Hampshire, and after a screening process, her horse, Chance, was accepted as well. She graduated at the top of her class, summa cum laude, and was hired by a large riding stable near her school. She was paid a good wage to teach riding lessons and manage operations. A small apartment and one free stall for Chance were included. Six years later, after Chance died, she entertained other employment opportunities and found one closer to home in Massachusetts. Eventually, she ended up at Willow Bend with her lesson horses, Jayden, Duncan, Brooks, and Flash. Susan saw herself in Jill and wanted to help her.

***

Carol returned home and went directly into the barn to sit quietly on the handmade wooden tack trunk Logan made for Jill. From the moment Carol saw Biz, Logan was alive in her mind. Her rational mind knew it wasn't Logan's fault that he got sick and died, but emotionally, she felt forsaken, and it made her sad and angry. *How could you leave me and our baby girl?* thought Carol. Two years passed since his death, and she still felt incredible sadness when she thought about him. She knew Jill still grieved him, too, but it was hard to get her to verbalize it. As she sat, thinking, she heard someone come into the barn. Without looking, she knew it was Caleb.

"I saw you come in here a while ago, but I didn't see you come out, so I thought I'd check on you."

When Carol turned to face him, she tried to hide her teary eyes, but she knew by the expression on his face that she was unsuccessful.

"Carol, are you okay?"

Carol couldn't hold it in. "Oh, Caleb. I love this barn, but I hate that it's empty. That *wasn't* the plan. This barn was supposed to be home to a tall chestnut with a white blaze and white socks. What happened to our dream? Why did Logan die? How could he leave us?"

Carol put her hands over her eyes and sobbed.

***

Caleb felt his eyes fill with tears as he walked toward Carol to hold her. "Life isn't fair, Carol. Logan was too young. He deserved a long and wonderful life with you and Jill. He was like a son to me, and my heart aches every day. Sweetheart, they say time is supposed to heal all wounds, but in my experience, especially with Logan and my dear wife, Marion, I found that time helps, but the wound never really goes away. It's always there. Somehow, you learn to manage it, but some days are harder than others."

Caleb nervously fished a tissue from his pocket. When he handed it to Carol, she took it and blew her nose. Caleb put his arm around Carol's shoulder and squeezed in an attempt to reassure her that things would get better. When she looked up at him, she smiled ever so slightly, and he touched his index finger to the tip of her nose. "You know, Carol, you have to let yourself cry to get past the pain. I think you try to stay so strong for Jill that you forget to take care of yourself. You have to let it out. Please believe me, I know from experience."

Carol nodded. "Thanks, Caleb," she said as she leaned over to kiss his cheek. "You're right. I don't allow myself to cry enough. I'm always afraid Jill will see or hear me, and I don't want to make her any sadder. I think she's brave in front of me for the same reason. I guess we stay strong for each other. I'm not sure if that's good or bad."

Caleb exhaled. "There's no right or wrong way to grieve. Everybody does it differently, but if you both act brave all the time, you're not allowing yourselves to go through the process. It's important. Talk about it. Let Jill know how you're feeling, and she'll do the same."

Carol sniffled. "I have to wash my face before Jill gets home. It's hard to hide anything from her. Thanks for checking on me. You always know when we need you."

Caleb shook his head. "Don't hide it from her, Carol. If she sees you cry, it might give her permission to cry, too. Tears help heal the soul. Please try to remember that."

Carol sighed. "I'll try, Caleb, but old habits die hard."

Carol went into the house, but Caleb stayed put in the barn. He, too, sat on the wooden tack trunk Logan made for Jill and remembered how meticulously Logan crafted it. He made it out of maple and lined the inside with cedar so everything would smell crisp and clean. He used an oil finish on the outside, rubber seals to keep moisture out, and even created special removable compartments for her grooming supplies and tack. The finishing touch was when he engraved Jill's initials on the top. Caleb marveled at how important Jill's happiness was to Logan. Everything was done with so much love. As Caleb reminisced, he felt unexpected surges of grief and ire. The loss of Logan's life was an injustice. For Jill. For Carol. And for himself. It wasn't fair that he lost his wife and the wonderful young man he loved and regarded as a son.

Caleb's mind went to Jill. He knew something was on her mind and whatever it was, it was close to her heart and weighed heavily on her. Caleb had known Jill since the day she was born. Over the years, they had many talks. He was aware that when she was upset, she had a tendency to over-think things, and as her mind spun, she got a distant look in her eyes. Caleb knew that look and when she got out of the car yesterday, she had it all over her face.

Caleb wished Jill was more forthcoming about things that bothered her, but she held things close to the vest, so Caleb learned to become a detective of sorts. Sometimes it was a lengthy process, but he knew how to get Jill to talk. He knew he would eventually get to the bottom of it.

* * *

After Carol left Caleb in the barn, she headed into the house to make tea. She grabbed the kettle from the stovetop and stared out the window over the kitchen sink as she filled it. Her tears started to flow again, but she didn't try to stop them. In the privacy of her kitchen, she took Caleb's advice and let them pour until she felt like she couldn't possibly cry anymore. She cried so deeply that her body shook, but she barely made a sound. When she finished, she was sitting on the floor in front of the kitchen sink, leaning on the cabinets, exhausted. She summoned enough strength to stand and washed her face with ice-cold water. In a panic, she looked at the clock and relaxed when she realized she still had a half-hour before Jill got home from school. She wasn't hungry, but knew she had to eat. She made a small plate of cheese, crackers, and red grapes and brought it into her office where she distracted herself with work until Jill got home.

* * *

Jill got off the school bus and ran up the driveway, hoping that her mother had already spoken to Susan. She entered the house with such force that she lost her grip on the kitchen door, and it slammed open. The house was quiet except for the sound of the printer in her mother's office.

"Hi, honey, what are you doing home?" asked Carol. "Shouldn't you be at the barn?" Jill dropped her backpack on the kitchen table and walked toward the office.

"It's a weekday, Mom. I only work on weekends."

"Not anymore. You better get down there if you're grooming Biz after school."

Jill entered the office and her mother looked up with a twinkle in her eyes. "I spoke with Susan, and we agreed that in addition to grooming Biz on weekends, you can groom him for one hour every day after school, as long as your schoolwork doesn't suffer."

Jill smiled, and then put her head down. She was disappointed because she hoped for more. When she looked up, her mother smiled slyly. "Oh, and I almost forgot, we also agreed that you can work late on Fridays to earn money to pay for Biz's extra grain."

Jill squealed with joy and ran to hug her mother. As Jill released her embrace, she looked up and saw her mother's eyes overflowing with emotion.

Her mother swallowed. "I met Biz today. You're right. He *is* beautiful. His eyes looked right into my soul. I think I already fell in love with him. By the way, young lady, you didn't tell me that along with being a tall chestnut with a white blaze, he has two white socks."

Jill burst into tears and her mother held her close as they streamed down her cheeks. "That's why I asked you to make time to see him. I knew you'd understand. I feel so close to Dad when I'm with him."

Jill felt safe in her mother's arms, so she stayed there until her tears stopped flowing. When she finished, her mother wiped the dampness from her cheeks and kissed her on the forehead. "That's a good thing, honey. I felt close to Dad when I was with Biz today, too. So close that when I came home, I sat in the barn and cried."

Jill took her mother's hand. "Sometimes, when I'm all alone, I think about Dad, and I cry. I miss him. So much that it hurts."

"Me, too. But you know what? Dad would want us to take care of Biz, so let's honor Dad by doing exactly that. Biz is part of our family now, so you better get moving if you're going to have time to groom him today. But don't forget that I want you home in time for supper."

Jill nodded. "Thanks, Mom. I love you so much."

"I love you too, honey."

Jill put on her jacket and asked if she could walk to Willow Bend if she promised to stay off the road and take the narrow path Caleb cleared behind the houses alongside the farm.

Her mother nodded. "If you promise to stay off the road. Be home by five-thirty."

Jill felt the excitement build within her. She was going to the barn to be with Biz. She bolted out the door and as she skipped across the yard, she saw Caleb, weeding in his garden.

Caleb let out a laugh. "What in the world are you so excited about, Jill?"

"I don't have time right now, Caleb, but I'll tell you all about it soon. I promise."

Jill could hardly contain herself. She couldn't remember that last time she looked forward to anything so much.

* * *

Carol went out on the porch and watched Jill run to the farm. She ran so fast that she looked like she was flying, and Carol was captivated by the joy radiating from her.

"Okay, what's going on, Carol? When that kid came home yesterday and today, she was twisted in knots and now she's happy as a lark."

Carol laughed. "Yes, she was, and now she's positively giddy. I want to tell you all about it, but I think I should let her do that. She'd want to be the one to tell you. I think the news will make you happy."

Caleb looked at Carol and then looked toward Willow Bend. "Well, then I guess I'll just have to wait. It's not fair, but I will," he said sarcastically.

Carol grinned as she excused herself and went back into the house to make dinner. She knew Caleb wanted to know Jill's secret at that very moment. She closed the kitchen door and laughed because she knew it was driving him crazy. He and Jill were buddies. Sometimes even partners in crime. It was a blessing that Jill had such a wonderful father figure in her life. Caleb helped fill a void after Logan died. Jill never said it out loud, but Carol knew she thought of Caleb as a grandfather. She could talk to him about anything and often did. If it was something he thought Carol needed to be concerned about, Caleb quietly told her, and Carol appreciated it.

***

Biz watched Jill run up the driveway to the farm. As she made her way to the paddocks, he heard Jonas chuckle. "Here comes Jill, and she's smiling to beat the band. It looks like you have a new friend. Gosh, she's a nice kid. I think you'll do fine together."

Jill ran to the paddock fence. "Hey, Biz, I'll be back in a minute to get you. From now on, every day after school, I'm going to brush you and check your feet." Then she whispered, "And there will be a little something extra in your feed bucket tonight from me."

Biz perked up. Hmmm, something extra in my feed bucket? He looked over at Jonas and noticed that his eyes were dancing.

A few minutes later, Jill led Biz into the barn. "Are you hungry, boy? Don't worry. We should be done before supper, and I have hay cubes for you." She put Biz in the cross ties and then went to the tack room to get his brushes, hoof pick, hoof brush, and thrush medication. While she was gone, Biz's head started to spin. Should he allow himself to get close to Jill? What if she went away like everyone else? And what if she rode him and got hurt?

Biz calmed a bit when Jill returned and started grooming. It relaxed him, and he had to admit that he liked the attention. He was grateful to Jill because his foot didn't hurt anymore.

Jill was so meticulous about how she groomed Biz that it took her a full hour. She walked him back to his stall just as the rest of the horses came in for supper. As Luis and Günter passed by, Jill brushed Biz's cheek with her fingers, and then kissed him on the nose and whispered, "You'll have extra food every day. I'm working to pay for it because you need it."

Biz was confused. He didn't understand why Jill was paying for his food and wondered why Ashley and her family weren't paying for it. If they weren't, did it mean that Ashley didn't own him anymore? If not, who did?

***

Jill's secret might have been safe from people in the barn, but Luis and Günter heard what she said, and Jonas was appalled by what he heard them say.

"Did I hear right? The *poor* girl is working extra to buy food for Biz?" asked Günter.

"I thought I heard that, too," said Luis with pursed lips. "I wonder why his owner isn't paying. If he still has one."

"Poor horse, poor girl. They're definitely a pair," gloated Günter.

"His owner can't care about him. He's more out of shape than any horse I've ever seen," quipped Luis.

"He's skinny, too. He needs to put on hundreds of pounds to look right," said Günter.

Luis grimaced. "That girl can't help him. She has *no* money."

Abdul was silent, but from the way he shook his head, Jonas was sure that he was embarrassed for his friends and taken aback by their meanness.

Opal walked closer to Aiyana. "Aiyana, did you hear? Jill's working extra hours to buy food for Biz. What's up with that? Where's his owner? Honestly, I don't know why Jill's interested in him. He looks terrible."

Jonas saw Aiyana turn her head away, but Opal didn't seem to realize that Aiyana had no interest in what she had to say.

"Günter thinks Biz needs to put on hundreds of pounds. Can that be right? I mean, if Daniella thought I lost just ten pounds, she'd be worried sick. I have to look good, you know." Opal flexed her neck up and then back. When she did, it tossed her long cream-colored mane high in the air, and then it floated back down over her neck.

Aiyana grunted. Jonas could tell she was tired of Opal's shallowness. It troubled Jonas that Opal never expressed concern about the fact that Biz had an uncaring owner or that he was underweight. Everything seemed to be about her.

Aiyana looked at Opal and Jonas sensed that she was about to let Opal have it.

"Opal, if you lost ten pounds, would Daniella be worried about *you* or losing blue ribbons?" asked Aiyana. "Remember, she only wins if you *look* beautiful."

Jonas felt his eyes pop open. Her comment shocked him because Aiyana was usually kind and caring. Opal looked hurt and Aiyana immediately seemed ashamed.

"That was mean. Are you saying Daniella doesn't care about me?" asked Opal.

"No, but does she do *anything* with you that isn't in some way about winning ribbons?"

Opal stomped her foot. "Daniella cares about me. What's your problem?"

Aiyana faced Opal. "Biz had nobody. Now he has somebody. Why can't you just be happy for him? Why do you think you're so much better?"

"If Jill can't afford a horse, then she definitely can't afford a horse like Biz," said Opal.

Aiyana sighed. "Money isn't everything. Biz's owner could probably afford to throw all the money in the world at him, but Biz still wouldn't have anybody. Jill doesn't have much, but she's there for Biz and that's what he needs. It's what all of us need."

Aiyana turned away again, but Opal walked closer. "Aiyana?"

Aiyana snapped her head around. "What do you want?"

Opal took a step back. "Geez, you don't have to be so nasty. I just want to know why you think you know what Biz needs. I mean, how would you know? You're a top western barrel racer. You've been in the show circuit your whole life."

Aiyana glared at Opal. "Not *all* my life, Opal. I'm a mustang."

Opal tipped her head. "So?"

"I was once wild."

Opal gasped. "Wild?"

Aiyana took a step toward her window and looked outside. "Yes, wild; a herd of horses living on their own in wide-open fields ... the wilderness."

Opal looked bewildered. "On their own? You mean you didn't have an owner? No barn?"

Aiyana looked at the floor. "No owner and no shelter. We ran free until we were captured. After that, the government watched over us, but I still didn't have anybody. I didn't have an owner and I was separated from my mother, father, sisters, and brothers because they were auctioned to the highest bidder. I know what it's like to be alone, Opal. I'd rather have somebody to love me than have lots of money and still be lonely."

Jonas was astounded. He never knew Aiyana was once a *wild* mustang. He wondered how that felt. Would he like it?

"Why didn't you ever tell me?" asked Opal.

Aiyana looked exasperated. "Have you ever listened to yourself? When you, Günter, and Luis get going, you look down your noses at everyone. I didn't want you to make fun of me."

"Make fun of you?"

"Yes, because I don't have the right bloodlines, enough money, or the right owner. Ellen comes to see me as often as she can. She's not rich, but she loves me and we're happy."

Opal put her head down. "I'm sorry. I know you don't believe me, but I'm very sorry."

Jonas was pleased to see some humility in Opal, but he could tell that Aiyana wasn't impressed when she turned her back to her. "I just want to go to sleep now. I have a big day tomorrow. Good night, Opal."

Opal stepped closer. "Aiyana? Can I ask one more question?"

"What?" replied Aiyana with irritation.

"Do you ever wonder what would happen if you couldn't barrel race anymore?"

Aiyana continued to look out her stall window. "No. I never worry about that. Ellen said she's getting tired of shows. She wants to stop, take care of me, and just do some trail riding. I like barrel racing, but I love trail riding. It reminds me of my youth. I love it out there."

Opal walked to the window in her stall. Jonas saw her swallow hard as she looked up at the stars. After a while, she turned to Aiyana and spoke softly. "I can't remember the last time Daniella took me on a trail ride. I'm not even allowed to roll on the ground because I might get dirty and ruin my coat. All year long, I go outside with some kind of blanket. One stops my coat from being bleached by the sun. Another protects me from bug bites, and another prevents me from cutting myself if I roll on the ground. I mean, heaven forbid that I get a scar. Another one stops me from growing a long coat during winter. Even my treats promote healthy skin and a shiny coat."

Jonas saw Aiyana's mouth drop open and her eyes widen, and then felt his do the same.

"Aiyana, you asked me if Daniella does anything with me that isn't in some way about winning ribbons. I can't think of a thing."

Jonas always thought Opal was beautiful. Heck, he gazed at her all the time, but he also knew she was deeply in love with herself and had little compassion for others. For the first time, he was hopeful that she discovered the meaning of grace and would learn to treat others with respect and decency.

~13~

After the school bus dropped Jill off, she ran up the driveway, dragging her backpack behind her. She was out of breath by the time she got to the porch.

"What's the rush, sweetheart?"

Jill turned and saw Caleb seated in the rocking chair on his porch. "I'm in a rush because I have to get to the barn to brush Biz."

"Biz? Who's Biz?"

Jill realized that days before, she promised Caleb she would tell him what she was so excited about. "Caleb, I'm so sorry. I promised to tell you, but I forgot."

Caleb grinned. "That's okay, sweetheart. It happens. Tell me all about it now or tell me the quick version and fill in the details later if you have to be on your way."

Jill thought Caleb deserved to know all the details, so she went over to his porch and told him everything. "I can't wait for you to meet him, Caleb. As soon as you see him, you'll understand why I love him so much."

"I'm sure I will, sweetheart. I'm *very* happy for you. Now, go see Biz."

Jill jumped up and kissed Caleb on the cheek. "I have to get changed. I'll talk to you later."

"Have a good time but be careful. It's easy to get hurt around horses, especially when you don't know them well ... even when they're wonderful horses like Biz. All they have to do is spook. I saw it time and time again at our family farm."

"Don't worry, Caleb. I'll be careful."

Jill looked over at Caleb before she opened the door to go into the house. He waved and smiled back at her, then took a sip of lemonade and opened up the newspaper. He wasn't usually on his porch at that time of the day. Jill wondered if he planted himself there at the precise time when she got home from school, just so he could get her to tell him what was going on. She laughed quietly to herself. She knew she was right. He had a way of getting her to tell him everything.

~14~

Luis and Jonas were in adjoining paddocks. Luis sunned himself while Jonas quietly munched on hay. As Jonas chewed, he looked up and saw Luis staring at him. When their eyes met, Luis walked closer. *Hmmm, I wonder what this is about. Luis never wants to talk to me*, thought Jonas.

Luis told Jonas he was moving up a level in dressage training and had to eat breakfast at 6 a.m. the next morning so Sharon, his owner, could have him groomed and warmed up for his trainer. He confided, during what Jonas presumed was a moment of weakness, that he was nervous about this step up the ladder in competition. Sharon hoped to get to this point, and he didn't want to disappoint her. Luis explained that each advance in dressage training required him to use his body differently. Forward movement was supposed to come from impulsion from his hind legs, so his hamstrings and glutes got quite a workout. Jonas sympathized because he had to learn to use those muscles to pull Noah's big wagons. Luis described how precise the movements were and explained that his neck had to be more elevated and flexed, which made his shoulders ache. And the two bits used in the double-bridle made his mouth uncomfortable.

"Two bits? Lordy, that sounds awful," said Jonas.

"It is awful, but when I see my reflection in the mirrors in the indoor arena, I look so impressive that I can't believe it's me, so I guess it's worth it."

Jonas wasn't sure that it was, but if it made Luis feel accomplished, then maybe.

The next morning, Jonas saw Luis heading to the indoor riding arena. He could tell by the bounce in his step that Luis was excited, but he also looked tired. Jonas assumed that Luis was nervous and didn't get much sleep. After breakfast, Jonas went outside, and from his paddock, he had a clear view of the inside of the arena because the big doors on each end were wide open. He could hear just about everything, too, because the wind was blowing in his direction. He stayed close by because he wanted to watch Luis and learn more about upper-level dressage. Luis looked impressive, but he seemed stiff even after warming up.

"Come on, Luis, pick up your feet," said Sharon. "I don't want you to take *more* steps. I want each step to be *longer*. Please lengthen your stride."

About fifteen minutes later, Sharon's trainer, Lynne, arrived. She watched for a short time and didn't seem pleased. "He's just being lazy. Get that whip on him and make him move."

"I don't like to do that," said Sharon. "Besides, Willow Bend has rules about how whips are used."

"*Your* horse, *your* rules," quipped Lynne. "Don't baby him. Make him listen. He's being stubborn and he needs to know who's boss."

It looked like Sharon tapped the whip on Luis's shoulder because he startled and then sped up. It was clear that the whip made Luis nervous because he kept bending his head and neck to the side as if trying to see where the whip was. He seemed incapable of relaxing and unable to focus. Jonas felt uncomfortable as he watched.

***

Abdul heard a loud voice as he entered his paddock. He looked in the direction of the voice and saw Jonas standing silently at the far end of his paddock alongside the indoor arena. The voice intensified as Abdul walked closer to Jonas and its harshness sent a chill up Abdul's spine. When he reached where Jonas was standing, Jonas was so focused on what was happening in the arena that he didn't seem to know Abdul was there. Abdul gently pawed the ground to get his attention. "What's going on in there, Jonas?"

Jonas swallowed. "Luis's dressage lesson. His trainer isn't happy with him, and the lesson is about to go south. You might not want to watch this."

Abdul squinted his eyes and peered into the arena. He remembered how it felt when Melissa screeched at him. He remembered how frightened he was when she threatened him with the whip. He remembered how it stung when she hit him with it. The thought of it made him break out in a cold sweat and he felt his body stiffen from anxiety.

Abdul stepped close enough to Jonas to make their shoulders touch and it somehow made him feel safer. "Jonas, I feel bad for Luis. I can't believe Sharon's allowing Lynne to treat him like that. It makes me angry. I'd like to bust into that arena and trample Lynne."

Jonas raised his eyebrows and widened his eyes as he looked down at Abdul. "I can't believe you said that, Abdul. It's not like you."

Abdul lowered his head. "I know it isn't, Jonas. I would never actually do it, but I'd like to because I have no patience for meanness anymore. I lost it after my accident with Melissa. What's happening to Luis right now is how it all started for me that day. I know something bad is going to happen. I hear it in Lynne's voice, and I feel it in my stomach. It frightens me. And it makes me angry because it doesn't have to be that way."

Jonas nodded. "You're right. It *doesn't* have to be that way."

Abdul hoped he was wrong. He hoped Luis would be okay. He hoped nobody would get hurt. He wished Biz was with him and Jonas, but he was still in the barn, waiting for the farrier because he was due to have his hooves trimmed.

Lynne's voice interrupted his thoughts.

"Okay, Sharon. He's moving forward. Keep that momentum. Now, sit deep. Let him know that you want longer strides. Don't put up with his stubbornness. Make him listen."

Abdul could tell that Sharon was uncomfortable with Lynne's tone.

"Let's take a break, Lynne. Let me walk him around for a few minutes to see if I can get him to relax and settle down," said Sharon as she quietly walked Luis around the arena. When they passed by the arena doors, Abdul heard her talk softly to Luis. She gently rubbed his withers and his body loosened. "Come on, Luis. We've practiced this so many times. I know you can do it. What's wrong?"

Lynne disrupted their chat with a sudden clap of her hands. "Let's get going, Sharon. I have another lesson to get to in an hour."

Abdul wondered why Lynne was in such a bad mood.

Sharon gathered her reins and Luis's chest expanded as he took a deep breath. She pressed her legs against Luis's sides and asked him to move forward. Luis walked for a few strides, and then picked up a trot. When he was moving along well, Sharon sat deeper and asked him to lengthen his stride. He did, but apparently, it wasn't long enough for Lynne because she marched toward them. "Let me get on him. *I'll* make him do it," she snarled.

Abdul hoped Sharon wouldn't let Lynne ride Luis. Her reluctance was plain as day, but for some reason, she dismounted anyway. She paused before she handed the reins to Lynne and then looked at Luis apologetically. Luis closed his eyes and was visibly shaking when Lynne got on his back.

"You'll do what *I* tell you," growled Lynne.

"Be easy on him, Lynne. He's usually good about doing what I ask. He's not himself today. I'm not sure what's wrong. Maybe he doesn't feel well," pleaded Sharon.

"Nonsense. He's fine. He's just lazy," said Lynne as she gathered the reins and squeezed her legs. Luis's eyes were large, and his neck and head were upright. When Lynne squeezed her legs, he hesitantly moved forward and then picked up a trot. When Lynne asked for an extended trot, Luis looked like he couldn't because he was so tense. Lynne asked a second time with the same result and then used the whip. Abdul heard it snap on Luis's shoulder. He darted forward and as Lynne readied to snap it a second time, Luis bolted with enough force that Lynne lost her balance and fell off. When she hit the ground, Abdul felt nauseous and turned away. By the time Abdul mustered the courage to look back, Lynne was sitting on the ground and Luis was at the far corner of the arena, breathing heavily. Abdul could see the whites of his eyes and the veins on his neck were bulging.

Sharon ran to Luis. Her hands were visibly shaking as she took his reins. Her teeth were clenched, and her voice was raspy. "I'm glad you're okay, Lynne, but that's it for today."

Lynne stood up and walked toward her. "I'm not done! You can't let him leave the arena without making him do what you ask. If you do, next time, it'll be twice as hard."

"I said this lesson is *over*. You're *fired*," yelled Sharon.

Lynne turned crimson. "I'm fired? For what? Trying to make your horse into something he isn't capable of becoming?"

Sharon stepped close enough to Lynne that their noses almost touched. "You're fired because you're incompetent. Luis is very capable, you're just not a good enough trainer to help him realize his potential. My horse. My rules. Nobody is allowed to treat my horse like that. *Nobody*. Get out!"

Abdul was proud of Sharon when she stood with Luis as Lynne stormed out of the arena.

***

The rest of the horses finished breakfast and were out in the pasture by the time Sharon finished tending to Luis. She gently walked him outdoors and opened the gate to the paddock. When she released the lead rope to set him free, Jonas saw Luis gently rub his nose on Sharon's shoulder, and then walk over to Günter.

"How'd the lesson go?" asked Günter as he sunned himself with his eyes closed.

Luis stretched his nose into the air. "Awful. That trainer is a *witch*."

"I guess upper-level dressage training is going to be more difficult than you thought, eh, Luis?" snickered Günter.

"I can take difficult, but not whippings."

Günter shifted his head in Luis's direction and opened his eyes just enough to see. "Whippings?"

Luis looked at Günter. "Yes, *whippings*. That witch whipped me twice. The last time was so hard that I bolted, and she hit the ground."

Günter faced Luis with an amused expression on his face. "You *dumped* the trainer?" he laughed, sounding half-shocked and half-amused. "Ohhh, you are in *big* trouble now. Wait until your next training session. That whip will have your name all over it."

"It already does, Günter. Look at my shoulder," barked Luis.

Günter glanced at his shoulder and seemed unimpressed. "That does look sore but get ready because the welts will be twice as big next time."

"There won't be a next time. Sharon fired her."

Günter pulled his neck back and scrunched his forehead. "*Fired* her? Why? Just because she hit you with the whip? My trainer uses a whip all the time. Sometimes as a reminder, and sometimes when he's mad. But he's the best show-jumping trainer around, so Thomas would *never* fire him."

"Well, isn't that just too bad for you," snapped Luis with a stare so intense that his eyes grew dark, and he lowered his head and walked to the far end of the paddock, probably to distance himself from Günter. Jonas could tell that Luis was disgusted with Günter. And from the way Luis lowered his shoulders, Jonas presumed he was bewildered by Günter's lack of support.

The next day, Jonas was out in the field with Noah, training with a plow for the annual pulling contest at the harvest fair. When finished, Noah hosed him off with cool water to get the sweat off of him, brushed him, and picked out his hooves. He pulled a carrot out of his pocket and gave it to Jonas before he walked him over to his paddock, opened the gate, and told him to relax for the rest of the day and enjoy some green grass. As Jonas entered, he saw Luis in the adjacent paddock. Luis, who usually stood tall, was hunched over. Jonas sensed that Luis needed to talk, so he strolled closer to the paddock fence.

Without making eye contact, Luis said, "Good morning, Jonas."

Jonas was surprised that Luis spoke first. In the past, Luis made it clear that an upper-level dressage horse like himself simply did not mingle with workhorses. Jonas felt his eyebrows raise. "Morning, Luis. What's up?"

Luis turned slightly toward him. "Nothing much."

Jonas glanced in Günter's direction. "How come you're not with your buddy, Günter?"

Luis stamped his foot. "Because there are some things he doesn't understand." Luis turned and glowered at Günter, who was staring defiantly in their direction.

Jonas figured that Luis didn't know he saw the whole thing, so he asked about the welts just in case Luis wanted to talk.

"Did Sharon do that to you?" asked Jonas.

Luis turned, saw Jonas staring at his shoulder, and immediately looked at the ground. "No, Jonas. Sharon would never hurt me."

"Then who?"

"That witch, Lynne."

"The trainer? What happened?"

Luis took a deep breath and his cheek muscles tightened like he was holding back tears. "It's a long story, Jonas. I wasn't on top of my game, so Lynne got kind of rough, and she eventually ended up on the ground."

Jonas spoke softly. "And how do you feel about that?"

Luis lowered his shoulders. "I don't feel bad about Lynne, but I'm afraid that I let Sharon down. Moving up a level is important to her. Now she has to find another trainer before we can start instruction again."

Jonas tipped his head. "Another trainer?"

Luis lifted his head into the air, shifted his gaze toward Jonas, and clenched his jaw. "Yes. Sharon *fired* that witch."

Luis was so animated that it made Jonas chuckle. "Well, that's good news. Maybe you'll like the new trainer and make progress."

Luis seemed lost in thought. "It is good news ... I guess. But I don't understand, Jonas. If Sharon would never whip me, why did she hire a trainer who thinks it's okay? Lynne hit me hard. My skin is broken."

Jonas was pleased to finally see the unassuming side of Luis. He understood what Luis was asking, but there was no easy answer. "That's complicated."

"It's complicated? Jonas, I have all the time in the world. *Please* enlighten me with your sage wisdom."

Jonas ignored his sarcasm. "I'm willing to bet that Sharon's gut told her not to let Lynne ride you, but she shut off her instincts and bowed to the wishes of the so-called expert."

Luis nodded. "She's an expert, all right ... in brute force."

Jonas sighed. "Not all trainers are good ones, but because they have that title, people listen to them instead of their gut. Your mind can play tricks on you, and your heart can lead you in the wrong direction, but your gut never lies. It *always* speaks the truth."

Luis rolled his eyes. "Spare me the poetics."

Jonas laughed. "It's true, Luis. If I had a flake of hay for every time I saw a trainer do something that made someone put a hand on their stomach, I'd never be hungry. Their gut tells them the trainer's wrong, but they don't stop it, and someone always gets hurt. The important thing is that Sharon fired her. She made things right. Try to focus on that. Everybody makes mistakes. What matters is whether or not you learn from them. It sounds like Sharon did."

Luis looked into Jonas's eyes. "Just exactly how do you know so much, Jonas? What makes you so wise?"

Jonas was taken aback because it sounded like Luis admired him. "Wise? I don't know about that. I just watch, listen, and learn," said Jonas as he meandered to the other end of the paddock. "Try to relax and enjoy the sun today, Luis. It's beautiful out. Live in the moment."

Biz's Journey Home

Jonas munched on the grass and thought about his life. Noah was good to him. He never yelled or swore at him. He never hit him, and he never carried a whip. Even before Noah owned him, he never had to deal with an abusive or neglectful owner or trainer. He wondered why he was so lucky. So blessed.

***

Jill finished her barn work just as Biz finished supper. She headed to his stall to put him in the cross ties but decided to take him outside first. "Let's take a walk, Biz. I'll show you where I live. Did you know that you can see my house from here?"

As they meandered down the driveway, Jill stopped and picked dandelions for him. "These are supposed to be excellent for aches and pains, Biz. They taste good, too. My mother sometimes makes a salad with them. I like the flower buds best."

At the end of the driveway, Jill pointed. "See that red house way over on the left? My mom and I live there. It's a small house with lots of daisies. Shasta daisies and my mother's favorite, Montauk daisies. Mom loves the Montauks because the leaves are beautiful, and they bloom from late summer into fall. My dad planted them for her. Just behind them, he planted a birch tree for himself because birches were his favorite tree. We have four acres of land and the two-stall barn my dad built so I could get a horse. We named our farm Tartan Glen because we're Scottish and our farm sits down in a little valley. My dad died two years ago, and the barn is empty, so it's just me and Mom. My dad would have loved you, Biz. He loved big chestnut horses with white blazes and white socks. My mom loves horses, too. She's the lady who came to see you the other day. My mom said you have eyes that look right into a person's soul. She said she couldn't help but touch your face."

Jill looked toward her house, and out of the corner of her eye, she saw Biz tip his head and look at her with his dark brown eyes. She turned and smiled at him. "I love you, Biz. If you ever need me and I'm not here at Willow Bend, that little red house is probably where I'll be."

When they got back inside the barn, Jill put him in the cross ties and headed to the tack room for his brushes, hay cubes, and a peppermint.

***

While Biz waited for Jill to return, he thought about their jaunt down the driveway. He was sad that Jill lost her dad. He wondered what he was like. He could tell that Jill loved him a lot. Biz knew he was a good father if he went to the trouble of personally building a barn so his little girl could have a horse. Biz liked the fact that Jill lived so close to Willow Bend and he liked her house. He could tell that it wasn't just a house. It was a home that looked warm and inviting. He wondered if he could live with Jill and her mother someday. The very thought thrilled him because, since he met them, he realized that he was tired of being alone. He needed someone like Jill, and he was glad that she kind of adopted him. The idea of being the only horse at a real home, not a stable, and being loved by *two* people, seemed wonderful. A dream come true. Since he was a year old, except for when he was with Maggie, he lived in one training barn after another. He wanted a home again … to belong.

~15~

As time went by, Susan became attached to Jill. She was a great kid. Polite, kind, and completely dedicated to Biz. Jill seemed to wear her heart on her sleeve when it came to Biz and Susan was beginning to feel protective of her. She wondered if Mr. Ellington would ever consider selling Biz to Jill. She worried that if he didn't, Biz and Jill would both end up with broken hearts.

As a businesswoman, Susan knew that the more Jill paid to feed Biz, and the more she walked him up and down the driveway for exercise, the more he'd be worth. She was afraid Jill would help improve his condition to the point that he'd be worth more than she could ever afford to pay. She knew that if Jill was going to buy Biz, it had to be soon. Very soon.

As Susan devised a plan, she asked herself why she allowed herself to become so committed to Jill, but she knew the reasons didn't matter. In her heart, she believed it was a mission somehow assigned to her and she intended to carry it out. Her first step had to be a phone call to Jill's mother, to ask if Jill could buy Biz if Mr. Ellington was willing to sell him. She knew it was a long shot because Biz wasn't part of the Ellington family; he was an investment, pure and simple, and Mr. Ellington would likely want top dollar. It would be an uphill battle to convince him that Biz wasn't worth much.

* * *

Carol was at her computer when Susan called. Her question took Carol's breath away. She didn't think owning Biz was a possibility. Her mind started to race. Of course, she wanted Jill to have Biz, but it was so unexpected. She had *so* many questions. How much would they sell him for? Could they afford to buy him? How much would it cost to keep a horse at home? What about veterinary bills?

"Susan, I don't know if we can afford a horse. I honestly don't. I guess I convinced myself a long time ago that we couldn't, so I never actually looked into how much it costs to purchase a horse and take proper care of it at home."

Susan laughed. "I'm so sorry, Carol. You must feel like this question is coming out of left field, but I think Jill and Biz belong together. They're like two peas in a pod and it's clear that they love each other. They *need* to be together and I'm ready to help any way I can."

Carol was excited about the possibility of having Biz become part of their family but scared to death about the financial commitment. "Susan, I want this for Jill more than anything, but this seems sudden. Rushed."

Susan sighed, and then explained why she felt Jill needed to buy Biz sooner rather than later. "Carol, don't worry about the cost of the horse. If we can get him for around one-thousand dollars, I'll buy him myself and let Jill pay me back a little at a time. As for the cost of owning a horse, it's much more affordable to keep one at home instead of a facility. I've seen your farm from a distance. If you can afford a couple of hundred dollars to put electric fencing around your pasture, you can save a fortune on stall bedding and hay."

Carol could hardly contain her joy. "Thank you, Susan. I would never expect you to pay for Biz, but I do appreciate your offer. I can afford to pay that much for Biz. And we can afford to put up the electric fence."

Susan went on to explain that horses generally need shoes if they have weak hooves that break and chip easily, or they are worked so much that they wear their hooves down faster than they grow. "Biz has healthy strong hooves. If you let him go barefoot, you can save significantly on the cost of shoeing. A barefoot trim will cost forty or fifty dollars every six weeks or so."

Carol was feeling more enthusiastic by the moment. "We can afford that."

Susan continued. "Okay, then if you figure in a little bit of money for bedding, as well as hay, grain, worming medicine, fly spray, hoof trimming, and a little bit to set aside for the veterinarian, I'd say putting three-hundred and fifty dollars aside every month would do it, *but* don't forget that you can always rent your other stall for additional income. That money would cover all of your expenses with plenty left over, and Biz would have company."

Carol heard the excitement in Susan's voice as she presented options. "That's a *very* interesting idea, Susan. I never thought about renting a stall. I can't believe it. Maybe we really can afford it, but please don't say anything to Jill in case this doesn't work out. I'd hate to get her hopes up, only to find out that she can't have him."

Susan agreed.

Carol was so excited when she hung up the phone that she put on the radio and danced in her office. It felt good to turn the music up and move to the beat. She couldn't remember how long it had been since she danced in celebration, but she knew it was way too long. How wonderful it would be to have Biz at home! She walked to the kitchen window, opened it, and stared at the barn and the part of the yard that would become the paddock. It was so easy to picture Biz looking back at her from under the shade of the big oak tree. Carol knew Jill would be ecstatic if Susan could pull this off. Carol was elated for Jill, as well as her own inner child, who couldn't wait for Biz to be with a family that loved and cared about him. When Carol met Biz, it was love at first sight. Having him in the barn would fulfill a lifelong dream for her and make her daughter the happiest kid in the world. Carol told herself not to get her hopes up, but it was already too late for that.

***

Out in the garden, Caleb heard music. He stood and listened. When she was alive, he and his wife attended concerts all the time. They liked all kinds of music: country, folk, rock and roll, jazz, blues, classical, symphony, and even opera. In his house, he played the radio softly because it was soothing, but he hardly ever heard music when he was outside. He turned to figure out where it was coming from. When he realized the tunes were coming from right next door through the open kitchen window, he smiled. It was a good sign.

When Logan was alive, he played music all the time. He had a radio plugged in the whole time he built the barn. Caleb remembered that he tended to play rock and roll as he hammered. He wondered if the beat motivated him and helped him keep going even when he was fatigued.

Over the past few weeks, he thought about Logan much more than usual. But what he was experiencing was much more than just thoughts. He *felt* Logan's presence. Sometimes it was as if Logan was standing right in the room with him. It was comforting, but it still made his heart hurt because he missed everything about Logan. Caleb particularly loved it when Logan asked him for advice. Looking back, he realized that it made him feel more like a father than a neighbor. He missed helping him with projects. He missed the insightful conversations they often had. He missed Logan's smile. His laugh. The twinkle in his eyes. And he missed his music. But Carol's music sounded pretty good, too. Loud music meant she was happy. He hoped she was singing and dancing.

***

Susan called Mr. Ellington. No one answered so she left a message, asking him to call her back. She was surprised when he called back promptly. "Is there something wrong with our horse?" he asked. He seemed shocked when she asked if he would sell Biz. When he said he wanted ten thousand dollars, Susan was stunned and politely told him that was way too much.

"Do you have any idea what I paid for that horse?" asked Mr. Ellington.

Susan was beginning to understand that the conversation was not going to go well, but she continued. "With all due respect, Mr. Ellington, Biz is fifteen years old now. He's completely out of shape and underweight. He's not worth that much."

Mr. Ellington was silent for a second and then barked, "That horse is worth at least ten thousand and maybe more."

Susan took a deep breath. "Mr. Ellington, I run a show barn. I know what people pay for top show horses that are younger and in much better condition. I'm telling you that Biz is not worth that much."

"You're ridiculous. Are you trying to steal him from us?"

Susan felt her eyes pop. She wanted to scream at him for insulting her yet again, but she held her tongue because, in the back of her mind, she heard her mother saying that you get more flies with honey than vinegar. After a moment of silence, she said in a firm, but reasonable tone, "Mr. Ellington, why would you insult me like that? I don't need to steal horses. I run this farm, and believe it or not, people offer me good horses for free all the time simply because they can't afford to keep them anymore."

Susan heard Mr. Ellington take a breath. "I didn't mean to insult you. If you're so knowledgeable about the worth of horses, what would you estimate his value to be?"

Susan closed her eyes before she spoke. "At best, fifteen hundred dollars."

Mr. Ellington swore under his breath. "What? That's outrageous. If he's only worth that much, then tell me how he got in such bad shape. Are you not taking proper care of him? I send a check every month that should more than take care of his needs. There's money for his stall, food, horseshoeing, and grooming. This is preposterous. I should sue you for neglect. As a matter of fact, I should sue you personally, *and* sue your establishment."

Susan felt adrenalin course through her body. She was shocked by his threats and bewildered by his accusation. She counted to ten to calm down, but she heard the anger in her voice as she started to speak and decided to just let him have it. "Mr. Ellington, how *dare* you threaten me. If you want to sue someone for neglect, sue yourself. Biz came here in this condition. When he arrived, I was told by the driver from his previous barn, that they repeatedly asked you to pay for extra food because he was losing weight, but you refused. According to him, you said that if he wasn't exercising, there was no need for extra food. He said you accused them of trying to scam you. Sounds familiar, doesn't it, Mr. Ellington? I told you Biz needed more food, and you accused me of the same thing. Let's be clear. The only person neglecting Biz is *you*. Yes, you include a very small amount in his board check for grooming, but as you know, *because it's in the contract,* you send only enough to cover grooming once a week, and that's just not enough."

Mr. Ellington was silent, but Susan heard his labored breathing. She assumed it was because he didn't like her tone, but she didn't care. "Mr. Ellington, do you remember that I called you when Biz first arrived at Willow Bend? You told me you didn't want him outside with other horses. You said you were protecting your investment because you were afraid he'd get kicked or injured and lose his value. I had to *beg* you to let me pair him up with Jonas in the pasture. During that call, I told you that he was thin and needed extra food, but *you* refused. Then I called you to offer free exercise so he could build some muscle. *You refused again!* You said he could get hurt if he was exercised or used for lessons. Do you remember? Do you remember any of that? I hope you do because I have it all documented. What the driver told me and what you said to me is *all* documented."

Mr. Ellington remained silent, so Susan continued.

"The *truth,* Mr. Ellington, is that Biz loses value every day because he's wasting away. You're *making* him waste away because you *refuse* to let him have access to extra food and exercise. Tell me, Mr. Ellington, are you basing his value on how he looked the last time you saw him? If so, I understand why you think he's worth more. From what I've been told, you haven't laid eyes on him in years. When *was* the last time you saw Biz, Mr. Ellington? Can you even remember?"

Mr. Ellington cleared his throat. "I can't recall."

"*Shocking.* Take a ride down here and then maybe you'll understand. Can you do that, Mr. Ellington? Can you take a ride down here to take a look at your *investment*?"

Mr. Ellington was quiet for what seemed like an eternity. "Look, I have a busy office. I don't have time to go to a stable to look at horses. I'll send my wife. She'll call you to set up a time," he said before he slammed down the phone.

Susan visibly shook when she put down the receiver. *Sue me? Sue Willow Bend? For neglect? Seriously? Who does he think he is?* thought Susan as she paced around her office. She hoped she didn't blow it by exploding on Mr. Ellington, but what did he expect? She wondered what she would do if he retaliated and moved Biz to a different barn. The thought terrified her, and she wondered if he was ever accused of neglect in the past and moved Biz in response.

Since Noah owned Willow Bend, and Mr. Ellington threatened to sue the establishment, Susan knew she had no choice but to call Noah and tell him what Mr. Ellington said. Since she started working for Noah, they never argued. In truth, she couldn't ask for a better employer. She didn't want him to be angry with her, nor did she want to disappoint him. She felt sick as she dialed his number. After she told Noah the story, she could tell that he was not happy.

"Tell me again why you called him," said Noah.

Susan reiterated the whole story about Biz, Jill, Carol, and Mr. Ellington.

"I wish you consulted me about this, Susan. I understand that you're trying to do a good thing, but I should have been informed."

Susan tried to hold back her emotions, but she felt her throat tighten as she spoke. "I know that now. I'm so sorry, Noah. I never dreamed something like this would happen."

Noah sighed. "I know you didn't. Look, I don't disagree with what you're trying to do. I guess I even applaud your efforts, but I don't like being threatened with a lawsuit any more than you do. For the record, I looked at Biz when he arrived at Willow Bend, and I've seen him out in the pasture. He has a nice disposition, but I think he's the most out-of-shape horse I've ever seen. Mr. Ellington's dreaming if he thinks he's worth ten-thousand dollars. Your estimate is dead on. Thanks for calling so quickly to let me know what he said, even though you knew I might be upset with you."

Susan felt herself relax when Noah's voice softened. "Thanks, Noah. I'm sorry. I really am. The last thing I'd ever want to do is disappoint you. I respect you and enjoy working for you. I have no desire to find another job."

Noah took a deep breath. "Jeez, Susan. There's no need to be fearful. I'm not firing you. You're the best barn manager I've ever had. Listen, don't worry about him. He's a jackass and he doesn't have a legal leg to stand on. If he thinks he's going to sue us for neglect, he's barking up the wrong tree and he'd be wasting his precious money. If you hear from Mrs. Ellington, let me know, and please keep me informed. Now, put this out of your mind and try to have a pleasant night."

Susan felt herself smile slightly. "I will. I promise, Noah, and again, I'm so sorry."

"Susan, my father used to say that no good deed goes unpunished. Your concern for horses is what makes you good at what you do. Sit tight. Now we wait."

When she got off the phone with Noah, Susan sat for a few moments to collect herself, and then she called Carol to let her know what happened. Carol gasped when Susan told her what Mr. Ellington said. "He threatened to sue you and Willow Bend? Honestly, Susan, that man doesn't deserve Biz."

"I know, Carol. Now we have to wait for Mrs. Ellington to call. I'll keep you posted. Listen, I know the situation sounds bleak, but I still have a good feeling. Call me crazy, but I do. I'll call you as soon as I know anything."

Susan was grateful that Noah was so understanding and forgiving. His words echoed in her head. It was time to sit tight and wait. But waiting was the hardest part.

A few days later, Susan finally heard from Mrs. Ellington, who said she would be down the following Saturday around four o'clock. Susan knew she had to make sure Jill was not at the barn when Mrs. Ellington arrived, so she asked Carol to keep her busy. She figured that Jill wouldn't be happy about being away from the barn on a Saturday, but if all went well, it would be worth the sacrifice.

Mrs. Ellington arrived, and her smile dropped at the sight of Biz. "Oh my goodness. What happened to him? This horse used to be absolutely gorgeous."

Susan could see that she was truly concerned. "When Biz arrived here, he looked pretty rough. He was very underweight. The driver who delivered him to us said Mr. Ellington refused to pay for extra food, so Biz lost weight. And he didn't want Biz exercised, so he lost muscle. He said Mr. Ellington only included enough in the monthly board check for Biz to have his hooves picked out and his coat brushed once a week and he was moved here because the board was less expensive."

Mrs. Ellington looked like she wanted to cry.

"My instructions from Mr. Ellington were the same as what the driver explained. I told your husband that Biz needed to put on weight, but he refused to pay for extra food and accused me of trying to scam him out of money. I also asked if someone could ride him to help build up his muscles. He refused, saying he didn't want Biz to get injured and lose his value."

Mrs. Ellington clenched her jaw before she spoke. "I can't believe how bad he looks. Who would ever want him, looking like that?"

Susan was grateful that Mrs. Ellington understood that Biz needed more than was being provided and felt a slight smile form on her face as she started to tell her about Jill. "I'm so glad you asked that question, Mrs. Ellington, because a young girl who works here loves Biz. She even offered to work extra hours to pay for his grain because she knows he needs it."

Mrs. Ellington put her hand to her face. "She's willing to work to feed *our* horse? I feel so ashamed."

"She'd love to own him, Mrs. Ellington, but as I explained to your husband, in his condition, at best, he's worth fifteen hundred dollars. Your husband thinks Biz is worth much more than that, but he's not. Truly, he's not."

Mrs. Ellington looked deeply troubled as she nodded. "I have to discuss this with my husband, but I promise to get back to you within a couple of days, Susan. Thank you for calling. I'm so glad I came to see him."

Before Mrs. Ellington left, she took one more look at Biz and Susan could tell that she was truly remorseful. She was glad that she called Mr. Ellington because she knew Biz would at least get the extra food and exercise he needed.

Three days later, Mrs. Ellington called Susan and said she could not get her husband to go lower than three-thousand dollars. "He said we'll have to pay extra for his food and get someone to exercise him, so we can sell him for more money."

Susan closed her eyes. Three-thousand dollars was twice his worth, but at least Jill would own him, and his life would improve dramatically. She asked herself if she should accept the offer or stick to her original plan. As her mind raced through the many ways the situation could play out, she felt her hands start to sweat. When she looked down, she had unconsciously squeezed her hands into fists from anxiety because Biz's life and Jill's heart were both in jeopardy. "You can do that, Mrs. Ellington, but you're looking at a minimum of six months of work and food to help get Biz back into shape."

"That's okay. We've got the time," said Mrs. Ellington.

Susan exhaled. "Yes, but those six months bring added expenses. From a business perspective, it makes no sense."

"I don't understand."

"Mrs. Ellington, you're paying six-hundred dollars a month to keep Biz here. Over those six months, you'll pay thirty-six hundred for board, plus extra money for the farrier, additional food, the vet, *and* for someone to exercise him. You'll end up paying over six-thousand to make three-thousand" said Susan.

Mrs. Ellington sighed. "We didn't think about that. You're probably right, Susan. I'll have to call you back, but before I hang up, please tell me about the young girl who loves him."

Susan was relieved that Mrs. Ellington couldn't see her face over the phone, because she couldn't stop grinning. "Her name is Jill. She's thirteen years old and she cleans stalls here in exchange for riding lessons. She has taken riding lessons and worked in various barns since she was six years old, but she never took an interest in a horse the way she did with Biz."

"She cleans stalls in exchange for lessons?" asked Mrs. Ellington.

"Yes. Her father built a barn so she could get a horse, but he died two years ago."

"Can she afford Biz?"

"Her mother believes they can," said Susan. "Her mother can pay for Biz, but if you are willing to sell him, I'm also willing to pay for him, and let Jill pay me back a little at a time."

With warmth in her voice, Mrs. Ellington said, "You must really believe in this young woman and truly trust her, if you're willing to do that."

Susan felt her eyes glaze. "That goes without saying. She's a great kid, and I believe she and Biz are meant to be together."

"Is she a good rider, Susan? In his younger days, Biz was rambunctious."

"She's a very confident rider and an excellent horse handler."

"Our daughter, Ashley, got hurt on Biz not long after we bought him. He was too much for her and she became afraid to ride. I don't want another young girl to get hurt."

Susan wondered if that was the real reason Mr. Ellington didn't want Biz exercised. He was afraid someone would get hurt and they would be liable. "That's understandable and I appreciate your concern for her, but Biz is older now and much more sensible. He has impeccable manners and he's respectful."

"Yes, but as he gets in shape and feels better, he might get spunky again. Are you sure she'll be safe on him?" asked Mrs. Ellington.

"I'm positive that she'll be safe on him," said Susan. "There's a great deal of trust between them, and from what I've seen, he'll take good care of her."

"Then I'd like to meet her, if I may," said Mrs. Ellington.

"Of course, you can meet her. I would like that, too, but I must caution you that she knows nothing about this. Her mother and I didn't want to say anything until we knew whether or not you would consider selling Biz. We didn't want to get her hopes up."

Mrs. Ellington promised not to say a word, so Susan told her the days and times when Jill was at the barn. Mrs. Ellington said she'd come by the following weekend after Sunday dinner when Jill would be grooming Biz.

Before Mrs. Ellington hung up, Susan felt compelled to ask her about Ashley. "Mrs. Ellington, if you don't mind me asking, does your daughter know about this? I ask because I don't want Jill to get hurt, should Ashley decide to keep him."

"Oh, don't worry about that, dear. Ashley has no interest in horses anymore. It's been years since she even mentioned Biz's name."

"Then why did you keep Biz all these years?"

"The answer to your question is simple and complicated. Snuggles was her very first pony. To say that they were inseparable is an understatement. We bought Biz because Ashley grew too big for

Snuggles, but her attachment to Snuggles never wavered. She loved that pony with all of her heart and cried uncontrollably when he died. I guess I didn't want her to lose Biz too. I hoped she would ride again someday, but it's obvious that we waited too long, and Biz is the one who paid the price. I don't know if I'll ever get over how much we let him down. It feels unforgivable."

Susan didn't know what to say.

As soon as Mrs. Ellington hung up, Susan called Noah to fill him in. He was pleased with how things were progressing and wished her luck. When their conversation ended, Susan called Carol.

"Should I be there when Mrs. Ellington meets Jill? I want to be there, but I don't want her to feel like we're putting pressure on her. What are your thoughts?"

Susan told Carol that since Mrs. Ellington just wanted to meet Jill, she didn't see a need, but if there was another meeting, Susan wanted her present.

~16~

Around mid-afternoon on Sunday, Susan was out in the pasture when she saw Jill leisurely walking Biz to the end of the driveway, picking greens along the way. The greens were hanging out of Biz's mouth so Susan assumed they were dandelions. Biz loved them. As she watched Jill, a car turned into the driveway. She was pleased when Jill automatically guided Biz to the side to let the car pass. Susan didn't think it was Mrs. Ellington because it was still early, but she kept her eyes on the car, trying to see who was driving. The driver parked the car, but no one got out. When Jill started to walk Biz back toward the barn, the driver's side door opened, and an older woman got out. Susan assumed it was Mrs. Ellington, so she got back to the barn as fast as she could and reached the main entrance just as Jill encountered her.

"Can I help you?" asked Jill.

"Yes, I'm looking for Susan," said Mrs. Ellington.

"I'll get her for you right away," said Jill.

Jill turned toward the barn and saw Susan. "I was just about to go and find you, Susan. You have a visitor," she said as she walked Biz inside to put him in the cross ties. She was busy brushing Biz when Susan and Mrs. Ellington approached her.

"Jill, this is Mrs. Ellington," said Susan as she purposely raised her eyebrows.

Jill froze. "Biz's owner?"

Mrs. Ellington smiled. "Yes, Biz's owner," she said in a firm, but pleasant tone. "I understand you've been paying for extra food for Biz."

Jill looked frightened and turned to Susan before she answered. Susan nodded that it was okay to answer honestly.

"Yes, I have. I hope you don't mind," said Jill.

"No, dear, I don't mind. You must love him very much."

Jill's eyes lit up. "I love him *so* much. He just loves everything I do for him. He has a big heart and just needs someone to love him." Jill looked panicked as soon as the words tumbled from her mouth. Right away, Susan knew Jill was frightened that she offended Mrs. Ellington.

Mrs. Ellington reached out and touched Jill's shoulder. "Don't feel bad, dear. You're right. He does need someone to love him. Nobody in our family has been to see him in a very long time. If we had, we would have seen that he was losing weight and we would have found the thrush. I assume you're the one who found that and treated it."

Jill nodded. "Yes, I did."

"And I hear that you've been grooming him?"

"Yes, but I haven't ridden him," said Jill. "I wanted to, but the most important thing was to make sure that he was okay."

"And I thank you for that. You've taken such good care of him for us."

Jill put her head down. "You're welcome. I don't mean to be disrespectful, Mrs. Ellington, but I didn't do it for you. I did it for him."

Susan felt her eyes widen. She knew Jill was being honest, not disrespectful, but she wasn't sure how Mrs. Ellington felt about her comment. Mrs. Ellington raised her eyebrows, and then tipped her head and spoke softly to Jill. "I understand, dear. I would like to reimburse you for the time you spent grooming him, giving him medical care, and for his extra food."

Jill brushed Biz's cheek with the palm of her hand, and he rubbed her shoulder with the side of his nose. "I appreciate that, Mrs. Ellington, but I never expected to be paid. I did it because I wanted to. The love in Biz's eyes is payment enough."

Mrs. Ellington looked at the barn floor. "Jill, when Susan told me all that you've done for Biz, in my mind, I added things up, and I'd say we owe you about a thousand dollars. I insist on paying you."

Susan felt anxiety building within her because she didn't know where the conversation was going.

Jill swallowed hard. "I honestly don't think it adds up to that much, Mrs. Ellington, and I don't want any money."

Susan saw fear in Jill's eyes. She knew Jill was afraid Mrs. Ellington was going to tell her to stay away from Biz. Mrs. Ellington stepped closer and took Jill's hand. "Well, before you refuse my offer, dear, please hear me out. I assume you'd like to own Biz. Is that correct?"

Jill's eyes nearly popped out of her head. "I'd *love* to own Biz, Mrs. Ellington."

"So if we were to sell Biz for a thousand dollars, and we owe you a thousand dollars, we'd be even, right?"

Jill looked stunned. Her face turned white, then red, and then white again. Her smile was so wide that it almost looked like it hurt. "Are you saying I can have Biz?"

Mrs. Ellington smiled at Jill with deep affection. "Only if you promise to take very good care of him, dear. He seems completely taken with you. He's happy."

Panic crossed Jill's face and Susan immediately understood why. "Jill, your mother said you can have him, but before you can bring him home, you have to put up the electric fence, so he has a paddock and some green pasture."

Jill squealed and jumped for joy and Biz jumped on the cross ties. "Sorry, boy! I didn't mean to startle you," said Jill as she hugged Biz's neck and looked back at Susan. "Mom said I can have him? Oh my God. Really? Thank you, Mrs. Ellington! Thank you *so* much. I promise I'll take *very* good care of him. I love him so much."

Jill hugged Biz and tears poured down her cheeks. Susan started to cry and, as she pulled a wad of tissues from her pocket, she saw a tear gently flow down Mrs. Ellington's right cheek.

"I'm so very glad I met you, Jill," said Mrs. Ellington, grinning from ear to ear. Jill gave Mrs. Ellington a hug so big that it made her blush.

Before Mrs. Ellington left, she stepped closer to Biz. When he turned his head and looked at her, Mrs. Ellington reached up and brushed his cheek. "I'm sorry that we failed you, Biz. I thought you had everything you needed, but I know better now. You deserved so much more. Susan and Jill taught me that. You're in good hands now. This lovely young lady has promised to take exceptional care of you, and I don't doubt that she'll do exactly that. All I want is for you to be happy now, Biz."

Mrs. Ellington rubbed his neck and kissed his cheek before she lowered her head and turned away. At that moment, Susan felt sadness for Mrs. Ellington because she never witnessed such heartfelt remorse.

Susan heard Jill talk to Biz and stopped to watch them together. "Did you hear that, boy? You're coming home," said Jill as she hugged him and kissed him on the nose. Susan was proud of herself for having the courage to call Mr. Ellington. There couldn't have been a better outcome.

* * *

Biz's head was spinning. Jill owns me now? I'm going to live at the little red house right up the road. In the barn Jill's father built. Surrounded by the daisies he planted. He couldn't believe it. He felt like he won a grand championship. He loved Jill and her mother. He knew he would be in loving hands. Kind hands. Safe hands. He wondered if he would have a stablemate or be alone. Either way, he'd be fine. If he could see the house from the farm, then he would be able to see the farm from the house. That meant he could see his friends in the pasture and talk to them with loud whinnies. But he would miss his friends from Willow Bend, especially Abdul and Jonas. Hopefully, he'd be able to come back for lessons. *Jill will tell me. She tells me about everything when she grooms me,* he thought. For the first time, Biz wasn't nervous about having a new owner or going to a new place. He looked forward to it. He was going *home*. That sounded wonderful to him.

It was just about time for the horses to come in from their paddocks. Biz couldn't wait to tell Jonas. He couldn't wait to tell Abdul either, but he knew the news would be bittersweet for him. Abdul would be happy for him but saddened that he was moving away.

Biz didn't recognize Mrs. Ellington when she approached, but that didn't surprise him. He wouldn't remember Ashley either. He was grateful that Mrs. Ellington gave him to Jill. He remembered her as a kind lady, and he was pleased that she didn't change.

* * *

Out by the car, Susan and Mrs. Ellington talked.

"That was very kind of you. I wasn't expecting that," said Susan.

"Well, Susan, I thought about it. Here we are, Biz's owners, with plenty of money, and we refused to pay for what he needed, yet this young woman, who has nothing, was willing to work extra hours to pay for his food and take care of him, knowing she was not going to be reimbursed. She's a lovely girl and she deserves to have Biz. She'll be good for him. When I drove in, I saw right away that Jill was consumed with Biz. She acted like he was her best friend and Biz seemed blissful with her. It's a relationship I never saw between Biz and our daughter, Ashley." Mrs. Ellington sighed. "Now I have to go home to tell my husband that I gave him away. He won't be happy, but he'll just have to get over it. It's done. Here's the paperwork for her mother," said Mrs. Ellington as she handed an envelope to Susan. "Thank you, Susan. You'd never know it by looking at Biz, but I truly love animals and I like them to be well cared for. I assumed when we sent the check every month that his needs were met. I know better now, and I'm sorry. It's obvious that *we* neglected him, not you or Willow Bend Farm. My husband should never have accused you of neglect or threatened to sue you or the farm. I told him that, and I told him he was reprehensible."

Susan was astonished and impressed by Mrs. Ellington's honesty. "I'm glad I got to know you, Mrs. Ellington. It has been a pleasure. Thank you for coming."

Mrs. Ellington started her car and began to pull out of the driveway, then stopped and put down the window. "Please give Jill everything in the trunk that arrived with Biz."

Shocked, Susan asked, "Are you sure?"

"Yes, I'm positive. And let her know that Biz's board is paid through the end of the month, so she has time to get her barn and pasture ready."

As Mrs. Ellington pulled away, Susan waved goodbye to her and the unhappy chapters in Biz's life. Wonderful days were ahead for Biz, and Susan felt honored that she played a role in it.

Susan thought about how easily everything fell into place. It felt amazing, but it also puzzled her because the driver who delivered Biz to Willow Bend told her that others offered the Ellingtons thousands of dollars for Biz, but they never sold him. That seemed unbelievable, but in a way, it made perfect sense because Biz and Jill were meant to find each other and be together. In her mind, Susan heard her grandmother's words: "When things just fall into place, it's simply meant to be."

Susan felt unbridled happiness when she went back inside the barn and told Jill that everything that arrived with Biz now belonged to her. "Let's call your mother and then go check it out. I never unpacked the trunk, so I don't know what's inside," said Susan. That was a little white lie because Susan knew exactly what was in the trunk and couldn't wait to see Jill's face.

***

Carol paced around the house, waiting to hear how the meeting with Mrs. Ellington went. The suspense was killing her. Why didn't they call yet? When the phone finally rang, Carol jumped and answered it on the first ring. Caller ID said it was Susan, so she was surprised to hear Jill's voice. "Mom? You're never going to believe it. She gave him to me. Mrs. Ellington *gave* Biz to me."

Carol was shocked. "What do you mean, she *gave* him to you?"

"She said she added up how much I spent for extra food and the money she owed me for grooming and said we were even. She said we were *even*, Mom!"

Carol was speechless. In her wildest dreams, she never thought this would happen. She anticipated paying at least two thousand dollars for Biz. "Oh my God, Jill. I'm so happy. I'm happy for him, happy for you, and happy for me. We're really going to have a tall chestnut with a white blaze and two white socks in our paddock, waiting for you to come home from school. It's a dream come true."

As the words poured out of her mouth, Carol felt her throat tighten. She tried to hold back tears, but it was useless. She sobbed openly on the phone and heard Jill sniffling too.

"Mom, you've got to come down here. Mrs. Ellington gave me Biz's trunk and everything in it. I won't open it until you get here. Hurry. I can't wait!"

Carol grabbed her keys. "I'm on my way, honey."

Carol squealed out loud as she grabbed a handful of tissues. The door slammed behind her as she ran for her car.

"Carol, is everything all right? Is Jill okay?" asked Caleb, who turned pale as he glanced between her teary eyes and the wad of tissues in her hand.

When he got close enough, Carol took his hand. "Nothing is wrong, Caleb. Jill's fine. It's good news. Get in the car with me. I'll show you."

The quick drive to Willow Bend was a quiet one. Carol didn't initiate conversation because she knew Caleb had questions that she couldn't answer. She wanted Jill to tell him.

* * *

Jill put Biz in his stall and waited for her mother to arrive. She ran out of the front entrance when her car pulled in and paused when she saw Caleb. "Does he know, Mom? Did you tell him?"

"No, honey. I didn't tell him. I thought you should."

Caleb looked confused, so Jill wrapped her arm around his. "Caleb, I have something to show you." Jill walked Caleb to Biz's stall with Susan and her mother in tow. "Caleb, this is my horse, Biz."

Caleb saw Biz and said, "Oh my *gosh*," in a way that sounded like a cry.

Jill looked up at him. The expression on his face was one of happiness mixed with pain. "I know, Caleb. He looks exactly like the horse Dad pictured in our barn. Isn't he beautiful? I love him so much."

Caleb seemed so overcome with emotion that he couldn't speak, but he managed to put one foot in front of the other as he made his way to Biz's stall. Biz walked over and rubbed his cheek on Caleb's shoulder and Caleb openly sobbed. Her mother handed him a wad of tissues.

"He's your horse, sweetheart? When did that happen? You left me in the dark again?" he said with a grin as he wiped his eyes.

"No, Caleb. I didn't leave you out. Mrs. Ellington *just* gave him to me. I called Mom as soon as Mrs. Ellington left, so except for Mom and Susan, you're the first to know."

"Wow. Look at that face. What a handsome bugger. He sure is a beauty, Jill."

Jill felt a rush of warmth through her heart when Caleb said those words. All she could think about was her father. She knew that was all Caleb was thinking about, too. After some time with Biz, they all made their way to the tack room so Jill could open Biz's trunk.

Jill howled with joy when she found a very expensive hunt seat saddle and girth made of soft brown leather. Under them was a bridle, as well as a martingale with attachments made of the same leather, but it was braided. Jill held up the martingale. "Susan, will we need this?"

Susan raised her eyebrows. "I don't think so."

"Then why are they here?"

Susan walked over and picked up the martingale. "Sometimes a martingale is used just to prevent a saddle from slipping back on a high-withered horse like Biz. And sometimes it's used with attachments to give the rider better control over behavioral problems. The martingale attachments can either give the rider leverage on the bit for extra control or prevent the horse from lifting his head too high to evade the bit. Some trainers use them to try and stop a horse from rearing, but I've never found that to be effective. I'm not at all concerned, though. You're not going to need the attachments."

"What makes you so sure?"

"Because it doesn't look like the attachments have ever been used. There are no wear marks. They look like they just came out of the package. The Ellingtons probably bought them when Biz was young and energetic but didn't use them because their daughter got hurt and never rode again."

Jill inspected them further. "You're right. They've never been used." Jill felt like she was in a treasure trove. She found boots to protect Biz's legs and hooves, a couple of blankets to keep him warm during cold weather, electric clippers, a few medical supplies, shampoo, conditioner, and extra brushes. "I can't believe she gave all of this to me," squealed Jill.

Her mother held one hand to her face. "Honey, I don't know a lot about saddles, but I recognize the brand on that one. It's extremely expensive."

Jill nodded. "I know it is, Mom. I don't know why she gave it to me. I can't believe it. Mrs. Ellington is such a nice lady."

Susan put her arm around Jill's shoulder. "Yes, she is. And thanks to her, you have pretty much everything you need. Now we just need to get the electric fence up, buy water buckets and some shavings, hay, and grain, and your barn will be ready to welcome him home. And it wouldn't hurt for you to have a lesson or two on him *before* you bring him home, so you're more confident in the saddle when you ride him down here for lessons. We should probably start by just walking him around the arena so he's not too sore afterward. It's been a long time since he carried anyone on his back. We need to gradually build up his muscles."

Jill burst into tears. "This is all I ever wanted. I can't believe it. I *really* can't."

Jill was extraordinarily grateful to Mrs. Ellington for her generosity and help in making her dream come true. For a few moments, she tried to sit quietly because she sensed her father's presence. From the very center of her being, she knew her dad was watching and aware of all the wonderful things happening. Her heart told her that he played a role in it and she felt loved.

***

Caleb was beside himself on the ride back from Willow Bend because

Jill and Carol could not contain their joy. Before Carol parked the car by the barn, she let Caleb out alongside his porch. When his feet were firmly planted on the ground, he tried desperately to hold on to his composure as he thanked them for including him. "Ladies, this was a wonderful afternoon. I had a great time. Meeting Biz is among the highlights of my life. I'm so happy for both of you. Heck, I'm even happy for myself."

Caleb made his way to his porch and opened his kitchen door. When he stepped inside, a waterfall of tears erupted. He finally understood why he felt Logan around him so much. He was working hard to bring his little girl the horse he promised her. That was the Logan he knew. A man of his word. A man who was so devoted to his family that he was determined to work a miracle even when he was no longer there. Raw emotion flowed through Caleb's body because he understood the true depth of Logan's love for Jill. He should have known that Logan would never leave anything unfinished. Not something like his little girl's heartfelt wish. Her dream.

When Jill was just a little girl, Logan told Caleb about his plan to build a barn for her. As Logan revealed his plans, Caleb relived his childhood and told Logan about his first and only horse named Copper, a chestnut quarter horse with a small white blaze and white socks. Caleb didn't talk about him very often because Copper was his dream and memories of his death still tugged at his heart. Caleb surprised himself when he shared the story with Logan, and he vividly remembered the expression on Logan's face as he described Copper. Caleb sometimes wondered if Logan pictured a chestnut horse with a white blaze and white socks because of Copper. That question would probably never be answered, but Caleb was okay with it because even the possibility made him smile.

***

The news that Biz belonged to Jill spread around the paddocks like wildfire. Jonas was ecstatic and could not stop happily pacing. When he finally settled down, he watched the others to see how they received the information.

Aiyana seemed at peace. Jonas figured it was because she knew Biz was finally going to a real home. Opal was weepy. Jonas hoped it was because she finally understood how important it was for Biz. Luis appeared pleased. After his unpleasant experience with his trainer, Jonas was positive that Luis knew Biz was safe and in the care of loving and kind hands. Abdul seemed to fluctuate between happiness and sadness. Jonas knew he was happy for Biz, but also sad because he was losing the only stablemate who completely related to him. Günter was visibly agitated. He shifted most of his weight to his rear right hip and turned to Luis. "Well, I guess water seeks its own level."

Luis pinned his ears back and snarled. "What the heck does that mean?"

"They're two peas in a pod. The *poor* girl wins the *poor* disheveled horse. He'll *never* be anything. You know that, right?"

Luis rolled his eyes and walked away from Günter. He seemed disgusted and Jonas realized how much Luis was growing tired of Günter's maliciousness. The more Jonas thought about it, the more he wondered why Günter seemed to have it in for Biz. There simply had to be more to it than any of them realized. He knew the truth would eventually come out.

***

At suppertime, flakes of hay and grain were put in the stalls, and then the horses were led in from their paddocks. Biz was already eating when the rest of the horses came in. After they were all safely in their stalls, Jill gave Biz a hug and a kiss on the nose, and then she gave a kiss to Jonas and Abdul. Jill seemed to be walking on clouds and Biz felt peaceful. Content.

Jonas looked at Biz and chuckled. "Man, that's one happy kid."

Biz replied, "Did you hear, Jonas? Jill owns me now and I'm going to live with her."

"That news is all over the barn," said Jonas with a twinkle in his eyes. "Luis's owner, Sharon, heard what was going on in here and told Luis, so naturally, the news made its way around the paddocks. Everybody's happy for you. How are you feeling, brother?"

"I'm happy, Jonas. Having a home with someone like Jill is what I want. I'll live at a real home and be part of a real family. But that means I have to leave you and Abdul, the best friends I ever had and that makes me sad."

Jonas walked closer, put his head down slightly, and looked reassuringly at Biz. "Now hold on, son. How far away do you think you're going? You'll be right up the road. Heck, we'll be able to see each other and whinny to each other every day. And I bet Jill will ride you down here every week for her lesson. You'll see us *all* the time."

Biz tipped his head. "I guess you're right. I'll probably see you a lot. Thanks for reminding me about that, Jonas. I feel better now."

"Son, we'll see each other every week. I'm sure of it. Besides, you're not gonna be leaving Willow Bend for weeks. I heard Susan tell Jill that the Ellingtons paid your board through the end of the month, so she can take her time getting the barn and pasture ready."

Biz felt less anxious, knowing that he had time to mentally prepare himself for the move, and he was thrilled that he would see his Willow Bend friends regularly. What he knew for certain was that Jill would fill in the blanks. She talked to him like he was her best friend and confidante. He relished their chats.

Biz glanced at Abdul and saw that his head and neck hung down so low that his nose almost touched the ground. He looked like he was going to cry so Biz walked closer to him. "This is the first week in September, Biz, so you only have three more weeks with us. I wish I was going with you. I'm going to miss you."

"Don't be sad. I'll be just a few strides up the road. I'll never be so far away that I can't help you if you need me. All you have to do is whinny. I'll be far enough away that you won't be able to hear my actual words, but you'll hear my voice. I'll miss you, too, but I'll be back every week for a lesson. Jill will let me visit with you."

"It won't be the same. I'm used to having you right here. Beside me."

Abdul's eyes seemed full of worry. "I wish I could bring you and Jonas with me, Abdul. I really do. Nothing would make me happier. Somehow, the three of us ended up at this farm together and we're a perfect fit. We're family. I will always be here for you, but if something happens and you can't wait to talk to me, I'm sure you could talk to Jonas."

Jonas looked at Abdul and nodded. "You sure can, and I'll be happy to help. Always."

A tear dripped from Abdul's eye and Biz realized that although Abdul loved Jonas, Abdul wanted to be with him.

~17~

It was an exceptionally warm September day, so Jill decided to take advantage of the eighty-degree weather and give Biz a much-needed bath. With shampoo and conditioner in hand, she walked Biz to the barn's indoor wash stall. She used warm water to wet Biz's coat and then she scrubbed and lathered him until he was covered with suds. After she got all the dirt off of his coat, she worked meticulously to clean dry flaky skin and excess oil from every layer, especially on his white socks. When she finished scrubbing, she rinsed him until nothing but clear water ran off his body. She could tell that he loved his bath by the way he stood with his eyes closed. "For the first time in years, you're squeaky clean, Biz," said Jill as she squirted conditioner into a big bucket of water. She sponged it all over him and left it on for ten minutes so his skin would get an intense treatment. As she rinsed him off, she was filled with pure satisfaction because he seemed content. The best part was that her time and energy were being spent caring for her very own horse, not somebody else's. She intended to take her time and savor every moment.

Jill rinsed off the conditioner and led Biz outside. She placed him in cross ties mounted where there was hot afternoon sun because she didn't want him to become chilled as he dried off. While Biz basked in the sun, Jill headed back inside to get his grooming supplies, but stopped in her tracks and looked around.

Look at him, Jill! He sure is a beauty. And he's all yours.

Was there someone nearby, or did she hear the words in her head? Her heart skipped a beat when she smelled Old Spice. There wasn't a soul around, so she didn't understand where the smell came from, but it didn't matter because it comforted her. Grounded her. She drew in a deep breath and memories of her father filled her mind.

She returned to Biz, and he was almost asleep. His eyes were closed, and his body looked incredibly relaxed. Limp. Peaceful. She felt so happy that she hummed as she groomed.

She began with his tail, gently brushing it, starting at the bottom, until all the snarls were gone, and then she trimmed the ends and put it in a French braid. She stepped back and admired her work. Next, she trimmed his mane, braided it, and put a white rubber band around the end of each braid as if he was a fancy dressage horse. Once his mane and tail were braided, she used the electric clippers to trim his whiskers, the hair on his ears, and his fetlocks. Biz didn't seem to take exception to any of it. He just stood there like he enjoyed every second.

Jill knew what she was doing because, in the past, she sometimes washed and groomed other people's horses for shows. "No one is ever going to groom you but me ... or maybe my mother, Biz. From now on, you are solely in the care of your family. That's what a family is about. As she groomed, thoughts of her father continued to fill Jill's head. "I wish my dad could have met you, Biz. He would have loved you. You know, he built the barn you're going to live in. He even pictured a horse that looked just like you in our paddock. I know you were meant to be mine, so that means he built our barn for you. You'll have a nice big stall, and you can go in and out all day long."

Biz looked intently at Jill as she spoke, and it warmed her heart.

"You can go inside to get out of the wind, rain, or sun. And if it's chilly in the stall, you can go outside to stand in the sun."

She picked out his hooves when she finished clipping him and was relieved to see that her daily cleaning of his hooves continued to keep his hooves clear of thrush. She polished his hooves with hoof conditioner because she thought it was healthier than hoof polish, and by the time she was done, Biz looked like he was about to go into the show ring.

"You don't have to go to a show to look fancy, boy. You deserve to look spectacular every day," said Jill. She looked into his eyes and saw so much love that it took her breath away. Goosebumps formed on her arms as a rush of warmth ran through her body. It felt like he sent a wave of love to her, and their souls touched. She hugged Biz and thought about nothing except how happy she was.

After a long hug, Jill put a lead line on Biz's halter and walked him past the paddocks to the end of the driveway and back. As he walked, Jill noticed that his head and neck were elevated, and his legs lifted high as if they were weightless.

Susan walked out of the barn and let out a soft whistle. "Wow, doesn't he look gorgeous! That's amazing. He still needs to put on weight and build muscle, but he glistens. He doesn't even look like the same horse. Great job, Jill!"

Jill knew she was beaming with pride. "Thanks, Susan."

Jill assumed that Biz felt handsome. She wondered if he was eager for the other horses to catch a glimpse of him.

***

Jonas knew Biz was handsome, but even he was shocked at the transformation as Biz pranced past the paddock fence.

"*Man*, he looks good. Squeaky clean and gussied up," said Jonas.

"Very distinguished," said Opal.

"And *happy*," said Aiyana.

"How can you tell?" asked Opal.

Jonas interjected. "Look at the spring in that boy's step. He's not walking. He's prancing all the way down that driveway."

Luis turned toward Günter with a devilish grin. "It looks like you may have some competition, Günter. Biz was a hunter-jumper champion. Maybe you two will meet in the show ring."

With his eyes at half-mast and furrows in his forehead, Günter stared at Biz with disdain. "Maybe, but perhaps this time, *I'll* win."

Jonas quickly realized that Günter had just revealed a secret. He waited patiently to see if Luis picked up on it. It took only a minute for Jonas to see a glint in Luis's eyes.

"Ohhhhhhh. *That's* why you say mean things about Biz! You competed against him, and he *beat* you. Hahaha! It all makes *so* much sense now." Luis laughed as he trotted around the paddock with what appeared to be enormous satisfaction.

Jonas couldn't help but chuckle, but it didn't make him proud. Günter was mean to Biz, so he deserved some needling, but Luis seemed to be having way too much fun. And it was painfully obvious that Günter didn't appreciate it.

"It was *one* show," barked Günter. "It certainly doesn't mean he was the better horse. We all have an off-day in the show ring."

Luis walked over to Günter, stuck his nose right in his face, and said, "Well, if you truly believe that, *why does it bother you so much?*"

Günter turned his head away, scrunched his face, and pointed his nose in the air like a pouting child. "Because it does, and that's all *you* need to know."

Jonas felt a small amount of compassion for Günter because he recollected when competing was important to him too. But during a competition, someone always won, which meant that someone always lost. It went with the territory. Jonas was never a sore loser, and he never held a grudge.

~18~

Carol walked around the barn with a measuring tape, trying to figure out how much fencing she needed, when Caleb wandered over and asked if he could help. "Caleb, the day I cried about our empty barn, I had no idea this was going to happen," said Carol while explaining what she needed to do. "I guess each day brings new promises. If we're bringing Biz home by the end of the month, we need to put up an electric fence, so I need to get some measurements."

Caleb smiled and gently took the measuring tape from Carol's hand. "I have some spare time today and I'm happy to help. If you don't mind, I'll talk to my friend at the hardware store. Maybe I can get a deal on the fencing. And by the way, I'm more than happy to install it."

Carol knew that buying the materials for the fence would be expensive, and hiring someone to install it might be cost-prohibitive, so she was eternally grateful for his help. "Thank you so much, Caleb. Sometimes I don't know what I'd do without you."

Caleb always seemed touched when people complimented him, so Carol was not surprised when he blushed. He explained that his tractor had an attachment called a post hole digger, so he suggested that they buy cedar posts instead of metal stakes. He said horses are much less likely to injure themselves on wooden posts, plus, they were sturdier and more attractive, so the property would look nicer.

For the same reasons, he suggested three-inch wide black electric fence tape instead of wire. Lastly, he suggested a solar fence charger, because the paddock was in an open field with lots of sunlight.

Carol agreed with all of Caleb's suggestions, and within a week, thanks to lots of elbow grease and savvy price negotiations, they installed the fence, charger, and gates. Carol was with Caleb when he bought the materials and could tell that he *loved* to haggle.

Once everything was installed, Carol bought water buckets, hay, grain, and shavings. Caleb picked it all up with his truck and delivered it right to the barn. Caleb didn't stop smiling as he unloaded the supplies and carried them inside with Carol and Jill.

"My goodness, Caleb, you're smiling as if you were bringing your own horse home," laughed Carol.

"I'm so excited. I can't wait to see that horse when I look over here in the morning," he said. "He's such a beautiful animal. All horses are."

"Have you ever owned one?" asked Jill.

Caleb hesitated, and Carol thought he sounded emotional when he answered. "My dad had a team of draft horses. Belgians. I loved them," said Caleb. "Big, but gentle. That's where I learned what I know about horses. I loved the smell of horses back then, and I still do. Those Belgians are among my fondest memories of childhood. Gosh, I can't wait to see Biz next door."

***

While they readied the barn, Caleb sensed Logan's presence. He figured that Carol did too, because now and then, she stopped working, looked off in the distance, closed her eyes, and took a deep breath. She didn't appear physically taxed. Her chest just seemed heavy from emotion, and he understood why.

Carol and Logan moved to the neighborhood fifteen years before, right after Caleb lost his wife, Marion. They never had children and Caleb was an only child, so he didn't have much family. To get through his grief, Caleb surrounded himself with friends and he had many, including Logan. Caleb was about twenty-five years older than Logan and he regarded him as much more than just a neighbor and a friend. Logan was like a son. During the months when Logan built the barn, he had several heartfelt conversations with Caleb about Jill, horses, and his dream to complete the barn so Jill could get a horse and bring it home. Caleb's emotions were running high as they put up the fence because he knew he was helping to bring Logan's dream to fruition. He felt honored to be part of it. He met Jill when she was a newborn and got to know her as a toddler, running happily around the yard. He watched out for Jill and Carol and was grateful to have them next door.

It took Caleb by surprise when Jill asked if he ever had a horse of his own. He wanted to answer her honestly, but couldn't seem to keep his emotions in check, so he decided not to talk about Copper. He didn't want to get weepy and ruin everything. It was a happy day and he intended to keep it that way. Someday, he would tell Carol and Jill about Copper, just like he told Logan.

He didn't realize how much he was grinning as he worked. Carol had no idea how right she was when she said he was smiling enough to make her think he was bringing his own horse home. In his mind, he was. Just like Copper, Biz was a chestnut with a white blaze and two white socks. It seemed surreal and he couldn't wait to look out his kitchen window and see Biz in the paddock. Was there a better way to start or end his day? He intended to visit Biz often, with carrots in his pocket, just as he did with Copper. There was nothing he loved more than a horse standing at attention with his ears up, waiting for a special treat. It couldn't happen soon enough for him. He felt giddy. Like a little kid. He couldn't wait.

~19~

Several times during the next week, Susan saw Jill walk Biz around the riding arena with just a saddle and saddle pad on his back, to help his muscles get used to carrying weight. Susan admired Jill's dedication and her commitment to his recovery. She was patient, and she had a lot of common sense when it came to horses.

Saturday was an unusually quiet day at the barn and Susan had some free time, so she asked Jill if she wanted to have her first lesson on Biz after she was done with her barn work.

"Really?" squealed Jill. "That would be awesome! Thank you!"

"Let me know when you're ready, and I'll meet you in the arena."

Susan chuckled as she watched Jill move quickly through her chores and then get Biz from his stall, place him in the cross ties, and groom him. She put on his protective boots, and then placed the saddle pad and saddle on his back and tightened the girth. Before putting on his bridle, Susan saw her walk toward her office.

"I'll be ready in ten minutes, Susan."

"Perfect. Don't get on him until I'm in the arena because we have no idea how he will react to being ridden or to the weight on his back."

Jill was hand-walking Biz around the outside edge of the arena when Susan got there. She looked elated, but also a bit apprehensive.

"Ready?" asked Susan.

"I am!" said Jill.

"This is your first time riding your own horse! Nervous?"

"A little," laughed Jill. "I can't wait to get on him, but I'm afraid it might hurt him."

Susan nodded. "That's why we're going to take it slowly. Just walk. No trotting or cantering. I don't want any bouncing on his back yet. It will take time to build his muscle strength. But there's plenty that we can accomplish as you walk and get to know each other."

Susan walked to the corner of the arena to get the mounting block - a set of heavy plastic steps - and asked Jill to bring Biz to the center of the ring. "Jill, it's important to be able to get on your horse without a mounting block, but in my opinion, you should use a mounting block whenever you can because it's much kinder on a horse's back. Visualize it. When you put your foot in the stirrup and grab the saddle to mount, it puts a lot of pressure and torque on the horse's shoulder and back. Biz doesn't need that right now."

Jill nodded. "That makes sense."

Next, Susan put a lunge attachment on Biz's bit and attached the lunge line. Jill raised her eyebrows, so Susan quickly addressed what she assumed was her concern. "Since we've never seen anyone ride Biz, and we don't personally know anyone who has, we don't know how he behaves under saddle. I thought this might be the safest way to start. It offers us a little more control, should he start to run."

Jill climbed the steps of the mounting block and looked euphoric as she gently lowered herself onto his back for the very first time. Biz blinked when Jill first sat down, but his ears stayed upright and he didn't widen his stance to brace himself, so Susan thought he was holding his own. But she planned to watch him closely for signs of distress during the lesson.

"How does that feel?" asked Susan.

Jill's smile was large, and her eyes sparkled. "Awesome!"

"I thought you'd say that," laughed Susan.

Susan told Jill to walk Biz around the arena and hug the outside edge. At various places, she instructed Jill to ask him to stop, walk a few steps backward, walk forward, walk faster, slow down, and bend into the corners of the arena. Susan was amazed at how well Biz responded. He seemed relaxed and eager to please. With pleasure, Susan observed how gently Jill used her legs and how softly she worked with her hands, being careful not to pull on the bit in his mouth. Biz was so well-behaved that halfway through the lesson, Susan removed the lunge line.

At the end of the lesson, Jill thanked Susan and walked Biz over to the mounting block, where she gently dismounted. Once her feet were on the ground, she stepped back, looked into Biz's eyes, and thanked him for being a good boy.

"That was a terrific first lesson, Jill. You two are great together. Just remember that we have to move forward with baby steps," said Susan.

"Yes, baby steps," repeated Jill.

Susan laughed as they left the arena because they both had a spring in their steps. Susan was around horses her whole life and knew how to read them. She was just about positive that Biz was going to behave during the lesson, but she had to make sure. She was overjoyed and grateful that Jill and Biz were a good fit for each other.

***

Jill was ecstatic as she walked Biz back to the cross ties. Her first lesson on her horse! She was nervous because of his physical condition. She was afraid that her weight on his back could hurt him, but the idea that she could get hurt never entered her mind. She was surprised when

Susan used the lunge line, but when she explained why, it made perfect sense. *It was best to be sure,* Jill thought as she relived every moment.

Her first lesson on Biz was unlike any other riding experience. There was something majestic about him. She felt like royalty on his back. She was exceptionally careful not to hurt him and she sensed that he wanted to take care of her too. Every move he made was smooth and gentle. The way he responded to her and the way he looked at her communicated how much he loved her. It felt amazing.

Biz was bigger than any horse she rode. She felt like she was on top of a skyscraper, yet when she looked down, she wasn't the least bit scared. Biz's back was wide beneath her legs. She expected it to get wider as his health improved and he put on more weight. She looked forward to it.

After the lesson, while Jill groomed Biz, she whistled and hummed. Biz's ears went back and forth like he was keenly interested in each note and every word said in between. It made her giggle. Several times, she took a step back and looked at him because she still couldn't believe that he belonged to her. She remembered the day she first saw him and felt a tug in her heart that never went away. Was it written in the stars that they belonged together? She thought so.

Before she put him in his stall, she put her arms around his neck and hugged him. "I love you so much, Biz." After she released him, she stepped back and gazed at him, trying to hold on to the moment. When she was ready, she fed him a hay cube, took him out of the cross ties, and walked him to his stall. Once inside, she kissed him on the nose and gave him a peppermint. She couldn't wait for her next lesson.

Before she left the barn, Jill went back to the tack room to make sure she put all of Biz's equipment away and ran into Erinna, a hunt seat rider who had one of the most expensive horses. Jill tried to avoid Erinna whenever possible because she was mean and took every opportunity to let people know how expensive her horse was, and even told other riders that their horses didn't measure up. If a rider made a mistake in the show ring or ended up on the ground during practice, Erinna laughed at them - even at the youngest ones. It enraged Jill when she made little kids cry. Jill tried to mentally prepare herself because she sensed that she was about to become one of Erinna's targets.

"So I hear that Biz is your horse now?" quipped Erinna.

"Yes," replied Jill with unbridled enthusiasm.

Erinna scrunched her face. "Why? Nobody understands why you want him. I mean…he's not worth anything."

Jill was not going to let Erinna get the best of her. "He might not seem worth anything to you, but he's worth a lot to me."

Erinna took a step closer and shifted her weight to her right hip. "Well, good luck trying to win anything with him. He looks like a lost cause." Erinna smirked as she headed toward the tack room door.

Jill tried to hold her emotions in check, but she couldn't. "You know what, Erinna? You might have one of the most expensive horses at Willow Bend, but that doesn't make him a better show horse or make you a better rider. I know what Biz is capable of. I know his worth. Wait and see. He already looks better than when he got here. Have you seen him?"

"Yes, I've seen him, but shampoo and conditioner don't make a horse better, Jill. It's like putting lipstick on a pig, don't you think?"

Jill put her hand on her stomach. How could anyone say something like that about Biz? She felt hurt, but anger soon took over. She spun around, glared at Erinna, and then took a few steps toward her. "Lipstick on a pig, Erinna? I'm sorry ... were you talking about yourself?"

The look on Erinna's face made Jill instantly regret her words, but she felt no desire to apologize. As Erinna swiftly left the room, Jill wondered if anyone was ever bold enough to stand up to her before. Jill was furious, but it didn't take long for her to regain her composure and remember how much she believed in Biz. She knew all things were possible for him. There was no doubt in her mind that Erinna and her snooty friends would soon understand why she wanted Biz. They saw the outside of Biz. Jill knew what was inside. Biz had heart. Sure, he still needed to put on weight and build muscle, but the foundation for all that was achievable was already there. It would take time, but everyone would eventually understand what she already knew.

***

A full week later, on the following Saturday, Jill had a second lesson with Biz and Carol watched. Carol was completely in love with Biz and so proud of Jill. Proud of her confidence. Proud of her kindness. Proud of her compassion. And proud of her humility.

Jill always wanted a horse and her commitment to Biz helped accomplish her dream, but what made Carol proudest was Jill's deep understanding that Biz was important. After all, without the horse, there was no equestrian experience, so the horse was the most important part of the equation. Jill seemed to instinctively understand that Biz had to be treated with respect, love, and kindness, and in return, he would treat her the same way.

When Jill's lesson was over, Susan asked Carol if she was ready for her first lesson on Biz. Carol was taken aback because, in her mind, it was too soon. Jill and Biz were just getting to know one another. She thought her lessons would begin in the spring.

"Do you mean right now? I-I-I don't know," stuttered Carol.

Susan laughed. "No, not right this minute. That would be way too much for Biz. But I think he can handle a short half-hour lesson in the coming week."

Carol looked at Jill. "Honey, are you okay with me having a lesson on Biz so soon?"

Jill smiled fondly at her mother. "It's better for you to have your first lessons while he's here, so you can safely ride him back to the farm for the rest of your lessons."

Carol was hesitant. "Well, if it's okay with you, and Susan thinks it's a good idea, then I guess I'm ready!" Carol felt excited as the words flowed out of her mouth. "Oh my God! Am I ready? Yes, I'm ready!" laughed Carol.

Susan suggested Wednesday afternoon at five o'clock. "Nobody's here at that time, so the barn will be nice and quiet. And Jill will be home from school, so she can watch."

Carol looked at Jill and nodded enthusiastically. "Yes, I want Jill to be here. After all, I'll be riding her horse."

Jill looked lovingly at Carol and Carol hoped the happiness she saw in Jill's eyes would remain for a long time.

The sight of Jill riding her horse didn't leave Carol's mind for days. At night, she lay in bed, picturing the joyous expression on Jill's face. It was something Carol would cherish forever because it was an experience she was able to give her daughter that her parents never offered her. Was it that they couldn't offer it or wouldn't? Carol knew her father would do most anything for her, but her mother ruled the roost. She controlled the checkbook and was much more stingy with Carol than her older sisters, Brianna and Abigail, who pretty much got anything they wanted. The hurt caused by her mother's favoritism created a wound that Carol carried throughout life. She never understood why her mother was so hard on her. It felt like her mother loved Brianna and Abigail but tolerated her.

Abigail died of cancer in her late twenties and Carol's father became the glue that held the family together. He passed away shortly after Carol met Logan and following his death, Carol didn't feel compelled to visit her childhood home. What was the point if her father wasn't there? As a result, she never saw her mother. Her relationship with Brianna was always strained, so they completely drifted apart. It was bad enough that her mother rejected her, but what Carol couldn't deal with was how much Brianna seemed to revel in the pain that their mother inflicted on her. Carol was happier after she distanced herself.

Carol didn't worry about her mother after her father died. She knew she would be okay as long as Brianna was alive. They were a pair. It didn't bother Carol that Jill didn't know her grandmother or her aunt, but she wished her father and Abigail lived long enough for Jill to know them. Carol wondered if she would ever see her mother or her sister again. But then again, did she want to? Over the years, Carol learned to surround herself with people who were good for her. People who made her feel good about herself. Sadly, her own family wasn't good for her.

Except for her father's love, Carol's childhood was laden with rejection and pain. Her biggest fear was that she would be the same type of mother. She was afraid to have children until she met Logan, which was the best thing that ever happened to her. He loved and accepted her for exactly who she was. He knew her whole life story and welcomed her strengths and weaknesses with open arms. On days when she felt bitter and angry, Logan never judged her, but he did sometimes remind her that people change. He suggested that she keep her heart open, should her mother or sister call. She promised that she would, but they never did. After Logan's death, Carol thought she might hear from them, but they never attended the wake or funeral, called, or even sent a sympathy card. She thought about reaching out to them, but in the end, decided against it, knowing that if she reached out during such a time of need and was rejected again, it would have devastated her. She proactively protected herself by never picking up the phone.

Carol truly missed her father. He always found a way to let her know how much he loved her. A hug, a kiss on the forehead, a token gift that had to be their secret. When her mother treated her unfairly, he often shook his head and looked at her with compassion. Sometimes, he put his arm around her shoulder and squeezed her, letting her know in unspoken words that he felt terrible about it. But he only did that when her mother wasn't in the room to see it.

When Carol married Logan, they eloped. It was the two of them against the world and they were happy. She knew Logan was the one for her the moment she set eyes on him. He desperately wanted a child, and it didn't take long for him to convince Carol to have one. He doted on her the whole time she carried Jill. After Jill was born, she became their world and neither of them felt a need to have another. Looking back, Carol would have agreed to a second child if Logan truly wanted one, but she was at peace with just Jill because there was never a possibility of favoritism. Carol promised herself that she would do anything to help her daughter achieve her dreams. Anything.

Carol doubted that her mother ever investigated the cost of owning a horse. She refused to even consider Carol's proposal to get a part-time job to pay for one all by herself. Carol was the responsible kid in the family. She never did anything halfway. She was all in, or not in the game at all, so her mother had to know that she would keep her word. But maybe it was never about money. Was it possible that her mother simply didn't want her to be happy? If so, Carol would never understand why. As a mother, all Carol ever wanted was for her daughter to feel loved and cherished. How could a mother not want that for her child?

When Carol saw Jill on Biz, she was thrilled for her, but she also felt sadness for herself. Suddenly, she was a little girl again, asking herself why she was deprived of the same experience. Was she deprived or robbed? For the first time in years, Carol allowed herself to feel anger. She blamed her mother, and even though it was hard for her to be angry with her father, she couldn't understand why he never stuck up for her. Why was he so powerless when it came to her mother? What didn't she understand about their marriage?

Carol shook her head. If it wasn't for Susan, Jill would not have experienced riding her own horse at the tender age of thirteen. She berated herself for not investigating the cost of owning a horse after Logan died. Did she not look into it because she thought it was pointless? Was she overwhelmed as a single parent and afraid to put one more thing on her plate? Or did she repeat a pattern from her childhood? Was she her mother? The thoughts made Carol sick to her stomach, and she wanted to cry. Thank goodness for Susan. She showed Carol that it was possible to afford a horse and helped her every step of the way. She seemed fearless. Carol would never forget how much Susan did for her and Jill. She felt indebted to her and would eventually figure out a way to properly thank her.

Carol took a moment to think about Biz. She let out a long slow breath and pictured his face. So handsome. So loving. So kind. Riding him was going to be amazing. Biz belonged to Jill, but Carol could not shake the feeling that he belonged to her too. Maybe it was because a horse at home was also her lifelong dream. But no matter the reason, Carol knew she had to keep that feeling in check so she didn't overstep. Biz was the center of her daughter's happiness and Jill was the center of Carol's universe. Nothing mattered except Jill, her precious daughter, and the only piece of Logan still with her.

***

Luckily, Jill and Carol wore pretty much the same size helmet, breeches, and boots, so Carol didn't have to go shopping. Jill told her mother to go through her riding clothes and pick out something to wear. On Tuesday night, she did, and it excited her so much that she had a hard time sleeping. Each time she woke and looked at the clock, she heard a barred owl outside her window and remembered how Logan used to smile, even in his sleep, when they hooted at night. She awakened before her alarm had a chance to ring. It was still early, so Carol worked quietly in the kitchen so she didn't disturb Jill. As she ate breakfast, she felt butterflies in her stomach but couldn't figure out whether she was excited or nervous. If she was nervous, was it apprehension about riding for the first time in years, or was she nervous about riding Biz? Maybe it was both. She thought about how much their lives changed over the past couple of months as she glanced over the newspaper and sipped her tea. She stood up and went to the window to look at their barn and the new paddock. Biz's new home. Life was going to be different for all of them. A much better life for Biz. And for her and Jill, a new chapter of dreams that came true, wounds that could heal, and the promise of a new adventure.

Carol hoped the void from Logan's passing could somehow be filled with Biz's presence. With Biz at home, it might feel like a piece of Logan was still there. Biz would bring their barn back to life. The barn Logan built. Was it a coincidence that the horse he envisioned looked exactly like Biz? Was it possible that Logan somehow brought Biz to Jill?

Carol's thoughts were interrupted when Jill came into the kitchen. "Morning, Mom."

"Good morning, honey."

"Today's the big day. Nervous?"

"A little, I guess. What would you like for breakfast?"

"I think I just want cereal this morning. Sit and relax. I can get it."

Carol watched Jill make her breakfast. Her little girl was becoming an independent young woman. Where did the years go?

Jill finished her breakfast and headed back upstairs. "Mom, I'm going up to shower and get dressed for school. I'll meet you here when I get home and we'll go to the barn together, okay? We should be at the barn no later than four o'clock, so we have time to get Biz ready."

Jill was grinning and it made Carol happy. "Okay, that sounds good."

Jill left to catch the bus, and Carol washed the breakfast dishes, took a shower, got dressed, and then went to her office to get some work done. Her morning was productive, but after lunch, it was hard to concentrate because she was distracted. She could hardly wait to get on Biz and experience how it felt to ride him. She weighed about ten pounds more than Jill and worried that the extra weight might negatively impact Biz. Would it be too much for his back? Would two lessons in one week overwhelm him?

At three o'clock, Carol gave up trying to concentrate and got dressed for her lesson. She changed into the hunter green long-sleeve Henley shirt she chose from her closet and matched it with the tan breeches and tall black boots Jill let her use until she could buy her own. The outfit looked good, and she felt wonderful. Carol was standing by the sink in her riding attire when Jill came into the kitchen door after school.

"Wow," said Jill. "Those look amazing on you. You look like one of those fancy horse owners from the big expensive dressage barn across town."

"Oh, stop it. I do not," laughed Carol. "I'm certainly not going to look fancy once I get in the saddle. It's been years since I was on a horse, and I don't remember much. Plus, I rode western back then, so I'll have *no* idea what I'm doing in an English saddle."

Jill giggled. "You'll do fine, Mom. Don't worry. Just relax and enjoy it."

Jill grabbed a snack and then they got in the car and headed to Willow Bend. They arrived exactly one hour before Carol's lesson. Once inside the main entrance of the barn, Carol stopped to take in everything, especially the smell of horses. She realized that Susan was right—Wednesday afternoons were very quiet. Carol was blissful until Jill told her to get Biz from his paddock and meet her by his stall.

"The lesson isn't just riding, Mom. It includes grooming and tacking up the horse. You're going to get a little bit dirty." Jill snickered.

Carol didn't have a poker face, so she was aware that Jill could see how surprised and nervous she was about the animal husbandry part of her lesson.

"Okay, Mom. Just this one time, I'll go with you to get Biz from the paddock. When we come back inside, we'll go to the tack room and get his brushes, hoof pick, saddle, and bridle, and I'll walk you through everything."

Carol laughed to herself. She was going to get dirty and smelly. Just as dirty and smelly as Jill was every time she came home from the farm.

With Biz in the cross ties, Jill showed Carol how to brush him with the hard, medium, and soft brushes to remove mud and dirt from the different depths of his coat. Then she demonstrated the correct way to brush his mane and tail to avoid breaking the hairs, and lastly, she cleaned his hooves. Once groomed, Jill showed Carol how to put on the saddle and bridle, explaining everything along the way. They finished just in time for Carol's lesson and Susan was walking into the arena when they arrived.

"Good afternoon, Carol," said Susan. "This is an exciting day."

"Yes, it is," replied Carol. "I didn't sleep much last night, and I've had butterflies in my stomach all day. I'm excited and nervous. It's been a long time since I've done this, and I never rode in an English saddle, so I have a lot to learn."

"Ah, okay, then we're going to start with the basics and build from there," said Susan. "I'm confident you'll do fine."

When Carol took the reins and started to lead Biz to the mounting block, he stopped for a second and looked at Jill as if confused. "It's okay, boy. Mom's riding you today," she said.

Biz looked deeply into Carol's eyes and then walked willingly to the mounting block. Carol's heart skipped a beat when she stepped onto the block and climbed into the saddle. What a wonderful feeling! Biz was so tall. When she looked down, she realized it was a long way to fall, so she better stay on.

Susan instructed Carol through some of the same exercises that she did with Jill during her Saturday lesson. Carol was comfortable on his back, and she hoped Biz felt comfortable too. Susan told her to sit deep and let her hips gently rock left and right with the motion of his walk. A couple of times, Carol lost her balance and lightly squeezed his trunk with her legs to stay on. Biz picked up a small trot each time, but quickly settled back into a walk. Carol was pleased to experience his trot, even for a second or two.

Biz behaved so well that when the lesson was coming to a close, Susan asked Carol if it was okay to remove the lunge line so she could walk around the arena on her own. Carol felt a huge smile form on her face as she nodded. Biz stood completely still for Susan and remained standing until Carol lightly squeezed his sides and asked him to walk. Carol was surprised that she wasn't the least bit nervous, riding him on her own. Perhaps it was because Biz seemed calm. He waited for her to tell him what to do before he moved. Without question, it was one of the best experiences of her life. It wasn't like lessons in the past. This time, it was Biz, a treasured member of their family. She was enamored with him.

When the lesson was over, Carol dismounted, and Biz gently brushed his nose on her shoulder. It felt like a lovely gesture on his part. Acceptance of her. Filled with emotion, Carol walked Biz back into the barn and placed him in the cross ties so she could remove the tack, brush him again, and clean his hooves. As Carol brushed, she fed Biz hay cubes, told him how beautiful he was, and gushed about what a good boy he was during their lesson. When they finished, Carol and Jill walked Biz to his stall so he could enjoy some hay while the rest of the herd came in for dinner. After she closed the stall door, he looked at her with loving eyes and it almost made Carol cry.

***

Biz entered his stall, but quickly turned around to face them because he wanted Jill and Carol to stay. The love he felt engulfed his heart. After a few moments, he rubbed his face on their shoulders and then walked over to the side of his stall closest to Jonas.

After Carol and Jill were gone, Jonas approached. "You've been busy, my friend. This week you had two lessons in four days. How are you holding up?"

"I'm a little bit sore, but I feel fine," said Biz. "Susan is a good instructor. She's making sure I don't do too much, and Jill and Carol are very careful."

Jonas tipped his head. "That's good to hear. The three of you seem like a real family."

Biz felt emotional. "Jonas, how did I get so lucky?"

Jonas turned to face Biz and blinked. "I don't know. But is it luck? You suffered a lot and came through it with a kind heart intact. You earned happiness and you deserve it."

Biz pondered what Jonas said. "Thanks, Jonas. I guess I never looked at it that way."

"Don't overthink it. Just enjoy it and be happy."

Biz hoped Jonas was right. Since he arrived at Willow Bend, his life changed dramatically. He was finally happy and dreamt about a wonderful future with Jill and her mother. He looked forward to the first of October when he would leave for his new home just up the road. He couldn't wait to live at the little red house that looked so welcoming. The house with the lovely Montauk daisies and birch tree, planted with love. He was going to miss being with his friends every day, but he relished the idea of a family and a home. He hoped he'd adjust to seeing his friends only when he returned for lessons.

During his lessons, Biz saw himself in the indoor arena mirrors and couldn't believe his eyes. He loved looking and feeling handsome again. He understood that he still needed to put some pounds on, but he couldn't get over how much better he looked already. What a difference from how he felt the day he arrived at Willow Bend. All eyes were on him as he walked from the trailer into the barn with his head down. He felt awful that day and didn't ever want to look that bad or feel that depressed again.

~20~

On the first day of October, Biz moved home. Before he departed from Willow Bend, Jill brushed him, tacked him up, and led him to the arena where she used the mounting block to get in her saddle. She was pleased to see how much muscle he had already started to build. His back was higher. Stronger. As they walked down the farm driveway and up the back path, heading for home, all the horses whinnied goodbye, and Biz whinnied back. Jill laughed out loud because it felt funny when he whinnied while she was on his back. His whole body shook, and it made her body shake along with it. All the whinnies sounded like a choir of horses.

Jill couldn't wait to walk him into their yard. It was her mother's birthday. What a wonderful gift for someone whose dream was to have a horse at home. Before they left the barn for their journey home, Jill placed a big blue bow on Biz's halter because blue was her mother's favorite color. Jill knew her mother would give him just as much attention as she did, and sure enough, when they arrived, she greeted them with an iced tea for Jill and a big juicy apple for Biz.

"Happy birthday, Mom," said Jill.

Her mother saw the bow and immediately hugged Jill. "Biz is going to be such a big part of both of our lives now," said her mother as she took a deep breath and gazed at Biz.

Mom seems happier and more content than I've seen her in a long time, thought Jill as she walked Biz to his new paddock. When his saddle and bridle were off, Jill saw Biz look toward Willow Bend as if checking to make sure he could see his buddies. When his ears went up and he whinnied, it was confirmation that he saw them. When they answered, he stared in their direction for a moment, whinnied again, and then quietly ate his hay.

Her mother laughed. "I guess they're determined to stay in touch!"

Jill rubbed Biz's neck. "Don't worry, boy. You'll see them every week when we go back for lessons."

Her mother walked to the paddock fence. "I'm glad you took the back path home, honey. The road can be dangerous."

Jill exited the paddock and locked the gate. "Don't worry, Mom. Susan talked to the neighbors. They all said it was okay for me to ride the back property line down to the farm as long as I stay off their lawns. And Caleb said I can ride on his farm anytime, as long as I stay on the edge of the fields."

Her mother's eyes twinkled. "Susan talked to the neighbors? That's great. And it was very nice of Caleb to permit you to ride on the farm. He didn't have to do that, so make sure you abide by his wishes."

"Don't worry, Carol. I'm sure Jill will do just that," said Caleb, sneaking up behind them. "She's always been a good girl." Caleb looked at Biz. "And welcome to the neighborhood, Biz. I think you'll like it just fine here. Boy, he sure is a beauty, Jill."

Dad's words again, thought Jill.

"Such a magnificent head," said Caleb, examining Biz's profile. "He's even more handsome outside in the sunlight."

Jill knew she was beaming with pride. "Thanks, Caleb. We're so happy to have him."

Caleb seemed enthralled with Biz. He took a few steps forward, looked at Biz squarely from the front, and whistled softly. "Wow. He's just so handsome." Caleb seemed lost in thought until Biz leaned forward with his ears up and sniffed his pocket. Caleb laughed. "Oh. Do you smell your carrot?" Biz stared intently at the pocket until Caleb gave it to him. Caleb's eyes glazed over as he smiled.

"I know a lot about horses, so if you have any questions, just ask," said Caleb. "I truly mean that."

"Thank you, Caleb. I will. I promise," said Jill. Caleb waved goodbye and as Jill watched him walk away, she gave thanks for all that was good in her life. At that moment, she had a lot to be grateful for. Biz, her mother, Caleb, and Susan. It was wonderful to have so many people in her corner.

***

Back at the farm, the barn felt empty without Biz. Biz didn't talk much, but from the moment he arrived, he had quite a presence. Partly because he was a champ. Partly because of what happened to him. And partly because of how he handled it. Abdul thought he was amazing because he never seemed bitter or angry about the unhappy times in his life. He liked everyone and, no matter how deep his pain, he was always kind. Abdul would never forget how much better Biz made him feel after his accident and he was grateful. When Biz arrived at the farm, he said very little to anyone, yet he cared enough to tell Abdul that he completely understood and explained why. Abdul knew he did it because he was compassionate. "I wonder how Biz is doing?" Abdul said to Jonas

"I'm sure he misses having his friends around, but I'm willing to bet that boy is happy as heck. All he wanted was a home with a family. He told me that."

Abdul's eyes moistened. He was happy for Biz, but sad that he would only see Biz once or maybe twice a week. He needed Biz around all the time.

"Don't worry about Biz, Abdul," said Aiyana. "He's happy. He looked a little bit sad when he left, but I'm sure it was because he had a hard time leaving us. But when he headed up the path to his new home, his pace picked up. He was prancing. And it looked like he couldn't wait to get there. But I want you to know that before he left, Biz told me he was going to miss you the most."

Abdul stood up straight and looked directly at Aiyana. "He *did*? Are you just saying that to make me feel better?"

Aiyana laughed. "No. He said it. He was worried about leaving because he knew you'd be sad. He asked me to keep an eye on you and report to him when he comes back for lessons."

Abdul jumped up and down. "So he's really coming back every week?"

"Yes, for Jill's lesson *and* her mother's lesson," said Aiyana.

Abdul knew that Biz's first visit back to Willow Bend was going to be a grand homecoming and he couldn't wait.

~21~

The night Biz arrived at Tartan Glen, Jill sat down with Carol and explained how much to feed Biz and at what times. She seemed like a teacher as she detailed the importance of a routine feeding schedule and why sticking to it helped avoid colic. She even wrote it all out on the whiteboard so there would be no mistakes. By the time Jill was finished, Carol thought she seemed tired, so she offered to get up early and feed Biz his first breakfast at home. Carol wasn't shocked when Jill adamantly refused her offer. With her arms firmly across her chest, she said, "Are you kidding? No way. If you said it was okay, I'd sleep in the barn with him tonight. I don't want to leave his side. *I* want to be the one who greets him on his first morning at his new home, and *I* want to put his first breakfast in his feed tub. It *has* to be me."

Carol laughed out loud. "Okay, okay! I tried, but I didn't think for a second that you'd actually go for it."

Jill laughed.

Carol was excited that they were finally going to have horse smells in their barn. She drew in a deep breath, let it out, and felt her stress level drop.

In the morning, Carol heard Jill's alarm go off. As soon as it rang, she heard Jill run down the stairs, and then the kitchen door slammed. Carol jumped out of bed and from her bedroom window, she watched her little girl run to the barn and open the door. She laughed when she realized that Jill slept in sweatpants and a sweatshirt, probably so she could jump out of bed and see Biz as soon as possible. Carol opened her window just in time to hear Biz grunt for his food. He sounded hungry. Carol heard Jill talking to Biz, but she was too far away for Carol to understand what she was saying. Carol put on her robe and walked downstairs to make tea. When her cup was ready, she took it to the barn because she couldn't wait to see Biz, either.

Jill's smile was wide when Carol entered. "Morning, Mom."

"Morning, honey. You look like you're walking on clouds."

"Oh my gosh, Mom. Look at him. My own horse, in my own barn. This is *amazing*. Awesome."

Carol chuckled. She couldn't agree more. It *was* awesome. Carol couldn't help but admire Biz's handsome face as he ate. He looked so much better than the day she first saw him. Jill was doing a wonderful job. His gait was better since the thrush was eradicated and his coat was beautiful, now that he was being shampooed and groomed regularly. His mane and tail in braids made him look dapper. And his weight was better. He still needed to gain weight and build muscle, but that would come with time. Carol exhaled, walked over to Biz, and rubbed her hand on his cheek. "Enjoy your breakfast, Biz. I am *so* happy you're here. I'll be out to see you again later. Want some tea, honey?" asked Carol.

"Sure. I'll be done in a few minutes, Mom."

Carol walked back to the kitchen, picked out a mug for Jill, and reboiled the water. She was grateful that Biz's condition was improving, but she was still concerned about his overall health. She wondered when he last had a routine checkup and made a mental note to ask Jill.

When Jill came in, Carol was drinking tea and watching Biz out the kitchen window.

"Can it get any better, Mom? I'm so happy. He's only been here for one day, but he acts like he's been here forever. He's not a bit nervous. He looks completely at home. He's calmly eating his hay and seems ... content."

"He does seem relaxed. And you're right. It is wonderful to have him here. He's looking so much better, honey. Do you have any idea when he last saw a veterinarian?"

Jill turned and looked at her with concern. "Do you think there's something's wrong?"

"No. He seems fine, but I was wondering when he had his last routine checkup. Should we set one up so that if he gets sick, he already has a doctor?"

Jill scrunched her eyebrows. "I guess that's a good idea. There you go, thinking like a mother, even for Biz."

"This family has grown, and I have to look out for both of you now. Who's a good vet?"

Jill didn't hesitate. "Everyone likes Dr. Norris. She's really smart, experienced, and very nice. Plus, the practice is large, so there are always a couple of vets on call."

Carol trusted Jill's judgment, but she still ran it by Susan, who agreed whole-heartedly about the checkup, as well as Jill's choice for a veterinarian. On Monday morning, Carol called and made an appointment for Dr. Norris to come over late in the afternoon on the following Thursday, when Jill was home from school. When the day arrived, Dr. Norris seemed to recognize Jill because she got out of her truck, wearing a huge smile. She introduced herself to Carol and looked at Jill.

"You finally got a horse of your own, Jill?"

"Yes, finally," Jill said as she led Dr. Norris into the barn.

Carol was pleased that Dr. Norris knew Jill's name.

Dr. Norris walked into the barn and stopped as soon as she saw Biz. "Is this the horse that arrived at Willow Bend back in March?"

Jill beamed. "Yes. His name is Official Business."

"I was at the barn, stitching up a horse, the day he arrived. He seemed depressed and I couldn't believe how thin and out of shape he was."

The expression on Dr. Norris's face, as she recollected that afternoon, made Carol weepy. She was impressed by Dr. Norris's compassion. Then, in an instant, Dr. Norris's expression changed to happiness. "What a difference. His eyes are bright. His coat is nice and clean, and he put on weight. He looks great, Jill. You've done a marvelous job."

Carol felt enormous pride. She thought Jill was doing a great job, but when the veterinarian confirmed that, it was an incredible feeling. Carol could tell that Jill was proud of herself too. She grinned from ear to ear.

Dr. Norris listened to Biz's heart and lungs and then placed her stethoscope on different parts of his abdomen. She said she was making sure the sounds coming from his stomach and intestines were normal. After she checked his eyes, ears, teeth, and gums, she asked Jill to lead him outside for his lameness exam. She asked Jill to trot him in a straight line up and down the dirt driveway, and then in a circle, clockwise and counter-clockwise. Lastly, she tested his hooves for tenderness. When the exam was over, she said she saw some minor issues with all four of his legs, especially his front right foot.

Jill nodded. "He had thrush in all four feet. It was deep in the heel of the front right foot, but I think the infection is gone."

Dr. Norris closely inspected his feet. "You're right. It's gone. Splendid job," she said as she knelt and pointed to the heel of his front right foot. "See how he has more heel on that foot?"

Jill looked closely.

"He has a club foot. We evaluate them with a grading system from Grade 1 to Grade 4. Grade 1 is the mildest. Grade 4 is severe. This is mild."

"Will it interfere with showing?" asked Jill.

"Not at all. Lots of horses have them. Some are born with them, and others develop them. A good farrier will know the right way to trim the foot, but I don't want you to show him until he's back in shape and that will take time. You've already made great strides. He's coming along nicely. You should be proud."

Jill smiled and nodded.

Dr. Norris put her hand on Jill's shoulder to reassure her. "I don't see any reason to worry. He's healthy, and all in all, I'd say he's seventy percent serviceably sound. He has some issues, but as he gets back in shape, he'll likely work out of them. His hind end definitely needs to get stronger. But he has a *wonderful* disposition. I think he's a good horse for you, Jill. He certainly has a lot of potential."

After examining his teeth, Dr. Norris estimated that Biz was fifteen years old. She told Jill that he was still too thin and suggested that they feed him as much hay as he wanted, add an extra pint of grain to each feeding, and make sure he had plenty of water. She also suggested that she always keep an eye out for thrush. "Once they get it, they can be prone to it, so it's best to stay on top of it. Please be patient to allow his muscles to build gradually. If you do that, he'll be okay," said Dr. Norris as she got back in her truck. "Oh, and don't forget to give him plenty of love. He needs that, Jill. He's needed it for a very long time."

With that, Dr. Norris winked at Carol and backed out of the driveway. Jill and Carol gave Biz a big hug before going into the house for dinner. Carol knew that as each day passed, Biz would become a bigger part of their family. She felt content. At peace. And filled with love.

***

On Saturday morning, Biz knew Jill would be up early so they could be at the farm in time for their lesson. As they walked past the neighbor's yards on their way to the farm, Biz anxiously looked for his friends. He let out a loud whinny when he saw them, and they whinnied back. Biz chuckled when he heard the excitement in Abdul's voice.

"Look, it's Biz," said Abdul, running to the edge of the fence. Jonas walked over to Abdul, and they waited for Biz to make his way to them. Jill tried to steer Biz to the arena, but he wanted to go over to the paddock instead and hoped Jill wouldn't mind.

"Hey, you have a lesson to get to, son," chuckled Jonas.

"I know, but I wanted to say hello to you guys first," said Biz.

"What's your new barn like?" asked Abdul.

"It's *so* nice. I have a big stall and I can go in and out all day long. There's plenty of bedding, lots of food, and a big pasture. They're taking very good care of me, but I miss you guys."

"We miss you too," said Abdul.

"I know you do. I told you I would be back for lessons and here I am," Biz said as he reached his head over the fence and affectionately rubbed his nose on the top of Abdul's head. Abdul looked up and Biz saw how much emotion there was in his innocent eyes. It appeared to be a mixture of sadness, fear, and affection. "I'm always here for you, Abdul. You know that, right?"

It broke Biz's heart when Abdul nodded, and a small tear dislodged from his right eye.

Biz felt Jill nudge him toward the arena. "Come on, Biz. We have to get in there or Susan will give our lesson time away."

Biz looked at Abdul and their eyes met. "Sorry, little buddy, but I have to go."

Abdul slumped his shoulders and then his neck and head dipped down. "I know you do, Biz. It's okay. Enjoy your lesson."

Biz looked intently at Jonas before he turned. Jonas seemed to understand the message because he walked close enough to Abdul that their shoulders touched.

Biz bowed his head to Jonas in thanks. "I'll see you guys when the lesson is over. Abdul, I should be back on Saturdays for Jill's lesson and hopefully another day of the week for Carol's."

When he was halfway to the arena, Biz stopped, looked back at his friends, and purposely locked eyes with Abdul because he wanted him to know that it was hard for him to walk away.

~22~

Biz was part of everything Carol and Jill did. When the weather was nice, they ate supper in the backyard alongside the paddock as Biz ate his grain and hay. Sometimes Biz finished before them and became interested in what they were eating. One day, he walked behind Carol and grabbed a chicken wing out of her hand. Laughing, she jumped up and grabbed it back. After dinner, Carol loved to bring him slices of different types of fruit to see which ones he liked. Based on his reaction, she was sure peaches were his favorite. For vegetables, he seemed to love carrots, sugar snap peas, and corn husks. But his favorite seemed to be his hot bran mash on Friday nights with apples, carrots, molasses, and a peppermint. It was fun to see his excitement. As soon as he saw the steaming pot come out of the house, he started grunting and paced until it was in his feed bucket. He savored every morsel.

Carol came to realize that she was as much in love with Biz as Jill. She had one short, but wonderful lesson on Biz when he was at Willow Bend. She wanted more as well as some riding time on the trails, but she needed to make sure it was still okay with Jill, so she asked.

"Are you serious?" asked Jill.

"Yes. Are you mad at me?"

"Mad at you? No, I think it's great. I'd love it if you spent more time with him. Mom, I love Biz so much, but he needs more than just me. When he was at Willow Bend, I wanted to see him every day after school so he knew he wasn't alone. Since he came home, all he has is us and Caleb because there are no other horses in the barn. I don't go anywhere after school because I know he needs company. He's all I think about. He comes first. Always."

Carol didn't realize that Jill passed up opportunities to socialize. Since Jill was a toddler, she was content to be by herself. She loved to be at home, especially when Logan was there, and she *loved* Caleb. Jill liked other children, but she was particular. If a child knocked on the door or called and asked her to play, she wouldn't go if she didn't want to. She had a mind of her own. Carol always felt bad for the child that faced rejection, so she encouraged Jill to play, but once Jill said no, it was no.

After Logan died, Jill socialized with friends at school and went to birthday parties, but other than that, she just wanted to be at home. Carol's mind drifted. After Logan died, did Jill stay home because *she* needed to be with me? Or did she stay home because she thought *I* needed her?

Carol knew Jill was well-liked because when they were out shopping or at an event, kids went out of their way to say hello and stop to talk. While they talked, Carol heard them giggle and laugh. Her thoughts were interrupted when she realized Jill was talking to her.

"Mom? Did you hear me? Promise me you'll take more lessons before you even think about going on trails. And please don't go on trails alone. Biz is feeling better, so he might get frisky."

Carol nodded. "I will. I promise," she said, still preoccupied. The next day, Carol called Susan to ask about another riding lesson and arranged to have one on Wednesday afternoon, the only day of the week when she stopped working at noon. Jill asked her mother not to ride Biz on the road to get to her lesson, but instead, use the path behind the neighbor's houses. Carol chuckled. *Who's the parent?* she thought.

On Wednesday, Carol put Biz's saddle and bridle on, then put his halter over the bridle and attached a lead line before she hand-walked Biz down the path to Willow Bend. The horses whinnied and whinnied as they made their way down and Carol understood that Biz was missed.

***

Susan was already in the indoor arena when Carol arrived. She watched Carol leisurely walk Biz to the center. Her body was relaxed, and the lead line was loose. Susan was pleased that Carol seemed so comfortable with Biz. He was a big horse, so Carol could easily have felt intimidated in his shadow. Susan could barely see the top of Carol's head at his withers. It was more challenging to handle a horse from the ground as opposed to his back if he wasn't trained. A well-trained horse tried to keep an eye for where his handler was. Susan noticed that when Carol took a step closer to Biz, he took a step away in the same direction, keeping the appropriate distance between them. Biz appeared to be a perfect gentleman and it was apparent that he wanted to take care of his owners just as much as they took care of him.

Susan realized that she needed to know more about Carol's experience with horses, so she began the lesson with a few questions. "I probably should have asked you a few things during your first lesson, but we only had a half-hour, so I just observed. You said you rode horses when you were younger, but how many *lessons* did you have?"

Carol laughed. "I don't think I ever took an actual lesson. Back then, you just got on the horse and rode. I rode a lot as a teenager, but it was trail riding."

Susan tipped her head. "You told me that you rode western, but did you *ever* ride in an English saddle?"

Carol scrunched her lips and shook her head. "No. Not ever. English saddles scared me. They seemed too small ... like you had nothing underneath you. I liked a big western saddle because I had something deep to sit in and a horn to hold."

Susan smiled. "I can understand why you'd feel that way."

"Anyway, now I want lessons in an English saddle because I'm pretty sure Jill will show Biz someday. We should probably ride him the same way so he doesn't get confused."

Susan nodded. "Yes, that's true. You definitely should be riding him the same way. You did well during your first lesson in an English saddle, so now you're aware that there are differences, especially with how you hold your reins, but we'll start from the beginning. Don't worry about a thing. I teach beginners all the time, and a surprising number are women with children who ride. In truth, from the conversations I've had, I think they give riding lessons to their children, so they have a good enough reason to be around horses themselves."

Carol grinned as she rubbed Biz's neck. "You may be on to something with that theory."

"Okay. Let's get started. Get on Biz, using the mounting block, please."

While Carol mounted, Susan watched how Biz reacted to the weight on his back and explained the importance of using the mounting block, just as she did with Jill. Over the years, Susan saw so many horses refuse to stand still while their rider mounted, but Biz stood exactly where he was supposed to and didn't move a muscle while Carol positioned herself in the saddle. For the next half-hour, without the lunge line, Susan coached Carol through some of the same exercises from her first lesson, plus a few more. Biz seemed more comfortable with the weight of a rider on his back, and he moved differently. He seemed more agile. More willing. She wondered if Carol was able to feel the difference.

At the end of her lesson, Carol directed Biz back to the center of the ring and dismounted on the mounting block. As soon as her feet hit the ground, she turned to Susan. "Oh my goodness, Susan, that was amazing. It was so much fun, and it felt like Biz enjoyed himself too. No matter how many times I ride him, I'll never tire of the excitement."

Susan laughed. "It looked like both of you had a good time."

Carol rubbed Biz's cheek with her hand. "He is so comfortable to ride. I swear, he felt even more comfortable than the first time. Did he look different to you, Susan?"

"How do you mean?"

"I don't know. It felt like he was moving better."

Susan was impressed. "I'm surprised that you noticed that. Yes. He seemed less stiff, and his stride was a bit longer. He's coming along."

Carol took such a deep breath that it raised her chest. "This may sound crazy, but his trunk felt wider beneath my legs. Is that even possible? Could he have gained enough weight for me to notice a difference?"

"He is steadily gaining weight. I can see it. If I can see it, it's possible for you to feel it."

Carol seemed emotional. She put Biz's reins in one hand, reached out to Susan with the other, and rested it on her shoulder. "Susan, I want to thank you. All along the way, Jill told me how much you helped her with Biz while he was at Willow Bend. Your advice and your assistance, especially with groundwork before anyone got on his back, were so helpful for her. I want you to know how much we appreciate all you've done, and how much we value you and your friendship. You're our instructor, but we also regard you as a very good friend."

Susan felt herself blush. "Thank you, Carol. It was my pleasure. Jill's great. She's different from most of the kids here. They act so entitled. Jill is gracious and eager to help just about anyone, so it's kind of natural to want to help her."

Carol smiled. "Thank you for saying that, Susan. I think she's a great kid, but she's mine, so I'm biased. It's wonderful to hear it from someone else, especially you. I know how much she likes and respects you. You are a role model and mentor to her. I'll never feel I've done enough to thank you for all that you've done for us."

Susan was beginning to understand where Jill got her big heart. Lots of parents thanked Susan, but none were as heartfelt and sincere. "Carol, there is no reason to feel indebted. I helped because I wanted to and I'm glad I did. It was the right thing to do."

Carol's eyes glistened. "We wouldn't have Biz if it wasn't for you."

Biz took a step toward the arena door and then turned to Carol.

Susan chuckled. "I think that's your cue."

"I think so. It's time to head home and take a hot bath. I'll see you soon, Susan."

"Same time next week?"

"I'll be here," Carol said as she loosened Biz's noseband and then took off the bridle, put on his halter, attached the lead rope, and kissed his nose. "I'll carry your bridle, Biz. We'll make the trek home with just your halter so you can munch grass without a noseband or a bit in your mouth." Biz nuzzled his nose into her shoulder, and she responded with a hug around his neck. As they started to walk past the paddocks, Susan heard him whinny to his friends and they answered. Susan sighed. She never felt better. The unending love and attention Biz got from Jill and Carol warmed her heart.

As Biz and Carol approached the pathway, Susan felt a flood of anxiety course through her body because she realized that she broke the rules, and once again, it had to do with Carol, Jill, and Biz.

When Noah hired Susan, he said horses were not allowed to be trucked in because lesson time was only for boarders, or a barn worker or student having a lesson on one of Susan's horses. Biz didn't belong to Susan, and he no longer boarded there. Susan should not have given Jill and Carol lessons on him—they already had four. Susan felt a knot in her stomach because she knew she had to call Noah, tell him the truth, and ask him to make an exception. She hoped he would. If not, she'd ask if he minded if she gave Jill and Carol lessons at their house. Susan put her head down, closed her eyes, and walked to her office. Once inside, she closed the door, took a deep breath, sat at her desk, and dialed his number. He picked up on the third ring.

"Hi, Noah, it's Susan."

"Hi, Susan. What can I do for you? You sound a little somber. Is everything okay?"

"Well, I have a confession to make, and I need a favor."

Noah laughed. "Now that's the Susan I know. Straight to the point. So tell me, what have you done and what do you need?"

By the tone in Noah's voice, Susan could tell that he was in a good mood. She figured that he was going to have fun with what she was about to tell him. "Noah, I broke the rules, but I didn't realize it until just now, so I'm calling to confess, explain, and ask you to make an exception."

Susan heard Noah inhale. "Okay, continue. But I have to ask, does this have anything to do with the lessons you're giving Jill and her mother on Biz, a horse that is no longer boarded at Willow Bend?"

Susan was astounded. "You knew?"

Noah roared with laughter. "Yes, I saw Biz's name on your lesson schedule. The schedule on the *big* whiteboard in the barn."

Susan squinted her eyes and then shut them. "Ugh ... Noah, I'm sorry." She felt the corners of her mouth curl down. "The lines got blurred. Biz did board here and Jill is technically still a barn worker. But Biz no longer boards here, and since he left, Jill and her mother had lessons on him at Willow Bend."

Noah cackled with what sounded like delight. "Okay, so I have your confession. What's the favor?"

Susan felt her heart beat faster and then her mouth went completely dry. "Noah, please don't make me send them away. Biz is doing well, and I'm emotionally invested in Biz, Jill, *and* her mother. I want to be a part of it. I *need* to be part of it. I don't know why, but I do. If you ask me to stop, I will, but it'd be like asking me to sever a limb."

Noah was quiet for a moment, then he spoke softly. "Well, we can't have you managing the barn and teaching without a limb. Go ahead and give your lessons. If anyone complains, tell them to talk to me. You have my full support. Biz is a good horse and Jill and her mother seem like nice people. They're our neighbors and part of the Willow Bend family. All I need, Susan, is a release and hold harmless form signed by each of them in case they get hurt on the property."

Susan gasped with delight. "Really?"

"Really." Noah chuckled. "Thanks for being honest with me, Susan. You know how much I appreciate it."

"Thank you for being so understanding, Noah."

"You bet."

Susan exhaled when she hung up the phone. She was relieved and grateful to Noah, the most amazing person she ever worked for. She pulled out the drawer where she kept the release and hold harmless forms because she planned to bring a couple to Jill and Carol, explain the situation, and get them signed. She placed the forms on her desk and then sat back in her chair and snickered. Noah knew. And he never said a word. It was a good thing she told him as soon as she realized her mistake, otherwise, his trust in her would have been damaged.

***

Caleb saw Carol leave for her lesson and let out a sigh of relief when he saw that she decided to hand-walk Biz to Willow Bend. He knew she could ride, but it was a long time since she was in the saddle, except for one short lesson. Caleb was around horses enough to know that it didn't take much to spook them, and it was much better to be able to let go of the reins than get thrown off their backs. But truth be told, he was just as nervous about Carol hand-walking Biz down an open trail. He was a big horse. Powerful. If he got spooked, it was hard to hold on to the reins and try to control his fight or flight response. Until horse and rider were used to one another, Caleb preferred that Carol handle him in a fenced outdoor ring or an indoor arena, not an open field or trail. Caleb kept a watchful eye as Carol and Biz made their way to Willow Bend, and when he figured it was time for them to come back, he positioned himself so he could watch them come home.

He was amused when Carol let Biz stop and munch on mounds of lush green grass as they made their way up the path back home. When they reached the edge of his yard, Caleb pretended he wasn't watching by acting surprised to see them. He jumped up from his garden and skedaddled over to their yard and opened the paddock gate. In the paddock, Caleb held Biz while Carol took off his saddle and protective boots. After Carol put his tack away, she brushed Biz and picked out his hooves, and Caleb asked about her lesson.

"Biz is doing very well, Caleb. Thanks for asking and thank you so much for your help today. Our lesson was fun. I'm learning so much. Susan thinks Biz had a lot of training in his younger years, and he seems to remember it. He's not just beautiful. He's smart and very talented."

"He is a beauty, Carol."

Carol's smile widened. "He sure is. He's our handsome boy."

Caleb liked Biz and hoped his worries would dwindle as he got to know him better. He didn't believe Biz would ever intentionally hurt Jill or Carol. He worried about unintentional injuries. The kind that happened when you trusted so much that you didn't pay attention, forgot to follow safety rules, or dropped your guard.

Caleb's mind drifted back to when he was a young lad. Hannah, the little girl next door, had a small pinto pony. She was eight years old, and she rode her little tan and white companion everywhere. They were inseparable. Best friends. She didn't think her pony would ever hurt her.

As a youngster, Caleb learned two of the most important rules for barn safety. The first one was to never go in a stall with a horse unless you were the one closest to the stall door, just in case you needed to make an emergency exit. The second was to never lock the stall door while you were inside, so you could get out as quickly as possible. One day, Hannah went into the stall and disregarded the rules. While she was in there, the pony got stung by bees that built a hive in the wall. Hannah wasn't closest to the stall door, so she couldn't open it quickly enough to free herself and her four-legged friend as the bees swarmed. Both of them got stung over and over again. The pony spun in circles and blindly kicked out in all directions, trying to get away from the bees. He didn't mean to hurt Hannah, but she was kicked several times. She was covered in bruises and had several broken ribs. It was a terrible accident, but everyone knew it could have been a lot worse. Hannah could have been killed.

Caleb shook his head. He didn't understand why that memory came back to him at that moment, but he wasn't going to dwell on it while Jill and Carol got accustomed to Biz. He wanted them to be cautious, not fearful, so he decided not to tell Carol that story. Caleb understood that when people know all the bad stuff that can happen, it can prevent them from enjoying what's good. Biz was good for them. He preferred to think about that.

"Well, I'm heading back home. I'm around if ya need me," said Caleb. He turned and took a few steps toward the paddock gate and Biz whinnied, so Caleb stopped and looked at him. Biz was standing tall and looking right at him.

Carol affectionately ran her hand along Biz's neck. "It's pretty clear that whinny was for you, Caleb. I think he was saying goodbye."

Caleb tipped his head and smiled at Biz. "I'll see ya later, big fella," said Caleb and he headed toward his house. When he reached his porch, he looked back at Biz. He was still watching Caleb. Caleb's heart melted because it was obvious that Biz considered him family.

***

Carol finished grooming Biz, and then let him graze in the pasture so she could go in the house and take a hot bath. She needed one. In the saddle, she used muscles she hadn't used in a long time and knew she was going to be sore. As she lay soaking in the hot water, she thought about her lesson and the walk home. So many times in the past, when she saw someone riding or walking their horse, she would say to herself, *someday*, that will be me. It was finally her someday and it was an incredible feeling. As soon as she was out of the tub, she put on her most comfortable robe and slippers, and then she made a hot cup of tea. She grabbed the new horse magazine she ordered and sat on the sofa to read it. The magazine had a comprehensive story about horse massage that explained why it was beneficial, especially for older horses or horses with sore muscles from injury or increased levels of training. After one hour-long lesson on Biz, Carol felt like she needed a massage. She imagined that Biz needed it even more.

Carol loved to ride, but since they brought Biz home, she discovered that her true passion was taking care of him. She thoroughly enjoyed grooming Biz and tending to his every need. She was glad that her focus was his care because it meant that when Jill eventually showed him, she could be their groom. Grooms helped horses and riders during shows, making sure the horse was properly groomed, and that the rider looked polished. The very idea was satisfying. She wondered if she should take grooming one step further and learn how to do horse massage. That way, she could help Biz be more comfortable as he got back in shape.

The next time she was at the grain store, Carol looked for a book on horse massage. They always had a large selection of equestrian magazines and books, but she couldn't find one, so she asked if it was possible to order one. It came in a few days later and Carol quickly thumbed through it and bought it. After reading the book, she looked at Biz's body through a different set of eyes and started gently practicing what she learned. She wasn't afraid because the book explained that when massage was done preventively, it was gentle and could easily be described as modified grooming. If she thought Biz needed something deeper, she would consult with Susan, and if need be, Dr. Norris.

As Carol massaged Biz, she noticed that he seemed reactive around his hips. When she touched that area, his ears went back, and he looked at her inquisitively. If she continued, he took a small step away and looked back at her again. She got the message. It was uncomfortable, so she worked very gently in that area. Carol remembered that Dr. Norris said Biz's hind end needed to get stronger. And Susan once commented that Biz needed to pick up his back legs when he walked because he dragged his toes. She wondered if sore hips could cause him to do this and made a mental note to ask Susan. The next time Carol saw Susan, she told her about the horse massage book and what she observed.

"I had no idea you were interested in horse massage, Carol. I think it's great that you're doing that for him. Many horses need it, but nobody does it around here. The short answer to your question is yes, sore hips can make him drag his toes, but we can do some exercises during his lessons to help with that. We can have him trot over fence rails lying flat on the ground. He'll have to use his hips more, to get his feet over them. Walking backward also helps. He'll get a bit sorer before he gets better, so we'll start slowly and help him work through it. In the end, he'll be much stronger, and the soreness will eventually go away."

"Should we be worried about the amount of tenderness he has in his hips now?" asked Carol.

"No. Tenderness is to be expected, now that he's back in training. Horses are no different than humans. If you started exercising after years of inactivity, your body would hurt, too. Some places more than others. In time, it should go away on its own."

Carol nodded.

Susan sighed. "Carol, while I have you here, I need to ask you and Jill to sign a release and hold harmless form so you can keep taking lessons on Biz at Willow Bend."

"I have no problem signing a release, Susan. It's pretty common practice, isn't it? I signed one for Jill when she started working at Willow Bend and I'm happy to sign one for me as well."

"Yes, but I made a special one just for you and Jill since he's your horse and you're riding him at Willow Bend."

Carol felt her head tip to the side.

"Confused?" chuckled Susan. "Without meaning to, we broke the rules. Lessons at Willow Bend are for boarders or students riding *my* lesson horses. Noah is happy to make an exception for you, Jill, and Biz because you're neighbors, and as Noah put it, part of the Willow Bend family. He just asked that you each sign a release form. You will have to sign Jill's form, too because she's a minor."

"Of course," said Carol. She was more than happy to accommodate Noah's needs and she was grateful that he made an exception for them.

* * *

Biz looked forward to Carol's Wednesday lesson because he knew he received a massage afterward. It helped loosen him up, plus when Carol finished, she gave him a special treat, like peaches, if she had some. They were his favorite fruit, but carrots, apples, hay cubes, and peppermints were acceptable substitutes.

Biz felt like a big, spoiled horse. Anything he wanted or needed was his. Every day before work, Carol groomed him. Later in the afternoon, when Jill got home from school, she told him all about her day as she cleaned his stall and brushed him for the second time. She simply had to be the one to add the finishing touches at the end of the day. He *loved* it when she told him that. He loved the attention and treasured the fact that this family couldn't seem to live without him. For the first time in years, he felt like he meant just as much to his owners as they meant to him. He knew he would be with them for the rest of his life.

Occasionally, Biz thought about Maggie, but only to wonder how she was doing. He no longer had those awful pangs in his heart. His life with Maggie was over a long time ago, but he was okay with it because his new life was filled with more love than he ever thought was possible. It felt good to be able to trust again and it was wonderful to no longer feel afraid. He experienced what it felt like to be the center of the universe for the two people he loved most. He knew he was thought about in every decision Jill and Carol made. Whether they made plans to go shopping, run errands, or purchase supplies, he always heard them say, "Who will feed Biz?" or "Does Biz need anything?" Somehow, he wove himself into the fabric of this family and he wondered how on earth he became so lucky. How amazing it was to feel whole again.

~23~

Jill took lessons with Biz at Willow Bend and practiced at home in the pasture. She practiced so much that Biz's hooves started to wear a ring in the grass. She wished they could afford for her to take more lessons to help get Biz back in shape and ready for the show ring, but she figured that they would have to give up something to make that possible and she didn't want to be selfish. As it was, she didn't understand how her mother made everything work financially. She wondered if her mother was secretly working overtime to make ends meet.

On a Friday afternoon, while Jill was practicing in the paddock, a car pulled into the driveway. A woman got out and walked toward her. She approached cautiously, as if being mindful not to spook the horse, and introduced herself. She said her name was Sarah and she lived about four miles up the road. Sarah told Jill that years before, she watched the barn being built, and from the very beginning, liked the way it was set up. She added that when she saw the new paddock fence go up, she knew a horse was coming and couldn't wait to see it. "He's very handsome," said Sarah. "What kind of horse is he?"

"His name is Biz and he's an Anglo-Trakehner," said Jill. Right away, Jill knew that Sarah never heard of it, so she quickly added that it was a cross between a thoroughbred and a European warmblood.

"Oh, my. That's an interesting combination. The spirit and athleticism of a racehorse, combined with the strong bones and level-headedness of a warmblood. I bet he's wonderful."

Jill nodded. "He sure is. We love him very much."

Sarah sighed. "Well, when I watched this barn go up, I didn't know that I would someday ask if I could board my horse here. He's always been at my parents' house, but they're downsizing, and I don't have enough land where I live. I would like him to be close by and in a small barn, like the one my parents have. A place like this."

Jill felt excited. "Let me get my mother. She's the one you need to speak to." Jill dismounted and quickly removed Biz's tack before she put him in his stall. "I'll be right back, boy," she said as she sprinted toward the house and went into the kitchen. "Mom? There's a lady named Sarah here who would like to talk to you."

Her mother came out of her office. "Do you know what she wants?"

"She wants to know if she can keep her horse here. Come outside."

They walked outside together. "It's lovely to meet you, Sarah. My name is Carol, and you've already met my daughter, Jill," said her mother as she put her hand on Jill's shoulder. Sarah told her mother how much she loved the barn and explained her situation.

"Well, this is unexpected. Boarding a horse was suggested to me when we initially planned to bring Biz home, but I haven't given it much thought." Her mother looked over at Biz. "I guess it would be good for Biz to have company. He's Jill's horse. I also ride him and help take care of him, but he belongs to her. Do you mind if we discuss it and get back to you?"

Sarah's smile told Jill that she was pleased that her mother was even considering it. "Of course," she said, as she wrote down her full name and phone number on a piece of paper and handed it to her. "The quick sale of my parents' house has me in a bit of a dither. As you can see, I'm about to have a baby. I'd like to get my horse settled in his new home before the baby comes."

Her mother reached out and shook Sarah's hand. "I promise to get back to you as soon as possible. I'll call you no later than Sunday evening."

"That sounds wonderful," said Sarah, and she headed to her car.

Jill stepped forward. "Sarah, is your horse a stallion, gelding, or a mare?"

"A bay Arabian gelding," replied Sarah. "He's fourteen years old and stands just over fifteen hands tall."

During supper, Jill and her mother discussed Sarah and her horse. "I've been thinking about it ever since she left. It could be good for Biz, and the money would sure help with expenses, but I didn't want to say yes until we talked. What do you think?" asked her mother.

"Well, it's good that he's a gelding."

"Why is that important?"

"Because mares can be temperamental, and stallions can be aggressive. Geldings tend to be more level-headed, and they get along better with other horses."

"I have a lot to learn," said her mother, looking at her inquisitively. "You smiled and nodded when she told you his breed and size. Why do we need to know that?"

"We need to know because the bigger they are, the more it costs to feed them, and the more room they need. Plus, some breeds are jittery and nervous, so they can be a safety issue."

Carol laughed. "I think that having a horse at home is going to be one of the biggest learning experiences of my life. Why don't we call Sarah? We can ask those questions as well as any others you have. Better yet, why not have her come back?"

Jill didn't think that was a good idea. "I think we should talk to Susan first. We have to ask Susan how much to charge, and she might even suggest some more questions."

Her mother nodded. "Good thinking, honey. Of course, Susan should be included."

After the dinner dishes were washed, her mother called Susan and explained what was happening. Susan suggested that Sarah come back late Saturday afternoon when she could personally be there, so her mother called Sarah and set up the meeting.

On Saturday, when Sarah came back, Susan, Jill, and her mother were all there to greet her. Sarah had pictures of her horse, Sonny, and told them all about him. She said she got him when she was twelve years old. She was taking riding lessons at the barn where he was born and instantly fell in love with him. Sonny's mother, a black Arabian mare, belonged to her riding instructor and she let Sarah help take care of him.

Sarah explained that her instructor taught her how to train Sonny. When she saw how devoted Sarah was to him, she secretly asked Sarah's parents if they wanted to buy him because she knew Sarah would be heartbroken if someone else bought him and took him away. When Sonny turned two, her parents built a small barn in their backyard and brought him home. He was stabled there ever since. "My sister and I are both married now, and the house is too big for my parents. They put it on the market, and it sold faster than expected. Now, we're scrambling to find a home for Sonny," Sarah said.

Jill liked Sarah, and she could tell that Susan and her mother did, too. From what Sarah described, Sonny seemed like the kind of horse they'd want for a boarder. Jill saw her mother look at Susan for guidance. Susan asked if they could go to her parents' house to meet Sonny before a decision was made, and Sarah agreed without hesitation.

"If you have time, we can do it right now. He's only about ten minutes away," said Sarah.

Everyone had time, so they piled into Susan's truck and followed Sarah. When they arrived, Sonny was eating hay in his paddock. His ears went up as they approached, and he walked to the fence to greet them. Susan asked permission to enter his paddock. Sarah opened the gate and Sonny stood quietly as Susan approached him. Susan stroked his neck and talked softly to him, and then she reached down and touched his hay to see if he was food aggressive. He had no reaction when she touched his hay or when she picked it up and moved the pile. Next, she asked Sonny to lift his front left foot, just as someone would do when attempting to clean his hooves. He instantly lifted it and stood calmly. Lastly, Susan asked Sarah for a lead line. Susan attached it to his halter, and he let Susan walk him around the paddock without resistance. Susan smiled and nodded at Jill and her mother.

Before they left Sarah's parents' house, her mother agreed on a price for the monthly board based on the parameters Susan gave them. Susan said to start high and negotiate lower if need be. Jill was surprised when Sarah jumped at the first figure. She seemed elated and said that as soon as she knew when Sonny had to leave her parents' house, she would call.

Jill was happy. If things worked out, Biz would have company. Her mother never talked about money, so Jill had no reason to think money was horribly tight, but she understood that having a horse at home was an added expense. A monthly board check would help.

* * *

Biz met Sarah the day she stopped by, and of course, Jill told him all about Sonny when she groomed him. From what Jill said, Biz wondered if Sonny knew how to behave around horses since he wasn't around them in years.

The afternoon before Sonny arrived, Caleb went over to help figure out the best way to divide the paddock. When he finished scribbling on a piece of paper, Biz watched him go into the barn and come back out with electric fence tape, fence handles, a cedar post, and a shovel. He asked Jill to drain the trough and then they moved it against the barn. He asked Carol to hand him the shovel, and then he dug a hole directly in front of the trough, inserted the fence post, and held it while Jill and Carol backfilled the dirt around it. Caleb packed the dirt around the pole, stood back to make sure it was straight, and then he inserted a screw eye about four feet up the post. Biz was amazed at how quickly and accurately Caleb worked.

Once the post was in place, they rolled out enough fence tape to cut the paddock in half. Caleb attached a fence handle to one end of the tape and hooked the handle onto the screw eye. Then they walked the other end of the tape to the far end of the paddock, attached another handle, tightened the tape through it until the line was taut, and hooked it to an existing fence post. "The way I did this, both horses can go in and out of their stalls all day long and have access to water. And the partition will be easy to take down when they can be outside together," said Caleb. Carol and Jill seemed grateful, and so was Biz, because the divider would give him the protection he needed if Sonny got out of control.

The next morning, Sonny arrived, and Biz watched Sarah guide him off the trailer. When his feet were firmly on the ground, he stood quietly and looked around, seemingly taking in his new surroundings. After a few minutes, Sarah walked him around the barn and paddock and then led him into his stall where a pile of hay and a bucket of cool water were waiting for him. Sonny locked eyes with Biz and softly whinnied when he entered the stall. Biz whinnied back. Sonny nibbled hay and drank some water, but he seemed much more interested in Biz. He even pushed his nose against a crevice in the wall that separated their stalls and inhaled Biz's scent. Biz could see Sonny's wet nose through the space between the boards and chuckled to himself when Sonny squealed and snorted. He knew Sonny wanted to get better acquainted, but for the moment, Biz was glad there was a wall between them because he knew it wasn't unusual for a new horse to nip and kick. Except for some squeals and a few snorts, Sonny seemed calm, so after a short while, Biz walked closer to the stall wall.

"Welcome, Sonny. I'm Biz."

"Hi, Biz. Nice to meet you. How long have you lived here?"

"I was at Willow Bend Farm, right down the road, until they finished fencing in the paddock and pasture. I moved here about a month and a half ago."

"Are the owners nice?"

"Yes. I'm very happy here. I think you will be, too. Relax and eat your hay."

Sonny nodded.

The rest of the day and the evening were uneventful. Sonny stopped whinnying, squealing, and snorting long before the horses ate supper. The next morning, Biz heard Jill and Carol discussing when to put the two of them in the paddock together.

"Susan said to wait a few days for Sonny to settle in and then try it. If it doesn't work out, we should separate them again," Jill said.

Carol sighed. "Okay, we'll see how it goes. I just don't want Biz to get hurt."

"Don't worry, Mom. We'll make sure he doesn't."

Biz was sure they would keep a watchful eye.

***

A few days later, after breakfast, they took down the partition and tried turning them out together. Biz noticed that Sonny was peeking at him while he ate his hay, and then he hesitantly walked over to Biz and sniffed him. Biz knew it was routine to be sniffed, so he stood still until Sonny finished checking him out from nose to tail. Biz breathed a sigh of relief when Sonny casually walked away and went back to his pile of hay.

About a half-hour later, Sarah arrived. Biz walked to the end of the paddock where she parked, and Sonny followed too closely. Biz turned, looked directly at him, and then stepped away from him. Sonny didn't seem to get the hint and stepped closer. Biz walked away, hoping Sarah might distract him, but it didn't work. Sonny chased Biz and nipped his butt. It startled Biz, so he ran, but Sonny followed, continually nipping. Frustrated, Biz turned and looked intently at Jill and Carol, hoping they would separate them again.

"Biz isn't happy, Mom."

"I know he isn't, honey. Should we give it more time or end this now?"

Sarah sprinted toward Jill and Carol. "I never saw him behave like this. I'm so sorry. What should we do?"

"I think we should separate them again," said Jill.

Sarah scrunched her forehead. "Okay ... I was hoping we wouldn't have to, but let's do it. Biz doesn't deserve this."

Biz heard the conversation and took a deep breath. He wanted to be patient because he knew Sonny just wanted to be friends. He hoped Sonny understood that they would never be friends if he kept biting him.

Biz was relieved when Caleb walked over. "I was hoping they'd work things out, but it's clear that's not going to happen right away," said Caleb as he retrieved the partition from the barn and quickly put it back up. "Hopefully, the nipping will stop soon. It usually does."

Biz observed Sarah as Caleb put up the partition. He thought she understood why separating him from Sonny was necessary.

Over the following days, Biz was pleased that Sarah visited Sonny frequently as he got accustomed to his new home. It was clear that she wanted Sonny to know that she was still his owner, and nothing changed except where he lived. He heard Sarah say that Sonny needed exercise to keep his stress levels down, but she didn't dare ride, being so far along in her pregnancy. Biz watched Sarah devotedly hand-walk Sonny down the pathway and lunge him in the field to calm his frayed nerves. Biz suspected that Sarah felt guilty because she knew that once the baby arrived, she would most likely have very little time for him.

Biz didn't talk to Sonny very much when they were outside because he didn't want to get too close. The partition helped, but if Biz was right next to it, Sonny reached his head over or under it and nipped. The most Biz ever said to Sonny was, "Hey, stop that. It hurts." He was discouraged when Sonny blankly stared back at him, like he didn't understand he was doing something wrong.

Biz understood that it wasn't easy to be in a new place surrounded by new people and new horses. He felt sorry for Sonny and decided it was time to talk things through.

"How are you doing today, Sonny?" asked Biz.

Sonny looked startled when Biz spoke. "Okay, I guess."

"Do you like it here?"

"It's nice. I like my stall, and I like that I can go in and out all day, just like at Sarah's parents' house. Everyone seems friendly, but it's all so different. Different barn. Different paddock. Different people. Different noises. I'm nervous. And I don't know how long it's going to take for me to feel like this is my home. The place I left was the only home I ever had after I left my mom."

Biz sympathized. "I understand better than you realize. I've been through it a few times myself. It will get better. I promise. Jill and her mother are wonderful. I know in my heart that this is my forever home and I'm sure you'll want to call it home too."

Sonny tipped his head and blinked so slowly that his eyes closed. "I miss my home and I miss Sarah's parents. They're the ones who took care of me after Sarah got married. Sarah says they're busy getting settled into their new house and don't have time to visit me just yet. It feels like they don't miss me, and it hurts. I feel ... abandoned."

"Abandoned? Why? Sarah comes to see you all the time.

"I know she does. I love her, but I still miss my home."

Biz was tall enough to look down at Sonny. "Give it a little more time. I'm sure they'll stop by soon. You'll adjust to your new home, Sonny, but in the meantime, please stop biting me. It hurts and it doesn't make me want to be around you. I know you're upset, but you have to find another way to express it. My patience is growing thin."

Sonny sighed. "Sorry, Biz. I'll try."

"Why do you nip me?" asked Biz.

Sonny shrugged his shoulders. "I don't know. It makes me feel good when I do it and then I feel awful. I can't seem to control it but I know I have to stop."

Biz nodded emphatically. "It's nasty aggressive behavior that won't be accepted or tolerated here. If you want to keep living here, you better stop."

Sonny's eyes grew wide.

"They're hoping you'll grow out of it. If you don't, I doubt they'll let you stay," Biz continued because he felt he had to make Sonny understand there would be consequences for his actions.

~24~

Over the next few weeks, Sonny settled in, and the nipping stopped, so Carol thought they should try taking down the partition again. At first, Sonny was well-behaved, but as time passed, he occasionally nipped Biz. Each time Carol saw it, she was disheartened because Biz, always a gentleman, just stood there and took it. She wondered if he would ever stand up for himself. He didn't seem to have an aggressive bone in his body. Carol and Jill discussed whether they made a mistake when they gave Sonny a stall. Did the benefits outweigh the disadvantages? They had extra money and Biz wasn't alone, but Biz had a smaller paddock, and his stablemate was a pain in the butt. Literally. In the end, they decided to hang tough and see how things panned out. Things did calm down, but six weeks after Sonny arrived, Sarah had a beautiful baby boy, and she wasn't able to get to the barn for weeks. During that time, Sonny nipped at Biz, and he even charged at Jill when she cleaned the paddock.

"Mom? Did you *see* that?" yelled Jill. "Sonny just tried to run over me. I had to jump over the fence to get out of the way. I think he wanted to knock me down."

Carol ran outside. "Are you sure? He's never done anything like *that* before. Has he?"

"No, but he did try to nip me the other day. I think he's upset because Sarah hasn't been around."

Carol's knees buckled as she realized how badly Jill could have been hurt. "You're right. He is upset, but the reason why can't be helped right now. Sarah has to recover. But even after she recovers, she's going to have less time for Sonny, so this behavior probably won't stop. If he keeps nipping and charging, we'll have to decide whether we want Sonny to stay or break Sarah's heart and ask them to leave. If we let him stay, we have to figure out how to properly deal with him. In the meantime, honey, you can clean stalls, but only if you lock both horses outside while you're in there. And I don't want you in the paddock at all. I'll take care of that."

Jill looked like she wanted to protest, and then her lips quivered. "How do you know *you'll* be safe in the paddock. What if he knocks *you* down?"

Carol instinctively knew that Jill was afraid of losing her, too. She walked over and hugged Jill, and then she held her face in her hands and looked deeply into her eyes to calm her fears. "I'll be careful. If he's being fresh, I'll lock him in his stall when I clean the paddock."

With wet eyes, Jill nodded. "Okay, Mom, but promise me that you'll be extra careful around him."

Carol agreed that she would. No shortcuts. No rule-breaking. Safety first.

Carol wondered if they did the right thing when they allowed Sonny to come to the barn. It was one thing after another since he arrived. Peace and tranquility seemed to be disappearing. The behavior they hoped was transient, wasn't, and Carol didn't know what to do about it except have a long talk with Susan and Caleb before it got completely out of hand.

Carol's mind drifted back in time. When Sonny first arrived at Tartan Glen, he didn't seem to care when Biz left for a lesson at Willow Bend, but since the baby arrived and Sarah stopped coming, he seemed agitated, especially when Biz left. The last time Jill left for her lesson, Carol coaxed Sonny into his stall with some hay and treats because he screamed and paced frantically as Biz disappeared from sight. His screams became shrill enough to cause Caleb to come out of his house, and Jill to come back up the path. When Carol saw Jill, she yelled for her to turn around because she had the situation under control. Jill turned around, but she did it hesitantly, and only after Caleb nodded and waved her on. It was clear that Jill was worried, and Caleb seemed unsettled. She didn't want Caleb or Jill to always be worried about her. It wasn't healthy.

The following Wednesday, as Carol got ready for her lesson, she worried that Sonny might get upset enough to break out of the paddock, so she kept him in his stall with plenty of hay and water. As she rode Biz to Willow Bend, she heard Sonny whinnying, and apparently, Caleb did too, because he stepped out of his house and promised Carol he would keep a close eye on him until she returned. The farther she got from the barn, the more frenzied his whinnies became. Carol's heart ached for him, but she understood that he had to get used to being alone, so she didn't turn around. She felt frazzled when she got to Willow Bend and she knew it was visible because Susan asked what was wrong. Carol told her about Sonny and asked for advice. Susan told her to ask Sarah to buy a calming supplement to give Sonny a couple of hours before she or Jill planned to leave the property with Biz. She explained that the medication would not take away all of the anxiety, but it would at least help take the edge off.

Carol and Biz arrived home an hour and a half later. Caleb was inside the barn and Sonny was dripping sweat.

"He ran in circles inside his stall the whole time you were gone, but he calmed as soon as he saw Biz coming back up the path," said Caleb. "He's soaked. You might want to talk to the vet about something to take the edge off while you're gone, just until he gets used to Biz leaving."

Carol tried to take a deep breath, but her chest was so tight from nervous tension that she couldn't. "Susan suggested the same thing," said Carol as she dismounted. Caleb seemed to be quietly assessing her as she removed Biz's tack, groomed him, and let him out to graze in the pasture. When she approached Sonny's stall, Caleb put his hand up. "I'll let him out. I don't want you in his path if he bolts."

Carol was relieved that Caleb was there, but to their surprise, Sonny calmly walked from his stall to the paddock, and munched hay as close to Biz as he could. They watched to make sure he continued to behave before they went into the house to call Sarah. Sarah said she would call the vet as soon as she got off the phone and pick up whatever was recommended.

"I'm sorry, Carol. I never expected him to act this way. He's not the same horse. I never thought a move to a new barn could change him so much. This has been a real eye-opener for me. I'm sure it's been difficult for you, too. I will get the supplement to you as quickly as possible. Please let me know if you see a difference. If not, the vet will help us figure out what to do next."

Sarah could not have been more cooperative, and Carol was grateful, but caring for Sonny was becoming overwhelming. Since the baby arrived, it seemed that Sonny attached himself to Biz in Sarah's absence. It was clear that he couldn't stand it when Biz left, and he wasn't able to calm down until Biz was beside him.

"Carol, I wonder if Sonny is desperate to be with other horses because he was alone for years, but now he's experienced what it's like to be part of a herd with Biz, and doesn't ever want to be by himself again," Sarah said.

"That makes sense," said Carol. Carol thought it was odd that when Sarah first arrived and took Sonny for his walks down the road, Biz never seemed upset. She wondered if Biz was more attached to his family than other horses.

~25~

Winter was unseasonably mild until mid-February when it turned freezing cold and didn't let up. The cold temperatures brought ice storms and ice-laden tree limbs became so heavy that they broke off. The big maple tree in Caleb's backyard lost multiple boughs. Carol could see that it broke Caleb's heart. Long ago, Caleb told Carol that he planted that tree for his wife, Marion, the year they bought the house. She loved maple trees because they were good for climbing, and she envisioned children sitting on its boughs. Carol felt a wave of grief as she wondered how Caleb's life might have been different if he and his wife were able to have children. There was no doubt in her mind that he would have been an amazing father. Loving. Kind. Helpful. Patient. Protective. Everything a father should be.

Caleb's maple tree and several other trees lost limbs and they blocked the path from the house to Willow Bend. The only other way to get there was the road. Carol didn't want anyone to get hit by a swerving vehicle, so to keep everyone safe, she refused to use the road and didn't allow Jill to use it either, so Biz was unavailable for lessons. Carol decided not to take lessons at all until she could safely use the pathway, and while Biz was unavailable, Jill rode Jayden. Jill tried to convince Carol to ride one of Susan's lesson horses too, but Carol had no interest. Truth be told, she wasn't a fan of cold weather. She gladly subjected herself to it to take care of Biz, but not to ride another horse. Carol wished she was talented enough to hop on any horse, but she needed a relationship with the horse to feel confident in the saddle.

The upside to winter was that everyone was calmer because Sonny settled down. Carol believed it was because Biz never left the paddock, so Sonny had no reason to get upset. Sonny wasn't nipping Biz at all, so they were outside together all the time. Quite often, they whinnied to the herd at Willow Bend and the choir answered. If the sun was bright, the ice and packed snow became spongy, so they romped in the pasture and got some exercise. To venture any further required winter shoes with snow pads and borium studs. The pads helped prevent snow and ice from sticking to metal shoes and balling up on the bottom of their hooves. The studs offered traction on ice. Carol, Jill, and Sarah all opted not to use them because the horses were perfectly safe within the barn, and safe in the paddock and pasture because Jill and Carol threw sand on icy areas for better traction. Plus, winter shoes were very expensive, borium studs didn't always stop a horse from slipping and falling, and the sharp studs sometimes caused nasty wounds if a horse did fall and struggled to get up. Plus, Biz and Sonny had strong barefoot hooves and they didn't want to drive nails into healthy hooves to attach winter shoes and risk damaging them.

Until spring arrived, Biz and Sonny seemed content to run together in the pasture on good days and hunker down on dismal days when it was too cold and windy to be outside. Carol enjoyed the slow pace and calmness of winter. She noticed that Jill used stormy days and long nights to dig her teeth into her studies and she read a lot of books. Since she was a little girl, Jill seemed to prefer a good book to television, but she did like a good movie, so Carol made a point of renting one at least once a week. If it was a movie she thought Caleb might enjoy, she extended an invitation. He always showed up with two big bags of hot popcorn. No microwave popcorn for him. Caleb did it the old-fashioned way on top of the stove, and he served it with lots of butter. One bag was just for Jill because she *loved* his popcorn. Caleb made it known that he hated horror movies and didn't want any tear-jerkers. He also let them know that he loved hot apple cider when it was cold out, so Jill always made some to go with the popcorn.

During cold months, Carol worked extra hours, but always made time to give Biz his weekly massage. She cleaned stalls and brushed Biz every morning, and Jill did the same at night. Sarah tended to Sonny whenever she could, but she didn't like cold weather either, so she often asked Carol and Jill to brush Sonny when they had time and agreed to pay extra for it. Despite the cold weather, both horses seemed warm in their heavy waterproof winter blankets, and they drank lots of warm water from their fancy heated water buckets. They grunted loudly on Friday nights when they got hot bran mashes with carrots, apples, and a peppermint. As soon as the hot sticky mixture was in their buckets, they dove in and ate as steam rose over their faces. When they finished, they always had bran stuck to their whiskers.

Carol missed riding Biz, but she filled the gap by spending as much time as she could with him in the barn. Her heart ached each time Jill told her how much she missed riding Biz, but they both agreed that it was best for Biz and worth the sacrifice.

***

In early April, when there were finally signs of spring, Caleb was eager to get out his chain saw and cut up the fallen tree limbs that blocked the pathway. Over the winter, he enjoyed seeing Biz and Sonny in the paddock or pasture every time he looked out the window, but he knew Biz needed more exercise. He wanted Jill and Carol to be able to ride him to lessons again and it pleased him to help make that happen.

Biz's Journey Home

Biz wore his warm blanket all winter except for when he was brushed and massaged, so Caleb didn't see how much weight he gained. The first time Caleb saw Biz without it on, he was thrilled. He no longer saw the outline of Biz's ribs through his coat. Biz was plump, thanks to lots of hay and grain, and very little exercise to burn up calories. His coat naturally glistened in the sun and his eyes sparkled.

Caleb felt himself smile. Biz looked like a masterpiece in the making. Wonderful care, lots of love, and great nutrition got him to that point. All he needed was more muscle. Caleb knew that would happen as soon as Biz was back in training. He couldn't wait for the show season to begin. Jill didn't tell him that she planned to show that year, but he knew it was going to happen. He felt it. And he planned to be there to watch. He wanted to see Biz prance around the show ring in all his glory. From the center of his being, Caleb understood Biz's potential. He felt his presence the moment he met him. Caleb was sure that Biz was something quite special when he was younger and would be amazing again. Biz was going to be a force to be reckoned with in the show ring, and Jill was going to be the equestrian on his back. Caleb couldn't wait to see the pride in Carol's eyes, the smile on Jill's face, and the many ribbons on Biz's bridle. Caleb knew Biz and Jill were going to bring home a ribbon from every class they entered, and he couldn't wait. He just couldn't wait.

It took a full week to clear all of the limbs out of the pathway. Caleb started at the back of his property, and then with permission from neighbors, cleared the way to the farm. He used his chain saw to cut the limbs and he pulled them into the open with his tractor. Then he cut the limbs up for firewood and hauled it away. Carol, Jill, and Susan offered to help, but Caleb thought he could do it with his equipment. He promised to let them know if he needed a hand, but he didn't. Once the firewood was removed, he used his friend's chipper to chip up the brush and he blew the chips into the woods. Mission accomplished. Caleb felt giddy when he put the chipper back on the trailer to return it to his friend. Before he pulled out of his driveway, he noticed Carol and Jill in the barn. "Go ahead and book your lessons. You're good to go. The path is clear," he yelled.

Carol and Jill yelled thank you and waved to him as he pulled away. Caleb was happy to get Biz back to his lessons because deep in his soul, he felt great things were about to happen.

***

Jill couldn't wait to ride Biz again, so she felt grateful for Caleb.

"My goodness, I love that man," said her mother. "He bailed us out of another jam, and he loved doing it. Sometimes I think he lives to help us."

Jill nodded. "He loves us, Mom. Just like we love him. There's nothing we wouldn't do for him, either, and he knows it. That's why he willingly does anything for us."

Her mother looked down at her, smiled, and then squeezed her cheek. "When did you become such a grown-up, young lady?"

Jill watched Caleb drive up the road until he was completely out of sight. "I'm going into the house to call Susan and let her know that we'll be ready to start lessons with Biz next week." she said as she skipped toward the house. "Same day and time for you, Mom?"

"Yes, honey, if it's available."

Jill booked their lessons for the following week. When she got off the phone with Susan, she was curious about the condition of the trails around Willow Bend, so she decided to take a walk to the farm and make a quick trip into the woods. She was pleased to find that the pathway from the house to Willow Bend was free of limbs, snow, and ice. And so were the trails surrounding the farm. Even the ones in the most shaded areas. On her way home, she stopped into Willow Bend to find Susan and ask if she could lunge Biz in the arena at a time when nobody was scheduled to use it. She found Susan in her office.

"Hi, Jill. Didn't I just get off the phone with you? What brings you here?"

Jill sat in the chair beside Susan's desk. "I just checked out the trails and they're clear. Would it be possible for me to lunge Biz in the indoor arena before we get on his back during lessons? I want to see how he's moving. And after having the winter off, it might help him get out his pent-up energy."

Susan smiled. "Let me check," she said as she pulled out the schedule. "If you want to do it today, the arena will be empty at five o'clock this afternoon. It will be dark around six-thirty, so you'll have to be done in an hour to make the trek home while there's still some sunlight."

Jill felt her heart skip. "Okay, I'll be back by five with Biz. Thank you." she said as she sprinted out of the office.

"I'm going to watch. I can't wait to see how he's doing," yelled Susan behind her.

Jill ran home so fast that she was completely out of breath by the time she got there. She raced into the house and took the stairs two at a time to get to her riding clothes. She was determined to ride Biz to Willow Bend and then lunge him in the arena.

"Why in the world are you in such a rush?" her mother shouted from her office.

"Susan said I can bring Biz down at five o'clock to lunge him. I have to get dressed and get him ready."

"That's great. Can I come? I'd love to watch."

"Susan asked the same thing. Of course, you can. Maybe Caleb too. Is he home?"

Her mother's voice was no longer coming from the bottom of the stairs when she responded. "His truck is outside, so he must be. I'll ask him if he's able to join us."

Jill moved like lightning as she got dressed because she couldn't wait to get a saddle on Biz. She knew he'd be happy to see his friends and she hoped he would whinny while she was on his back. When she ran outside, Caleb and her mother were waiting for her and Caleb had a big grin on his face.

"I'd *love* to accompany you today, sweetheart," beamed Caleb. "Are you going to walk him to the farm or ride him?"

"I want to ride him," said Jill.

Caleb frowned. "He might have a lot of energy after a winter without exercise. Are you sure that's a good idea?"

Jill thought about it. "I think he'll be fine, Caleb."

Caleb looked at the ground. "Let's compromise. You can ride him there as long as you walk, but I want to be by your side with a lunge attachment and lunge line on his bit. After you work him in the arena and he gets all that energy out, you can ride him home, but your mother and I will be with you."

Jill knew she wasn't going to win the negotiation, so she gave in. All she wanted was to get on Biz's back. Caleb's proposal allowed for that and kept her safe just in case Biz acted up.

"I'll meet you right here at four-thirty and we'll make our way down," said Caleb.

Jill went into the barn and gave Sonny a dose of his calming supplement in hopes that he wouldn't get too stressed. She meticulously brushed Biz, making sure she cleaned his coat right down to his skin, and then she cleaned and conditioned his leather tack and made sure it still fit him. Over the winter, he gained so much weight that she had to loosen his bridle and lengthen his girth three notches on each side. Jill could tell from the old impressions in the girth straps that Biz was once that wide. Her heart sank when she realized how much weight he lost over the years. She noticed that his back wasn't just wider, it was higher, indicating that he did build some muscle over the winter. Jill figured it was probably from romping with Sonny and carrying a heavy winter blanket on his back every day. She was sure his back would carry her nicely on their ride to Willow Bend, but she still planned to monitor how he was doing.

Before their departure, Jill put Sonny in his stall with hay and a bucket of water. She turned on the radio so Sonny would hear music and conversations between the DJs and not feel so alone. It was months since Sonny was without Biz. Jill was hoping for the best when Sarah unexpectedly pulled in.

"Where are you off to?" asked Sarah.

"We're starting lessons again next week, so I'm taking Biz down to the arena to lunge him and see how he's moving. Almost three hours ago, I gave Sonny a dose of his calming supplement. We just put him in his stall. Hopefully, he'll be okay."

Sarah smiled. "Hopefully, he'll be just fine. Have a good time. I plan to be here when you get back, so I want to hear all about it."

Jill walked Biz to the mounting block, positioned him properly, climbed the steps, and gently sat in her saddle. What a thrill to be on top of Biz again. His back and sides felt so much wider underneath her. She savored the moment while Caleb clipped on the lunge line, and then she asked Biz to walk. As they left, Sonny let out a few whinnies, but he didn't sound frenzied. Jill wondered if it was because of the calming supplement or the fact that Sarah was with him. Probably both.

Biz walked at a leisurely pace down the path to the arena. Jill could tell that Caleb and her mother were impressed. Each time Caleb looked at Biz, he smiled and shook his head in what appeared to be disbelief. As they approached the farm, Biz whinnied. Loudly. And Jill giggled with delight as her body jiggled in the saddle. The horses looked up, whinnied back, and ran to the paddock fence. All of them—Jonas, Abdul, Luis, Günter, Aiyana, and Opal—waited for him to arrive. Caleb seemed surprised when Biz pulled him and the lunge line toward the paddocks instead of walking toward the arena. Jill giggled at the expression on Caleb's face. "Don't worry, Caleb. Biz isn't being disobedient. This is our routine. Biz *always* gets to visit with his friends before we go into the arena."

Caleb raised his eyebrows and chuckled. "Oh, is that right?"

"Yup." Jill laughed.

Her mother seemed overjoyed by Biz's welcoming committee. "I love it when they run to see him. It never gets old, Caleb. They seem to miss one another."

"I'm sure they do," responded Caleb.

Once Biz's visit with his friends came to an end and they walked toward the arena, Caleb motioned for Jill to stop, and he removed the lunge line and attachment. "There you go, Biz. You're a good boy. So good that you even surprised me."

Biz turned his head toward Caleb and brushed his cheek against his shoulder. When he did, Caleb seemed a tad emotional. So was her mother.

"Sweetheart, I have no worries about this horse," said Caleb. "It's clear that he has a sound mind and will take exceptional care of you. I couldn't be happier. Now get in there and show us what he can do."

Jill looked at her mother. "I'm so happy, Mom. He's better. I can feel it. He built muscle on his back over the winter. I'm sitting higher."

Her mother smiled. "He looks good, honey, I can't wait to see how he looks when you lunge him."

Jill gathered her reins and entered the arena. Susan was already inside, waiting for them.

***

Biz was excited when he heard Jill say they were going to Willow Bend in the afternoon. He wanted to see his friends. He *needed* to see them, especially Jonas and Abdul. Biz never worried about Jonas because he knew he could take care of himself, but he did worry about Abdul. A lot. Though Jill went home from Willow Bend each week and told him all about the herd, Biz needed to see Abdul for himself. He was like a little brother, and he needed to know that he was okay.

While Jill got Biz ready for his jaunt, he pondered his friends. He remembered how emotionally painful it was the day he arrived at Willow Bend. He wondered what his life would have been like if Jonas wasn't there. Jonas was the one who made him feel welcome. Then there was Abdul. They instantly bonded. Jonas and Abdul got Biz through the lowest point in his life. It was an unspoken truth that the three of them would be friends forever.

Biz's daydream was interrupted when Jill attempted to put on his saddle. When she tried to cinch the girth, it didn't even reach. While she perfected the fit, the girth was sometimes so tight that Biz didn't want to expand his abdomen to take a breath. Each time that happened, Biz felt his body tense and Jill looked at him apologetically. "Sorry, boy. I knew the girth was going to be short because of all the weight you gained, but I never expected it to be this short. You gained *all* of your weight back. I can't wait for Susan to see you."

When the saddle was on, Biz walked out of the barn with Jill by his side and he was thrilled to see Caleb. Caleb stood a good distance away, but he was close enough for Biz to smell the carrot in his pocket. He felt his ears stand up as he stared, and Caleb smiled as if he knew why Biz was excited. Biz didn't beg for the carrot because he figured Caleb would give it to him when he was ready.

Biz wasn't completely surprised when Caleb gently secured the lunge line to his bit. He understood that Caleb loved Jill and wanted to make sure she was safe. He didn't blame him; most horses acted a little crazy their first time out of the paddock after having the winter off. But not him. He carried Jill. Precious cargo. He wanted to take care of her, and he respected the fact that Caleb did too. He was positive that, over time, Caleb would trust him, and he didn't mind proving himself.

Biz took in the sights as they meandered down the path. Carol and Caleb were by his side as he carried Jill to the arena, and he couldn't have been in better company. He was surprised at how light Jill felt in the saddle. She didn't look skinnier, so he assumed that she felt lighter because he grew heavier and stronger. He was excited when he saw his friends in their paddocks, so he whinnied. He loved the eager whinnies he heard in return. He couldn't believe how happy they were to see him.

Jonas was waiting when he got to the paddock fence. "Man, you're lookin' good! Your coat is a whole different color ... like a shiny copper penny. And you put on weight."

Biz stood tall. "Yes. My coat glistens in the sun now, Jonas. Jill says it's because they feed me well and have me on supplements to make sure I'm getting all the vitamins and minerals I need. I'm so happy, Jonas, but I miss you guys."

"We miss you, too, brother. A lot."

"Hi, Biz," whispered Abdul as he inched closer.

His sad little shuffle broke Biz's heart, but he tried to be upbeat. "Hey, little buddy, how are you?"

Abdul looked down. "I miss you, Biz. It feels like I haven't seen you in ages."

"I know. I'm sorry. It was a long winter. I couldn't come over because the path was blocked by fallen trees. And it was icy and I'm barefoot. But winter's over now, and I'll be back every week for lessons. I missed you too, Abdul. Very much. I hope you know that. You heard me whinny to you every day, right? So you know that you were in my thoughts."

Abdul lifted his head slightly. "I did hear you whinny to me, and I whinnied back. You honestly missed me, Biz?"

Biz looked down at Abdul and tipped his head. "Yes, of course, I did. You're my family, Abdul. I mean that. Now, tell me about Melissa. How is she? Has she come to see you?"

Abdul stared off in the distance as he swallowed and gently nodded. "Yes, but it's not the same. She brushes me, but she won't ride. She said she has to get up the courage to get back on."

Biz sighed. "It takes time. At least she came back. Ashley never did."

"Do you ever think about her, Biz?"

"Ashley? No. I don't think about anything from the past anymore. I'm happy now. Nothing else matters. I love my life. I have wonderful friends, like you and Jonas. And Jill and her mother take good care of me. They love me, and I love them."

Jonas's eyes sparkled. "I'm happy for you, brother."

"Thanks, Jonas," said Biz.

Biz glanced over at Aiyana, Luis, Günter, and Opal. "I miss you guys, too. It's good to see all of you. Now that spring is here, I'll see you more often."

Aiyana seemed peaceful. "You look happy, Biz. It makes my heart sing."

"I am happy, Aiyana. Very happy. Thank you."

Luis stepped forward. "You look great, Biz. Plumper. Physically fit."

"Thanks, Luis. I feel wonderful."

Opal winked. "Handsome. You look *so* handsome, Biz."

Biz felt himself blush. "It's very nice of you to say that, Opal."

Günter cleared his throat. "Welcome back, Biz. It's good to see you."

"Thanks, Günter. It's wonderful to be back amongst my friends."

Biz felt Jill gently press her leg against his side to direct him toward the arena doors. "I have to go, guys. Jill's going to lunge me in the arena, but I'll be back soon. Promise."

Abdul looked down as Biz walked away and it sent a shot through Biz's heart. Biz wanted to help him more, but he didn't know what to do.

Biz was honored when Caleb removed the lunge line because it proved that he trusted him. He would never do anything to violate that trust and he thought Caleb understood that.

He took a deep breath when he stepped into the arena. It felt good to be back. He didn't realize how much he missed it until he smelled the shaved leather footing and the myriad scents of the big barn. He took another deep breath and whinnied with Jill on his back. She giggled and rode him to the center of the arena, where she dismounted to lunge him. Susan made her presence known, but she mostly stayed to the side and observed.

Jill guided Biz through the motions and he loved it. Training made him feel alive. Purposeful. The shaved leather footing never created dust and it was deep, so it acted like a shock absorber for his legs. It felt good to be able to run without fear of slipping on snow and ice. About a half-hour into it, Susan stepped forward. "Jill, he looks so healthy and fit. His back is nice and high and he's round. Maybe even plump. And he's not dragging his toes anymore. What do you think? Are you ready to ride? I think he's ready," said Susan.

The smile on Jill's face was huge. "Of course I am," she said as she led Biz to the mounting block and hopped on.

At first, Jill asked Biz to simply walk, but he was soon eager for more, so she asked for a trot and then a canter. His transitions between gaits felt smooth and before he knew it, Jill asked him to do a twenty-meter circle in clockwise and counterclockwise directions, and then a figure eight with a flying lead change. He was elated that he not only remembered how to do everything but did it exceptionally well. When Jill finished, she let him cool down with a walk around the arena, then she asked him to stop and reverse direction. When he turned, he saw the expressions on everyone's faces and it made him feel proud.

"He looks amazing and the two of you look *so* good together, even after having the winter off. I can't believe the difference. I expect great things if you decide to show this year, but that's up to you, Jill. No pressure," Susan said.

Biz felt Jill's weight shift in her saddle as she turned to look at her mother and Caleb. "What do you think, Mom?"

Carol started to cry. "I think the sky's the limit, honey. I'm speechless. He looks so healthy and strong."

Caleb walked over and stroked Biz's neck. "Go for it, sweetheart. Just do it."

Carol nodded. "Susan, can we talk sometime soon about the cost of showing?"

Susan reassuringly put her hand on Carol's shoulder. "Of course, and there are lots of options we can discuss, based on any budget you give me. We have plenty of time. I don't expect them to be in the show ring for at least a couple of months."

Carol closed her eyes and smiled. "Oh, good. We have plenty of time to prepare. I'm excited, Susan. Thank you so much ... for everything."

"You bet."

Carol turned to Jill. "We better get going, young lady. The sun will be going down soon."

Caleb rubbed Biz's neck and laughed out loud when Biz stuck his nose in his pocket. "I knew you smelled that carrot, boy, but you can't have it now. Wait until we get home, and the bit is out of your mouth. We don't want you to choke."

Jill laughed as she escorted Biz toward the arena doors to begin the walk home. As he exited, he was excited to see his friends again. They would not be outside too much longer because darkness was coming, so Biz hurried to the paddock fence to say goodbye.

"How did it go, son?" asked Jonas.

"It was great. Jill lunged me, and then Susan asked her if she wanted to ride. She felt so much lighter on my back. I must be stronger, Jonas."

Abdul nodded as he walked beside Jonas. "You are bigger and

stronger, Biz. I'm glad your back feels better. Thanks for coming over to say goodbye. It was so good to see you again."

"You betcha. I'm happy to be back. And I'll be back for lessons. Bye, guys. I'll see you soon. I promise."

As they all walked the path home, Biz relived his training session. He felt accomplished. It was a long time since he felt that way. His chest felt wide, and his head was high as he made his way home. Home. What a wonderful word. He couldn't wait for his carrot.

~26~

As they made their way home, Jill heard a barred owl in the woods and stopped. As she listened, she looked at her mother and Caleb, because she knew they both understood why she wanted to hear every beat of its beautiful call. When she didn't hear it anymore, she asked Biz to walk, and the rest of the way home was in silence. A pleasant, upbeat silence. Then, as they entered the yard, Jill heard the owl again, but it was loud and very close by. They all looked around and then Caleb pointed to a tall pine tree at the edge of the property. Jill's heart melted because the owl was big. Tall. And it was looking directly at her. So intensely that it felt like it was looking into her soul. After a moment, it hooted again and then flew past her as it made its way into the woods. When she looked at her mother and Caleb, they both had grins. Big grins. Even Caleb knew it was something much more than just an owl.

When they reached the barn, Sarah walked out. Jill hoped she could stay for at least a few minutes to hear about Biz.

"How did it go?" asked Sarah.

"Awesome. He looked so good that Susan suggested that we show this year," Jill said.

"Wow. You must be excited. I want to hear all about it, but right now, I have to go. I showed a lot as a kid, so I'd love to hear your plans. I'll be back tomorrow mid to late morning. If you're here, you can fill me in."

Jill was disappointed that Sarah had to leave, but she didn't say anything as she took off Biz's bridle and put on his halter.

"The baby is finally old enough that I feel comfortable leaving him with my husband for longer chunks of time, so I'll be coming to the barn more often. I have a good block of time tomorrow. If anyone is interested in going on a trail ride, let me know, because I'm dying to go."

Carol nodded. "We will. But before you leave, was Sonny okay while Biz was gone?"

Sarah shook her head ambiguously. "He didn't like it when Biz left and it took a while for him to stop staring at the path, but other than that, he seemed okay. He let out a few whinnies, but no screams, thank goodness."

Sarah started her car and pulled away, and Jill saw a look of apprehension on her mother's face. "Don't worry yet, Mom. Let's wait and see what happens. Sonny might be fine. If not, we'll have to figure it out."

The next day was sunny and warm. Jill and her mother were in the barn, cleaning stalls and rearranging the tack area, when Sarah pulled in.

It was around ten o'clock in the morning, so Sonny was finished with breakfast and basking in the sun in the pasture right beside Biz.

"What a beautiful day," Sarah said.

"It is a lovely day," replied Jill. "It's too nice to be inside."

"My thoughts exactly. Is anyone up for a trail ride?"

Jill looked at her mother. "Mom, you should go."

"Me? But I haven't been on his back in months, honey. I'd rather wait. I want to have at least a couple of lessons on him before I venture into the woods."

Jill nodded. "Okay. Fair enough. Do you mind if I go?"

Her mother grinned. "I don't mind at all, and I'm not the least bit worried after seeing you ride Biz yesterday. Have fun, but don't forget to bring your cell phone just in case one of you needs something. Make sure you have it on mute, so he doesn't get spooked if someone calls."

"I won't forget," said Jill. "Sarah, I'll get dressed and be back in a jiffy."

"Great. I'm going to lunge Sonny for a few minutes before I get on him, so take your time. And during our ride, I want to hear every detail about yesterday."

Her mother looked at Jill questioningly. "If Sarah is going to lunge Sonny in the pasture, why did you bring Biz to Willow Bend to lunge him?"

Jill took a deep breath as she thought. "Because the footing in the indoor arena is better and it's a regulation size ring. Plus, Susan thinks it's best to have horses associate the ring with work and the paddock and pasture with leisure time. The ring puts them in the right mindset. Besides, Sarah is lunging Sonny to see if he needs to let off some steam. I wanted to lunge Biz to evaluate him and see how he was doing."

Her mother squeezed her chin between her thumb and index finger and squinted her eyes. "That's very interesting. And it makes perfect sense."

Jill went into the house to get ready. She was back in the barn in no time and surprised to find that Sarah was already brushing Sonny. "Did you already lunge him?"

"Yes, but not for very long. I've had him since he was a baby, so I know him inside out. He wasn't the least bit energetic, so I know he's fine to ride."

Jill and Sarah tacked up the horses in their stalls. Within fifteen minutes, they were both ready to go.

"Bye, Mom. We'll see you when we get back."

"Be careful. I love you."

"Love you, too."

Side by side, they made their way down the path to Willow Bend. Biz and Sonny appeared to be full of energy. Along the path, there were spots where it took some coaxing to get them to slow down and just walk. As they passed through Willow Bend on their way to the trails, Biz let out a big whinny. The horses looked up, whinnied back, and ran to the fence. Jill tried to steer him away, but Biz politely resisted and walked over to them. Jill chuckled as she gave in. "If you don't mind, Sarah, I'll let him visit with his friends for a few minutes."

Sarah followed, but when they got to the paddock fence, she turned Sonny toward the barn. "I want to check out the arena. Is it okay if Sonny and I meander over to the arena doors and peek inside? We won't go inside."

Jill glanced toward the arena entrance. "I'm sure it'll be fine. It's right there and Susan knows who you are. If anyone says something, just say that you're with me," Jill said.

Sonny looked toward the arena and took a step forward, but then he attempted to turn and stay with Biz. Sarah seemed amused at first, but then her tone became firm as she coaxed Sonny to turn.

Jill liked the way Sarah handled Sonny. Consistent. Firm. And most importantly, kind. She didn't use a whip, kick his sides, yell, or even raise her voice. She simply changed her tone. Jill knew she was going to enjoy trail riding with Sarah. She was excited. She was about to embark on her first trail ride of the season, and she was on her horse for the second time in two days. She took in the sights and felt blissful in her saddle while Biz visited his friends.

* * *

Jonas was so happy to see Biz again that he cantered to the paddock fence. Abdul and Aiyana followed and whinnied the whole way.

"To what do we owe the pleasure of seeing you two days in a row, brother?" asked Jonas.

"We're going on a trail ride. I wish you guys could come," said Biz.

"I wish we could go too," said Abdul.

Jonas looked toward the arena. "Who's your friend?"

"That's Sonny," whispered Biz. "He's okay, but he's not you guys." Biz winked at Abdul, who seemed to beam with pleasure.

Jonas chuckled because Biz always seemed to know how to make Abdul feel special.

"That's Sonny, my stablemate. I worry about him. If I leave the property, he gets upset. A few times last fall, I thought he was going to make himself sick."

Jonas nodded. "I remember his screams."

"Is he better now?" asked Aiyana.

"I don't know because we've been together all winter. I hope so. Jill's talking about showing this year, so I'll be gone all day," said Biz. "Where are Luis, Günter, and Opal?"

"It's show season. They were in the trailer at the crack of dawn this morning," said Abdul.

Biz nodded. "I remember those days. They were long, but lots of fun."

Jonas chuckled. "You were always in your element at shows. You never looked nervous."

Biz sighed. "I loved it, and I can't wait to get back in the ring."

Sarah and Sonny started to come back, and Jonas saw Jill lightly pull on Biz's reins. "Well, it's time to go, guys. I'll see you soon. Say hi to everyone for me," Biz said.

Jonas looked down. "We will, my friend. We'll see ya soon."

Abdul shuffled closer to the fence. "Bye, Biz. Please come back soon."

"Don't worry. I'll see you next week."

Jonas saw a small tear fall from the corner of Abdul's left eye. He could relate because he felt a tug in his own heart as Biz made his way to the trails. Selfishly, he wished Biz was still stabled at Willow Bend because he liked having him around. As Biz walked out of sight, Jonas recounted their many candid conversations. In all his years in big barns, Jonas never met another horse like Biz. He was special. He knew when to speak and when to be quiet. Biz had a lot of wisdom, a forgiving heart, compassion, and a profound sense of fairness. All those years ago in Virginia, when Jonas admired Biz from afar, he never dreamt he would someday be his friend. Biz was a true champion, inside and outside of the show ring. Jonas was proud to know him. And even prouder to be his friend.

***

Sarah turned Sonny away from the arena doors, so Jill knew it was time to hit the trails, Together, they headed toward the woods. The trail that began at the back of the pasture was wide, flat, and smooth, so they opted to begin there. They rode side by side until they got to the tree line, and then shifted to single file with Jill and Biz leading the way. The ride was enjoyable. Slow, leisurely, and conducive to conversation.

"Sonny was my best friend when I was growing up. When I started dating my husband, I felt guilty because Sonny had less time with me. When I got married and moved out of the house, he got even less. Now that I have the baby, it's even worse. I know it doesn't seem like it, but Sonny is a priority, it's just buried beneath so many other obligations."

Jill turned to Sarah. "I bet he's happy just to be with you right now."

Sarah shrugged. "I hope so. It's a huge weight off my shoulders now that the baby is old enough to be with my husband. But my husband doesn't know what's worse, hearing me complain about not spending time with my horse or babysitting."

Jill chuckled. "Does he call it babysitting? It's his child."

Sarah smiled. "Yes, it is. What I mean is that he's comfortable taking care of the baby without me around now. He's more confident about it, so I'm more confident in him."

"I understand," said Jill as she imagined what it would feel like to not have time for Biz.

Sarah giggled like a schoolgirl. "You know what I can't wait for, Jill?"

Jill laughed because Sarah looked so excited. "What can't you wait for, Sarah?"

"I can't wait until my son is old enough to be at the barn with me. I want him to ride. Maybe I'll even get him a pony. He can start with lessons and then do leadline classes."

"What's a leadline class?"

"You never heard of it? Leadline classes are for very young children. I think ages seven and under. They ride the pony and they're dressed for the show ring, but an adult has the pony on a lead line. I can't wait. I can even picture him in his little helmet."

Jill laughed. "I could help you, Sarah. I'd love to watch a leadline class. I bet the kids and the ponies are adorable. It sounds like fun."

Sarah smiled at Jill. "I'd love to have you there. I can't think of anyone who'd be better company or more qualified help."

Sarah sighed, and Jill felt her sadness. "What's wrong?"

"I'm just tired of feeling torn. I wish my husband was interested in horses. It's one thing we don't have in common and that's hard for me because it's such a big part of who I am."

"Does your husband like Sonny?"

"He does, but he doesn't understand the bond I have with him. My husband didn't grow up with animals of any kind, so he doesn't get it. Sometimes I think he's resentful because Sonny's always on my mind. Our life is very busy right now. My husband gets less attention from me because of the baby. And now I can spend time with my horse, so he'll get even less."

Jill groaned. "I'm never getting married."

Sarah laughed out loud. "Oh, Jill. If it was only that simple. You'll meet someone and fall in love someday. My only suggestion is to make sure he *loves* horses."

Jill giggled. "Definitely."

Jill felt sorry for Sarah. She didn't realize that Sarah was pulled in so many directions. She was glad Sarah confided in her because it helped her realize that she never wanted to be in that position. Whoever she ended up with, he would have to understand that Biz came first. Biz would win every time.

In June, after weeks of training, Jill went to her first horse show with Biz. Susan was there as her instructor, and Carol and Caleb watched every minute. During lessons before the show, Susan constantly commented that she and Biz were a perfect team, so Carol was hopeful they would have a good day. She was excited and nervous because Jill was competing against some of the girls who made fun of Biz when he arrived at Willow Bend.

At the show, when Jill got him off the trailer and tacked him up, Carol saw that they couldn't believe their eyes.

"Is that Biz?" asked one of the riders.

"It sure is." Jill said beaming with pride. "Isn't he handsome?"

The girl smirked. "Well, I guess he looks a *little* better."

Carol was irritated. She could tell that Jill was too, but somehow managed to ignore her. When the girl walked away, Jill looked at Carol and Caleb and rolled her eyes. "I don't care what Erinna thinks. He looks absolutely gorgeous. That's the expression Mrs. Ellington used when she described Biz in his younger days, and I think it has a nice ring to it."

Caleb winked at Jill. "It has a wonderful ring to it *and* it's accurate. Don't let mean-spirited people bother you, sweetheart. Concentrate on you and Biz and good things will come. This is going to be your day. I can feel it. You just wait and see."

Biz's body was full and round. His coat was such a rich shade of reddish-gold chestnut that it sparkled in the sun. His tail looked elegant in a French braid. His mane grew long enough for Jill to put it in a running braid that hugged his neckline from the back of his ears down to his withers. Jill even used a stencil to put a checkerboard pattern on his haunches, just to catch the judge's eye. Carol had the pleasure of watching Jill put the checkerboard on. She placed the stencil on the haunches and used a course brush and clear styling gel to brush the open squares in the opposite direction of the natural growth pattern. When the stencil was lifted, the checkers that were not brushed were light and shiny. The ones that were brushed backward with gel appeared darker. It looked snappy.

Jill looked good too. Carol helped her pick out a light sage green shirt with a gold pin at her collar, a hunter-green pin-striped blazer, sage breeches, and tall fitted black leather boots. The muted shades of green complimented Biz's reddish coat. They were a winning combination.

At the show, Biz carried himself perfectly. It was apparent that he was in his element at horse shows. As Jill worked her way around the practice ring, everyone stopped and watched—fellow competitors, instructors, judges, and spectators. Jill and Biz were completely in sync. Out of the corner of her eye, Carol saw Erinna, watching, and she didn't look happy.

At the beginning of each class, as she entered the ring, Jill seemed elated. She didn't look the least bit nervous, and Carol soon understood why. She and Biz won every single class they entered. It felt like a dream. At the end of the day, Jill said she felt a tad guilty because they won with ease. Their efforts melded in such a way that winning felt natural. They were a perfect team. Unstoppable. As the day progressed, Erinna seemed sad. Defeated. It was clear that she expected to win. Carol saw Erinna wipe her cheeks several times throughout the day and wondered if she wiped away tears.

The day was perfect but one thing puzzled Carol. Biz behaved perfectly until the very end of each class. Once the riders received their ribbons and started to exit the show ring, for a brief moment, Biz went in a direction other than where Jill directed him. Each time, Jill looked at Carol and Caleb, shrugged her shoulders, rolled her eyes, and giggled.

***

Biz felt at home as soon as he got off the trailer. He loved everything about shows. During his younger years in the show circuit, he met countless horses who hated showing. They hated the pressure, and they dreaded the way their owners acted under pressure. Grumpy. Impatient. Aggressive. Biz was a champion because pressure didn't bother him. It made him better. He loved a challenge and getting ready for shows made Biz feel alive.

At his first show with Jill, he cherished the fact that competitors thought he was handsome again. He saw it in their eyes. Biz felt his body elevate and his chest widen when he realized everyone was watching him and Jill in the practice ring. *That's right, people. Biz is back! With checkerboards on his butt and the most beautiful and kind rider in the world on his back. Stand up and take notice*, he thought.

It was Jill who gave that special feeling back to him, so it was very important to Biz that they do well. He entered the ring with panache for their first class, and when they won, he was ecstatic. His confidence grew with each blue ribbon they won during the day. He felt Jill's joy and heard the pride in her voice when she rubbed his neck and told him that he was a good boy.

Biz didn't recognize any of the horses at the show, except for a few from Willow Bend. As he looked around the show grounds, he used his senses to take it all in. It was wonderful to see all the horses with shiny coats, braids, and shoe polish. The riders looked exceptional, from their helmets down to their polished boots, and the show grounds looked lovely. Ahhhhh, the smell of the food trucks selling everything from greasy doughnuts, sausages, and submarine sandwiches, to sparkling water, pizza, salads, and soups.

Trainers moved about while watching the horses and riders under their instruction. Some riders wore a smile and others had frowns and tear-streaked cheeks, but that was to be expected. Horse shows were competitions. Somebody won, so somebody lost. Biz didn't think losing was a bad thing. The best lessons learned were often from mistakes made. But he didn't approve of tears born from nasty comments from parents or trainers. He had no patience for meanness.

The show wasn't an A-circuit show like the ones from years ago in Virginia, when Maggie owned him and he competed against some of the top horses, but he still loved everything about it. Less pressure. More fun. And he was with Jill. The only reminder of Virginia that was still in his life was Jonas. He lived at one of the farms where Biz competed. When Jonas told Biz that he remembered him, Biz was embarrassed that he didn't recall Jonas, but when Jonas described their conversation, it all came back to him. Jonas was in the field, watching the hunter jumper show from a distance. At the end of the day, when Biz was standing by the fence, Jonas walked up and told Biz that he was so athletic, he could probably jump the moon. Biz closed his eyes and replayed that conversation in his head. What were the odds that a big and powerful workhorse in Virginia would cross paths with him years later in Massachusetts? Probably slim to none, but he was glad that their lives intersected again. He felt blessed to have Jonas in his life and grateful that they became good friends.

***

At noontime, Caleb walked over to the food trucks to get lunch for everyone, while Carol took Biz for a quick walk around the show grounds. During her walk, she spotted Dr. Norris, who was serving as the on-duty veterinarian at the show that day. Dr. Norris looked at Biz but didn't seem to recognize him until she saw Carol, and then she quickly looked back at Biz. "I can't believe that's Biz! He doesn't even look like the same horse."

"Thanks, Dr. Norris. He's coming along. I can't tell you how much we love him. There aren't enough words," said Carol.

"It shows," said Dr. Norris. "The two of you are doing a terrific job."

Carol nodded. "That means a lot coming from you. I had no idea you would be here today. It's so good to see you. Biz and Jill are having a great day, so good that I have a couple of questions. Can I ask you here, or should we schedule a time for you to come by the house?"

Dr. Norris tipped her head and smiled. "I'm not busy. What's on your mind?"

Carol took a deep breath. "When you came to our barn for Biz's first checkup, you said he was seventy-percent serviceably sound. What does that mean? Before you answer, let me explain why I asked. Jill wants to jump, and I'd like her to be able to, but I don't want to do anything that could hurt Biz, and Jill doesn't either."

Dr. Norris seemed touched. "First, let me tell you how pleased I am that Biz has such a loving home."

"He's our world."

Dr. Norris's expression softened. "To answer your question, it can mean anything. Try jumping over fence rails laying flat on the ground. If he does well with that, try some low fences and see how he does. If he becomes lame, you'll have to stop."

Carol nodded. "Okay. One more question. It's been nine months since his lameness exam. With the care, exercise, and nutrition he's had since then, is there any chance he might do better on a lameness exam now?"

Dr. Norris grinned. "There's no question that he would."

Carol was hopeful. "Can we make an appointment for another exam and go from there?"

Dr. Norris put her hand on Carol's shoulder. "That's a great idea. Just call the office to set it up."

Carol thanked Dr. Norris for taking the time to talk with her and continued their walk around the show grounds. Her shoulders felt softer, and her body was lighter. Talking with Dr. Norris alleviated her concerns because she was sure that Dr. Norris would not have suggested that they allow Biz to start jumping if she didn't think he was capable.

***

At the end of the day, Biz glanced around the show grounds and let out a sigh of relief. He wanted to make everyone proud that day and he was successful. His mind drifted back to his performance. No mistakes. Not one. From the looks he got he was quite sure that he was fabulous. Jill was fabulous, too. And her riding was stellar. She didn't make a single bobble in the saddle. What a team. Biz could still see the grin on Caleb's face each time they finished a class. He saw abundant love in Carol's eyes, and Susan watched with pride.

He knew he baffled Jill a few times during the day, but he couldn't help himself. He heard Erinna's comment before the show and it annoyed him, so each time they won, he made sure he pranced right in front of her as they left the ring. He wanted her to have a bird's-eye view of the blue ribbon attached to his bridle and an up-close view of the team that kept her from winning it. The look on Erinna's face was a priceless combination of frustration and anger. She turned red. Her eyes widened. Her eyebrows rose to her hairline, and her mouth dropped open. Biz wasn't without a conscience, so he wasn't completely pleased with himself, but he wasn't disappointed in himself either, because Erinna was mean to Jill.

He chuckled as he remembered how Jill tried to steer him in a different direction as they exited the ring. He felt her confusion during that brief moment when he didn't listen and wondered if she understood what he was doing.

***

Jill, her mother, and Caleb, had a wonderful day at the show, but when they returned home, they found Sonny on the ground, thrashing. Colic. Without thinking, Jill jumped into action. She asked Caleb to get Biz out of the trailer and put him in his stall. Then she asked her mother to call Sarah while she called the veterinarian. Jill was on the opposite side of the barn when her mother called Sarah on her cell phone, but she still heard the panic in Sarah's voice. "I don't understand. I went to the barn twice to check on him. The last time was just two hours ago, and he seemed fine," said Sarah. "I'll be there right away."

Dr. Norris was at the show, so they had to wait for one of the two veterinarians on call. Jill was told it would be at least an hour before one of them arrived because they were both tending to other emergencies. The veterinary technician on the phone told Jill to try to get Sonny up and keep him walking.

When Sarah arrived and rushed into the stall, Sonny was startled and jumped up on his own. They all took turns walking him, but it was difficult because he kept trying to lay down. Jill knew he was in a lot of pain. When a vet finally arrived, almost two hours later, Sarah had blisters on her feet, and they were bleeding. She told Jill she was in such a rush to get to Sonny that she forgot to change out of her sandals.

When the vet finished his exam, he said Sonny most definitely had colic. "I'm going to give him some Banamine for pain and tube some mineral oil into his stomach. I didn't feel any blockages, but I still want to make sure everything passes through. I think he'll be fine," he said.

With what appeared to be incredible relief, Sarah sighed. "I've had this horse since he was a baby and he's never had colic. Why now? What caused it?"

Jill listened intently to what the vet had to say.

"Probably stress. From what I heard, today was the first time his buddy was gone all day. Any kind of change can cause colic. A new owner. A new stable. New grain. New hay. A change in stablemate. Being alone. Even changes in the weather can cause colic. He probably paced the whole time his buddy was gone and didn't eat or drink enough all day. The sounds coming from his gut seem normal now, so just keep an eye on him. Tomorrow, any stools he passes should glisten from the mineral oil, which lubricates stools and makes them pass easier. No food for the rest of the day, but make sure he has access to lots of water. Tomorrow, no grain, but he can have a handful of hay in the morning and a couple of handfuls for lunch and dinner. If all goes well, the next day, he can go back to his normal eating schedule."

As the vet packed up his equipment, his cell phone rang with another emergency. "I'll call you tomorrow to check on Sonny," he said as he jumped into his truck.

Jill knew Sarah was going to worry about Sonny all night, so she quietly moved closer to her mother and asked if Sarah should spend the night at the house. Her mother nodded and then suggested it to Sarah, who gratefully accepted the offer. Sarah had two baby monitors at home, so she quickly went home to retrieve one, and slept on the couch in the living room with the monitor by her head, so she could hear if Sonny was in any distress.

At the crack of dawn, Jill was up early to check on the horses. Sonny seemed fine, but the amount of food he could eat was restricted, so she had to divide the paddock to prevent Sonny from eating Biz's hay. As she divided it, her mother and Sarah came out of the house.

"I'm so worried about him. He's my baby," said Sarah.

Jill nodded. "I know just how you feel. Granted, we haven't had Biz as long as you've had Sonny, but he's part of the family. I don't know what we'd do if anything happened to him."

"Biz touches my heart in places I never knew existed," her mother said. "You'd think that people would be the most attached to a small animal that's easy to cuddle, like a small dog or a cat. I've had pets and loved them all, but I've never been as attached as I am to Biz. There's a deeper connection that I can't explain."

Sarah sighed. "When I saw this barn being built, I knew it was going to be a special place. It seemed surrounded in love and white light."

Her mother looked intrigued. "White light?"

"Yes. Positive energy that's full of love and good intentions. This is a place that's warm and relaxing where anyone can feel at home. When I come here, I feel peaceful. I've been around a lot of horses, and I've seen how people interact with them. I can honestly say that I've never seen love in a horse's eyes the way I see it in Biz's. It pours out when he looks at either one of you."

Jill put her head down and felt her eyes become wet with tears.

"Thank you for saying that. It means a lot," her mother responded as she put her hand on Sarah's shoulder.

Sarah looked at Jill and tipped her head questioningly. "Why did you take him? I mean, I heard Biz was in very rough shape when he arrived at Willow Bend. What made you decide to take a gamble like that?"

Jill felt her throat tighten with emotion. Her mother seemed to understand what was happening and answered for her. "Well, Logan built the barn so Jill could have a horse at home. He always envisioned a tall chestnut with a white blaze and two white socks standing in the paddock, waiting for Jill to come home from school."

Jill cleared her throat and walked to the paddock fence. As she looked at Biz, she felt her heart swell. "When I saw Biz, I fell in love with him, and I knew he was the horse I was supposed to bring home. I felt it. And I couldn't stop thinking about him."

Her mother sighed. "Jill was in love with him, so I went to see him myself. His eyes were so kind, and he stood proud like his mind forgot what his body looked like. Jill wanted to be the one to help him and I agreed with her."

"And we're halfway there," said Jill.

"Halfway? He looks wonderful," Sarah said.

Jill inhaled. "He does. He gained his weight back and his coat is gorgeous, but there's still work to be done. He needs to build more muscle. To get him back in tip-top shape, it will probably take another six months to a year."

Jill gazed at Biz and contemplated Sarah's question. Why did we take him? How could we not? He's supposed to be with us. Forever.

***

The day Sonny had colic the barn was full of angst as they waited for the veterinarian to arrive. Sonny looked extraordinarily uncomfortable, and Biz felt his pain. It made him remember a very bad bout of colic during his early years. It was so bad that the vet insisted that someone sleep in the barn to keep a close eye on him. Mr. Ellington refused, and Ashley was too young, so Mrs. Ellington stayed. To her credit, she slept on a cot right outside Biz's stall door so she wouldn't miss anything.

Biz thought he developed an intestinal blockage because he hurt his knee and was temporarily on stall rest. His hay and grain rations weren't reduced in consideration of his lack of exercise, which helped move food through the intestines. His stomach pain was so intense that he couldn't stand, and he could hardly breathe when he lay down. In the end, he was fine, but it took three vet visits and gallons of mineral oil to make sure he defecated.

Biz felt that pain over and over again as he watched Sonny. The poor guy looked rough. Biz didn't like to see horses suffer so he paced in his stall and swayed his head from side to side until the vet arrived. It was the first time he exhibited such nervous behavior in front of Jill and Carol, but he couldn't stop it. He felt helpless.

Horses expressed stress in different ways. They kicked walls, chewed wood, stopped eating and drinking, screamed, paced, weaved, and cribbed. Horses that cribbed grabbed something wooden between their teeth and sucked air into their stomachs. Weavers stood in one spot and swung their neck and head from side to side. When Biz was stressed, he paced. When he was very stressed, he weaved uncontrollably, swinging his lowered head and neck like a pendulum. It was his way of suffering silently.

It was obvious how much Sarah cared about Sonny. She pulled into the driveway on two wheels, threw the car in park, and jumped out. Biz saw Caleb shake his head as he walked over to her car and turned off the ignition. Sarah rushed into Sonny's stall, grabbed a lead line, and started walking him. Each time he tried to lay down, Sarah cried and begged him to get up. Sonny looked exhausted, but he somehow mustered enough strength to keep going. Biz knew he did it for Sarah. Biz whinnied to encourage Sonny, but his whinnies sounded shrill from his high level of anxiety, so they were far from soothing. He was grateful when the vet pulled in and overjoyed when he heard Sonny was probably going to be okay.

Biz instantly felt sick to his stomach when the vet poured a gallon of mineral oil into a stainless steel pail and then inserted a plastic tube down Sonny's throat to pump the oil down the esophagus and into the stomach. He knew it had to be done to help Sonny recover, but he remembered how awful it was.

After the vet left, Sarah put Sonny in his stall and hugged him. He looked physically and mentally drained. "Sorry, Sonny. I can offer you water, but I can't give you any hay until morning," said Sarah.

Sonny rested his chin on her shoulder and let out a deep breath.

Sarah cried. "I know. I was scared, too, but it's all over now. Try to get some rest." A short while later, Sarah returned with a baby monitor. "I'm sleeping here tonight so I'll be out to see you first thing in the morning, Sonny," said Sarah. She kissed Sonny's cheek, and then she pointed to the shelf. "See that, Sonny? It's a monitor so I can listen to you throughout the night. If you don't feel good, make some noise and I'll come out to check on you right away."

Biz thought the baby monitor was a sweet way for Sarah to show Sonny how much she cared. After Sarah left the barn, Sonny leaned against his stall wall and looked at Biz. "I never had colic before, Biz. It hurts ... a lot."

Biz walked closer. "I know. I've had it and I don't ever want it again. Feeling any better?"

Sonny sighed. "A little. I guess I need to calm down when you leave. The vet was right. I didn't eat or drink all day. And I paced while you were gone and worked myself into a frenzy."

"Why do you do that to yourself? You know I'm coming back, right?"

Sonny's shoulders slumped even more. "That's the strange part. I do know you're coming back. I just can't stand being alone. Something makes me panic inside."

Biz walked to the other side of his stall and looked outside. "I'm always here, Sonny, but sometimes I'm just not as close by. Try to remember that I'll always be back by the end of the day. If you feel yourself starting to panic, focus on that, and look forward to the great stories I'll have about my adventure. There's always something juicy to talk about after a day at a show."

Sonny smiled. "I'll try, Biz, but the stories better be good."

"I already have a good one, but I'll tell you in the morning after you get some rest."

Sonny nodded.

Biz looked out the barn window at the sky. The stars were beautiful. He hoped Sonny would have a good night.

***

The next night, Jill went out to the barn to check on the horses before she went to bed. Sonny's colic made her worry about Biz. The barn was quiet when she entered. She stood next to Biz's stall and gazed at him, wondering what she would do if he ever became sick and died. He walked over to her, and she stroked his cheeks and talked to him as tears rolled down her face. She needed to be closer, so she opened his stall door and stepped inside. As soon as she did, Biz walked over to his window, looked up at the sky, and then looked back at her, as if inviting her to follow. She did, and when she looked up at the sky, the moon was full, and stars twinkled brilliantly.

When she was a little girl, her father sometimes got her out of bed and brought her outside to look at the night sky. She remembered laying on a heavy blanket with a pillow in the middle of the field as her father pointed out the planets and stars and helped her see constellations. Big Dipper, Little Dipper, Great Bear, Little Bear, Orion, Taurus, Gemini. It was a long time since she thought about those nights. She stepped closer to Biz and hugged him. He felt so comfortable and warm that she didn't want to let go. "Thanks for calling me over, Biz. I might have missed the view if you didn't."

Jill gazed at the sky with Biz until she couldn't keep her eyes open. She needed sleep, so she kissed him goodnight and opened the stall door. As she stepped outside, she saw something out of the corner of her eye. She turned quickly and saw what looked like her father standing by the barn door. She blinked and looked again, but the image vanished. With a smile and warmth in her heart, Jill walked toward the door and whispered, "I know you're here, Dad. I just know it."

Jill quietly opened the kitchen door in case her mother was asleep. As she climbed the stairs toward her room, she felt peaceful inside. If her father was in the barn, could he possibly have watched her at the show? The thought made her smile, and she decided to make a habit of looking at the night sky with Biz more often.

A week after her first show, Jill reminded her mother that they needed to schedule an appointment for Biz's second lameness exam. She was hopeful that Biz would get a clean bill of health. "Please have her come when I can be home. I always learn so much from Dr. Norris."

Her mother made the call and was able to get an appointment that week. When the day arrived, Jill was filled with anticipation and waited in the barn for Dr. Norris. Dr. Norris had a bright smile when she saw Jill.

"Hi, Jill. Biz looked *incredible* at the show. You deserved every ribbon. He didn't look like the same horse. You're a miracle worker."

Jill felt proud. "Thank you, Dr. Norris. It's been quite a journey."

Dr. Norris looked at Jill with a warm smile. "So I'm here to see if Biz might do better on his lameness exam?"

"Yes. I'd like to jump him, but only if he can do it without injuring himself."

"Well, I can tell you without hesitation that he will test better this time. After I spoke with your mother at the show, I tried to watch your classes. He looked perfect."

Jill went into the barn to get Biz and a lunge line. When they came out, her mother was greeting Dr. Norris. She listened to Biz's heart and lungs, took his pulse and temperature, calculated his respiration rate, checked his ears and eyes, and placed the stethoscope on his abdomen to listen to his belly sounds. When she finished his checkup, she did the lameness exam, including a test where she held his leg joints in a flexed position and then asked Jill to trot him. "Flexion tests sometimes show a problem you won't otherwise see," said Dr. Norris.

When the exam was over, Dr. Norris looked at Jill. "I put him through the wringer, and I can't find anything, even in his front right foot. It's not unusual for a Grade 1 club foot to test differently on a flexion test. It did, but it was still well within what's considered the normal range. He's one hundred percent sound, Jill. Go for it. He can do anything you want, even jumping, but start small and work your way up."

Jill was beside herself with joy. "Oh my gosh. I knew he was better, but I didn't expect him to be a hundred percent." She looked at her mother. "Mom, did you hear that?"

Her mother grinned from ear to ear. "Yes, I did. I'm so happy for you, honey."

Jill hugged Biz and Dr. Norris's pager went off.

"I have to run. There's an emergency," she said as she jumped into her truck. "Carol, don't worry about paying me today. I don't have time to write the invoice. I'll have the office bill you. Good luck, Jill. I can't wait to see you at your next show. Hopefully, I'll be on duty."

Jill waved goodbye and walked Biz back to his stall. "Did you hear that, boy? We can jump." Jill was pleased that they got a green light, but what made her happiest was knowing that Biz was in such good condition.

The next day, Jill told Susan the good news and they planned their first jumping lesson for the following weekend. Jill jumped Jayden at Willow Bend, so she had enough experience to help Biz, but he didn't need any. During their first jumping lesson, it was Biz who guided Jill over the ground rails, and at the very end of the lesson, a few small fences. The fences were so small that Biz could have simply walked over them, but he didn't. His ears went up as he approached, and he jumped them like they were four feet tall. Jill couldn't believe how high and how well he jumped. He seemed to know which approach to take, how fast to go, and how many strides were needed before his feet left the ground. His body felt powerful, yet graceful beneath her. His gait was balanced and smooth, and his landing was comfortable. Jill was astonished.

Susan clapped. "That was a *great* lesson, Jill. He's *amazing*. And boy, does he like to jump. He'd have kept going if you let him. His ears were straight up."

Jill was beaming. "That was *so* much fun. I'll cool him down and check on him tomorrow. Dr. Norris said to take it slow. I want to keep an eye on him."

Susan smiled. "Good idea, but I'm not worried. He's capable of a whole lot more."

Jill said goodbye to Susan and headed home. As they made their way up the path, she heard Sonny whinnying. Thankfully, he didn't sound frantic. Sarah asked them to give Sonny calming medication every time Biz left for a lesson or trail ride. It seemed to work, but when they were away an entire day for shows, they still used prescription tranquilizers, just to be safe. As they made their way to the barn, Jill spotted Caleb.

"What are you so happy about, young lady?" he asked.

"Great news. We had our first jumping lesson today. He was awesome."

Caleb smiled. "Jumping, huh? Well, that's wonderful, sweetheart. I know Biz is a good boy, but please promise me that you'll be careful. Riding horses can be dangerous, but jumping can be even more so. Don't jump without your helmet and you should wear a protective vest."

Jill nodded. "Don't worry, Caleb. I'll be careful. I promise."

"Do you have a vest, sweetheart?" Jill shook her head. "No. Not yet. They're very expensive. I'm saving for one, but Susan has some at Willow

Bend that I can use," said Jill as she steered Biz toward the barn. "Gotta go, Caleb. Good to see you."

"You, too. Say hi to your mom. I didn't see her yet today."

"I will. I promise. Have a good day."

Sonny greeted Biz with a big whinny. Jill chuckled as she put Biz in his stall, took off his tack, and brushed him. From the stall, Jill could see Caleb outside. Now and then, he looked toward the barn, probably to make sure she was okay. It warmed Jill's heart to see how much Caleb worried about her.

***

Jill told Biz they were going to start jumping, but it didn't feel real to him until he walked into the arena and saw the ground rails and fences. He felt his eyes widen and his ears stand up. It was a long time since he jumped, but his body felt strong. He felt his nostrils flare from the thrill of it all. He was ready.

Susan started the lesson by asking Jill to put on a protective vest and then slowly warm him up. He walked and trotted for about fifteen minutes and then Susan told Jill to ask him to canter around the outside edge of the arena. He felt the wind part around his nose and his mane bounce on his neck. Nirvana. He was happy. And just when his body felt ready, Susan asked Jill to trot him over the ground rails. He moved forward at a good clip and easily lifted his legs high so his hooves didn't hit them. Wow. His hips felt good. He was thrilled when he heard Susan tell Jill it was okay to start jumping the fences. They were small for a horse of his size. He could have simply hopped over them, but where was the challenge in that? He wanted to fly. When Jill asked him to jump the first fence, he cantered toward it, tucked his front feet, and his back legs launched him off the ground. He soared over the fence and felt exhilarated. When he landed, he quickly looked toward the next jump because he was eager for more. When he heard Jill giggle with what sounded like delight, he could hardly contain himself. Jill must have felt his exuberance because she made him canter around the arena one more time before he jumped the second fence. He went over it like he was jumping the barn and felt like a bird in flight. Oh, how he missed that feeling over the years. It was the only time he truly felt free. He felt like someone was watching, so he turned and looked through the big arena doors and saw Jonas standing by the paddock fence. He whinnied excitedly to Biz and Biz answered. Biz wasn't ready for the lesson to be over, so he was disappointed when Susan told Jill she didn't want him to do too much. But he was thrilled when Susan said he was capable of doing a whole lot more.

After Susan and Jill talked about the lesson and said their goodbyes, Biz headed out of the arena and walked toward the paddock. It was their usual routine, so Jill didn't fight him. "Did you see that, Jonas? My first jumping lesson in years. I had so much fun."

Jonas stood proudly. "Yes. I saw you, and you looked amazing. Just like the old days. You've still got it, my friend. This is going to be a wonderful year for you and Jill."

"I can't wait. I feel so alive. Energized. And my body feels good. I'm ready. I want to do it for me, but especially for Jill."

"Dang it, I wish Abdul saw it. But he's in his stall, waiting to get his teeth cleaned."

"I wish he was here, too, Jonas. He would have enjoyed it."

Jonas looked up at Jill, sitting on Biz's back. "Jill looks proud as a peacock."

"Thanks for always being there for me, Jonas. You're the very best friend I have."

Jonas tipped his head slightly and looked back at Biz. "And you are the very best friend I have. Now you go on home and rest before supper. I'll see you next week."

Biz felt affection pour from his eyes. "Okay, Jonas. I'll see you soon."

Biz headed toward the pathway. All the way home, he thought about Sonny. He promised Sonny he'd tell him a story each time he came back from a lesson or show, so he planned to talk about his jumping lesson and how wonderful it felt. When they arrived at the barn, Sonny ran to the fence to greet them. He appeared to be full of nervous energy, but able to control it. Biz whinnied softly. "Do I have a story to tell you."

"Really? I can't wait. You'll be pleased to know that I was okay while you were gone. Nervous, but okay. Carol checked on me a lot and made sure I had plenty of hay."

"That's great. I'm proud of you. When Jill is finished brushing me, I'll tell you all about my lesson and we'll talk."

While Jill groomed Biz, Sonny waited in the paddock. Biz chuckled to himself because every few minutes, Sonny looked anxiously into the barn and then slumped his shoulders when Biz was still in the cross ties. When Jill finally led Biz outside, she dropped a flake of hay on the ground in front of him. "I'm going to take a shower, boy. I'll be out to feed you in a little while."

Biz told Sonny all about his day while they leisurely munched on hay, side by side, in the paddock. Sonny seemed to hang on to every word.

"That's exciting, Biz. When will you jump again?"

Biz said he was sure it would be the following weekend. He hoped so. Jumping was in his blood.

~29~

In late summer, Sarah found out she was pregnant again. Her morning sickness lasted well into the afternoon, and with a little one at home and another on the way, she was tired and needed rest.

Understandably, she spent less time at the barn and Sonny started to act up again. He charged at Jill in the paddock, so Carol put her foot down and told Jill she was no longer allowed in there. Cleaning the barn and paddock in the morning and the afternoon became Carol's chore, but she honestly didn't mind because she loved barn work.

While in the paddock, there were times when Carol noticed Sonny staring at her like he wanted to charge, but he didn't. Then, after a couple of weeks, he finally did and the menacing look in his eyes scared Carol. That night, she called Susan to tell her what happened. Susan was quick to tell her to never let a horse get away with that kind of behavior. She stopped by for a chat the next morning and Carol was shocked when Susan told her to buy a Wiffle ball bat. Susan explained that Wiffle ball bats were made of very thin plastic and hollow inside, so if she swung it at Sonny in self-defense, it would sting and startle him, but never injure him. She advised Carol to take it into the paddock with her, and if he charged, hit him right between the ears. She guaranteed he would never try it again.

Carol gasped. "I can't do that, Susan. That's terrible."

Susan sighed. "Carol, it's all about the pecking order. You and Jill are part of a herd. The question is, who is the alpha? At your farm, you and Jill have to be the alphas, or you run the risk of getting hurt. In the wild, if a horse charges the alpha, he either wins or loses. The alpha has seconds to react—often retaliating with force to maintain his status. Carol, horses don't understand how humans think. Trust me. The next time he does it, you have a few seconds to whack him once and then walk away. I promise it will be a long time before he tries it again."

Carol thanked Susan for stopping by, but she wrestled with the advice. It made sense, but it seemed barbaric, and it went against everything Carol believed about the proper treatment of animals. Carol didn't completely disregard Susan's advice. She bought the bat and brought it to the barn, but she wasn't sure she would ever be able to make herself use it. About a week later, while Biz was freely eating hay at the far end of the paddock, Carol decided to brush him outside and talk to him about her dilemma, hoping he'd somehow tell her what to do. "What do you think, Biz? I have no idea. I've never hit an animal like that, especially with a bat. I don't care that it's thin, plastic, and hollow. I'm not comfortable with it."

Biz turned his head and stared into Carol's eyes in a manner that communicated that what she felt was good, but there were exceptions. She rubbed his face and ears, kissed him on the nose, and walked over to the part of the paddock closest to the barn to clean it. She was deep in thought when out of the corner of her eye, she saw Sonny put his head down. She turned to face him just in time to see him paw the ground and run at her. Carol panicked. She didn't have the bat. *How could I have been so stupid? I should have listened to Susan*, she thought.

Carol looked for a way to get out of Sonny's path, but there was nowhere to run. The fence was too far away, and the barn wall was behind her. Fearing the worst, she closed her eyes and tried to brace for the impact.

With her eyes closed, she heard Sonny run toward her. She even felt his gallop as the ground rumbled under her feet. Waiting for him to physically hit her felt like an eternity, but he never did. When all was silent and she felt brave enough to open her eyes, what she saw astounded her. Biz pinned Sonny against the outside wall of the barn with his teeth in his neck. Biz, who wouldn't lift a finger to defend himself, attacked Sonny to protect her. When Biz removed his teeth, he backed away from Sonny with his ears pinned back. He placed himself halfway between Sonny and Carol and then stared Sonny down as if daring him to try it again.

Sonny was either unable to move or terrified to move when Biz had him pinned. He looked frozen against the wall and his eyes were wide. When Biz finally released him, Sonny kept his eyes on Biz as he backed away. Sonny shook his head and neck like he was shaking off tension. He looked scared. Biz seemed brazen, undaunted, and unwilling to back down.

When Carol was able to get her feet to move, she quickly separated the paddock because she didn't know if Biz and Sonny were still friends. Once they were separated, Carol walked over to Biz, wrapped her arms around his neck, and melted into him. He saved her from harm and might have even saved her life. If she was killed, what would have happened to Jill? Carol cried. She remembered the fear in Jill's eyes and her quivering lip the day she made Carol promise to clean the paddock with Sonny locked in his stall. She broke that promise, and the consequences could have been dire. Carol was in awe of Biz's loyalty.

From across the paddock, Carol looked to see if Sonny had any blood on his neck. She didn't see any, and though she wanted to get a closer look, she was afraid to go near him. She thought it was safer to wait until

Jill or Caleb was around. When Jill got home, Carol decided to be honest and tell her the truth.

"Mom, you promised," Jill said with tears in her eyes.

"I know. I don't know what I was thinking, but I learned my lesson. Never again. I'm sorry. I'm so very sorry."

Jill hugged her mother. "I'm glad you're okay."

"Me, too."

Jill went into the house to call Susan and tell her what happened. Within five minutes, Susan was at the door, asking for every detail.

Susan shook her head. "I've never witnessed anything like that. You have a *very* special horse out there. There is absolutely no doubt that he protected you, but I have to be honest, I'm having a hard time picturing Biz with his ears pinned back, never mind his teeth in another horse's neck. Other than Jonas, he's the gentlest horse I know."

Susan looked at Jill. "Don't ever doubt that he would have done the same for you, Jill. Both of you love and care for him. He would protect you and your mother at any cost."

Jill smiled. "I know he would."

Susan hugged Jill and reminded her that they had a lesson the next morning. "Be on time and ready for work. We have a show next week and we have to be prepared."

Jill nodded. "I'll be in the arena before you."

Carol cleared her throat. "Susan, before you go, can you help me check Sonny? I didn't see any blood, but I don't know if Biz broke the skin. I was afraid to get too close. "

Susan chuckled. "I don't blame you. You did the right thing by waiting until someone else was around. Let's take a look."

They all walked outside but only Susan went inside Sonny's paddock. He looked skittish as she approached, but he stood still. Susan looked closely at his neck and asked Jill to get a wet cloth and some antibacterial wash. "Biz's teeth scraped his skin, but it's not broken. There's no blood. We'll just wash it and be done with it," said Susan.

Carol watched Jill and Susan work together in the paddock. Sonny seemed calm, but she still didn't trust him. It would be a long time before she did. She dreaded that she was going to have to call Sarah and tell her what Sonny did. She knew it was going to upset Sarah that Sonny was regressing, but there wasn't much Sarah could do to change it at that time. Carol decided to always have a Wiffle ball bat with her in the paddock, but she hoped with all of her heart that Sonny would never give her cause to use it.

***

Jill went out to the barn after Susan left. As soon as she opened the door, both horses grunted for food, and she chuckled because it was clear that they thought she came bearing treats. The first thing Jill did was thank Biz for taking care of her mother. Sonny must have sensed her anger when she turned to face him because he took a step back. With purpose, she walked over to his stall and, in a stern voice, said, "I get it, Sonny. I understand why you're upset with Sarah, and I don't blame you, but it's not my mother's fault. You better not ever hurt her. If you do, you won't live here anymore, and I won't feel bad about it."

Sonny's ears moved back and forth, like antennas trying to crack a secret code.

"I mean it. Three strikes and you're out. One more incident and you're out of here."

Out of the corner of her eye, Jill saw Biz's ears perk up, and then he turned his stare to Sonny, who lowered his head to the floor. Sonny looked remorseful, so after Jill said what she needed to say, she let her anger go and hoped for the best.

**

Jill threw Biz and Sonny a flake of hay before she went back inside the house. When Biz heard the kitchen door open and close, he knew Jill was safely inside so he let loose on Sonny. "What the heck did you think you were doing out there, Sonny? You better understand that you're not allowed to hurt my family. *My* people. *My* world. *My* life would still be hell if not for Jill and her mother. I will protect them with everything I have. If you ever hurt them, I will hurt you. Today was a warning. Feel grateful. Next time, you won't be so lucky."

Sonny backed up until he was against his stall wall and cowered.

"Why? Why did you do it?" Biz demanded.

Sonny put his head down and whispered, "I don't know."

Biz bellowed. "You don't know? What have Jill or Carol ever done to you?"

"Nothing. They didn't deserve what I did."

Biz felt his shoulders drop and the tone of his voice softened. "Then why? I thought we were friends, but I can't think of you as a friend if you'd hurt my family. I just can't. I don't think I want you here anymore, Sonny."

Sonny's head snapped up. "What? You don't want me here?"

Biz shook his head. "I don't think you can be trusted. Since you arrived, it's been one thing after another. You charged at Jill—*twice*, but I didn't think you intended to make contact. What you did today is *unforgivable.*"

Tears streamed down Sonny's face. "Please don't give up on me, Biz. I'm sorry. I guess I'm mad at Sarah because she's not here. And I'm resentful because you have Carol and Jill around you all the time. I took it out on Carol. You're right. It's unforgivable. I'm not asking you to forgive me, but I do hope you'll give me another chance."

Biz turned his butt to Sonny.

"*Please*, Biz?"

Biz didn't answer. Whether Sonny stayed or not was up to Carol and Jill. If he stayed, Biz would have to accept it, but he wasn't sure he would be able to embrace it.

***

Dinner was quiet that night. Jill wasn't angry with her mother, but she was upset. Just the thought of her mother getting hurt was more than she could bear. After the table was cleared and the dishes were done, Jill excused herself and went upstairs to read and then get ready for bed.

Her mother walked to the bottom of the stairs and called after her. "Honey, I'm sorry. I know you're still upset. I don't blame you. It was a stupid mistake. I guess I never thought he'd do it to me, but now I know better. I promise you that it will never happen again."

Jill walked back down the stairs and hugged her mother. "It's okay, Mom. I'm not mad at you. I just need to calm down. It scared me."

"I know it did. Try to get a good night of sleep and I'll see you in the morning."

Jill got in her pajamas and started to get into bed when she heard her mother on the phone with Sarah. After she told Sarah what Sonny did, her mother spent most of her time comforting Sarah. It was clear that Sarah was appalled by his behavior and ready to move him if they wanted him out. Jill heard her mother tell Sarah that it wasn't necessary to move him yet. She wanted to give it some time. When she hung up the phone, Jill heard the kitchen door open and close, so she peered out her bedroom window and saw her mother walking toward the barn. She knew she was going out to thank Biz one more time for keeping her safe. The barn lights clicked on, and Jill was able to see her mother through Biz's stall window. She stood by Biz for a while and from the way she used her hands and bobbed her head back and forth, Jill knew her mother and Biz had an important talk. She was certain that Biz understood everything and wished she could have heard every word. Jill was positive that her mother told Biz how much she loved him and always would. She was also positive that her mother cried.

When her mother turned toward Sonny's stall, her body language shifted. She stood taller, and the index finger on her right hand went stick straight as she pointed in Sonny's direction. Her motions were harsh, so Jill knew he was getting quite a tongue-lashing. Jill watched until her mother came back into the house. When Jill finally climbed into bed, she turned off her light, rested her head on her pillow, and was instantly enveloped by the scent of Old Spice. She was comforted by it, felt herself relax, and whispered, "I'm glad you're here, Dad. We need you right now. Today was pretty scary for Mom and me. We miss you *so* much." The last thing she remembered before she fell to sleep, was tears streaming down her face, and the feel of a wet pillowcase against her right cheek.

~30~

Carol could hardly take her eyes off Biz. He looked better than ever. His body was round and full. Exercise no longer seemed to tax him. His muscles were strong. Powerful. And he likely felt like the athlete he was in his younger days. Carol suspected that he knew it because when he passed by the mirrors in the indoor arena, he looked at himself.

For weeks, Carol watched as Susan guided Biz and Jill through exercises to help him listen to the commands Jill gave with her legs, hands, and seat. They practiced so much that Biz knew exactly what Jill wanted and they performed like a fine-tuned machine.

At the last show, it was a very hot day. By noontime, the temperature was ninety-nine degrees. Biz was stressed from the heat, as were all the horses, but Jill made sure he was in the shade between classes, and they brought plenty of water with electrolytes to replenish the nutrients he sweated out. Jill called it horsey Gatorade. They also brought hay cubes soaked in the electrolyte water because Susan said it was a good way for him to get extra calories and extra water to keep him energized and hydrated.

Everyone took exceptional care of Biz at the show. Even Caleb. Carol saw him, sneaking carrots to Biz between classes. Susan told Jill to give Biz extra hay as long as he was drinking water. She said his heart was pumping faster to cool his body, and the more his heart pumped, the more calories he burned. Biz loved to eat. Horse food *and* people food. He always begged Carol or Jill for a piece of whatever they were eating, and at the show, that didn't change.

As Carol walked around the grounds, she saw Jill and Biz standing in the shade of a big oak tree. Biz's ears were pointing straight up, and he was intently looking at something in front of him. When Carol realized what it was, it was too late to warn Jill. He reached his long neck over and grabbed a doughnut right out of a spectator's hand.

When the woman turned and saw Biz, she laughed out loud. Jill looked embarrassed. Her body language told Carol that she was apologizing, but the woman didn't seem to need an apology. She kept laughing and she reached over and rubbed Biz's neck. Jill looked over and saw her mother laughing and put her hands up in the air as if to say there was nothing she could do.

The day was so hot that Biz started to fall asleep before the first class following the lunch break, and it appeared that he woke up halfway through it.

"Gee, I'm sorry your horse gets so stressed at shows. It must be awful for you," laughed Tim, the father of a student at Willow Bend. "Carol, you lucked out with Biz. We all thought you were crazy to take him, but I guess you saw something nobody else did. I'm happy for you."

Carol sighed. "We certainly feel lucky to have him."

Tim grinned. "You should. Look at how much we paid for our daughter's horse, and he never wins anything. She loves him, so we keep him, but if it was up to me, he'd be gone and she'd be riding something worth the money we spend."

"But if the horse makes her happy, the money's well spent, isn't it?"

Tim pursed his lips. "Well, when you put it that way ... her pony does make her smile."

"Maybe winning ribbons isn't important to her," Carol said.

Tim looked at Carol inquisitively. "What do you mean?"

"If your daughter and her pony never win and she doesn't want another horse, maybe she doesn't care about competing."

Tim scratched his head. "Maybe she doesn't."

Carol put her hand on Tim's shoulder. "Maybe all she wants is a buddy."

Tim looked up at the sky and then at Carol. "Maybe that *is* all that she wants."

Carol hoped she didn't overstep. Tim attended all of his daughter's shows and supported her in every way. He was a nice man who just wanted his daughter to be happy.

***

After Jill's last class, when all the riders had their ribbons, the judge motioned for Jill to stay, and then walked over to her after the horses and riders departed from the ring. From the sideline, Susan thought the judge wanted to offer some constructive criticism, but when she finished speaking, Jill turned and had an enormous smile on her face as she trotted over with a blue ribbon on his bridle.

"She knows him," exclaimed Jill.

"She knows who, honey?" asked her mother.

"The judge knows Biz. She said judges only have the numbers assigned to each horse and rider, not names, so after we got our blue ribbon, she asked if he is Official Business."

Susan was surprised. "How does she know him?"

"She said she knew him when he was Virginia Hunter Jumper Champion. He was so handsome and such an athlete that she never forgot him."

Susan couldn't peel the grin off her face. "*Biz* was Virginia Hunter Jumper Champion? Wow. That explains so much. I heard the Ellingtons paid a lot of money for him, so I assumed he was accomplished, but I didn't know he earned *that* title. Now we know why he has such incredible skill. He's had *lots* of training."

Jill nodded. "The judge was surprised to see him here because she hasn't seen him at a show in a long time. She said he looks just as handsome as he did back then and she's glad we're taking such good care of him."

Carol looked stunned. "He must have been quite special if she remembered him from that long ago. Think about it, honey. How many horses does she see in the show ring during just one year? Wouldn't it be normal for the horses to blur together in her memory?"

Susan nodded. "When I judged at horse shows, that's what happened to me. The horse had to stand out for me to remember it."

Jill squealed with joy. "I can't believe she remembered him. But we already know he's remarkable. Isn't that right, Biz? You're such a good boy. I'm so proud of you."

"Did she say anything else, honey?" Carol asked.

"She asked if we ever do jumper division shows. I told her we just started jumping lessons, so we weren't ready for jumping competitions yet."

Susan wanted to burst with happiness. She was proud of Jill for believing in Biz from the moment she saw him. She was also proud of Biz because he had so much heart. She knew it took enormous courage for Biz to trust after so many years of unhappiness, but his life was rich and full because he did. *Sometimes you just have to take risks*, thought Susan.

~31~

At the end of the day, as the herd made its way in from the pasture, Abdul heard yelling inside the tack room as he passed by.

"I can't believe we lost to Jill and her *deadbeat* horse *again*," someone bellowed.

When Abdul heard Jill's name, he stopped walking and peeked into the open tack room door. It was Erinna. Her face was beet red, and her fists were clenched. The last time Abdul saw someone that angry was when Melissa whipped him. It sent a chill through him and made him wonder if she ever whipped her horse. He made a mental note to look for whip marks on Excalibur the next time he passed by, but at that moment, all he wanted was to distance himself from her. He scurried away at such a fast clip that he tripped into his stall and bounced off the wall. The ruckus made Jonas jump. "What in the world is wrong with you, son? I darn near jumped out of my skin."

"Erinna scared me. She's really angry at Jill and Biz. She called Biz a *deadbeat*."

Jonas stopped chewing and stared at Abdul. "What? Why?"

Abdul walked closer. "She said she couldn't believe she lost to Jill and her deadbeat horse *again*."

Jonas laughed out loud.

"Why are you laughing, Jonas? It's not funny. Erinna was mad and she looked like she wanted to hit someone. She reminded me of Melissa. I hope she doesn't take it out on Excalibur."

Jonas stopped laughing. "Sorry, Abdul, I understand why that would upset you."

Abdul felt anger rise in his chest. "I'm pissed off, Jonas. Biz doesn't deserve to be called a deadbeat."

Jonas grinned. "I don't think I've ever seen you angry before, Abdul. And I know I've never heard you cuss."

Abdul chortled because Jonas was right. He never cursed and he was a little bit embarrassed. He pivoted on his heels and looked out his stall window. "Sorry I cussed, Jonas, but I'm angry. Biz is my friend and he's amazing."

Jonas sighed. "You're right, little man. Biz is amazing, and that's why Erinna hates him."

Abdul tipped his head. "You're confusing me, Jonas."

Jonas lowered his head and looked into Abdul's eyes. "Erinna has the best of everything. Her parents are rich, and they give her whatever she wants. She has expensive trainers, expensive tack, expensive show clothes, and Excalibur is a *very* expensive horse."

Abdul snorted in frustration. "What does that have to do with hating Biz?"

"Think about it. Erinna lost to the girl she mocked because she had to work to pay for lessons. *And* she lost to the horse she ridiculed because of how he looked when he first arrived. Erinna has egg all over her face and doesn't know how to get it off. Karma. It couldn't have happened to a more deserving person."

Abdul sighed. "What's karma, Jonas?"

Jonas shifted his weight. "If you do good things, you get good karma. If you do bad things, you get bad karma."

Abdul shook his head. "I'm still confused, Jonas."

Jonas chuckled. "It means that if you treat people badly, people will treat you badly, too. And if you do good things, good things will happen to you. Everything comes full circle. What you throw out to the universe eventually comes back and slaps you in the face or pats you on the back. It might not happen right away, but eventually, it happens."

Abdul inhaled. "Jill and Biz won because they worked hard. Erinna is mean."

Jonas grunted. "She's a spoiled brat. Her parents should wash her mouth out with soap."

Abdul wondered how many classes Biz entered, how many ribbons he won, and how many were for first place. He couldn't wait to get the details straight from the horse's mouth, so to speak. In the meantime, he wished he was able to see Tartan Glen from his stall window. He knew he would feel better if he could just lay eyes on Biz before he drifted off to sleep.

~32~

The following Wednesday, Carol rode Biz to her lesson at Willow Bend. They left the house around nine-thirty to get there by ten o'clock. Biz was excited to see his friends and tell them all the details about the show. He couldn't believe they won every class again. He hoped Sonny would be okay while he was gone. Sonny always whinnied when Biz left the farm, but it was the tone of the whinnies that told Biz whether it was going to be a good day or a bad day. It sounded like a good day. From moment to moment, things could change, but overall, Sonny was much better.

On the ride down to the farm, Biz kept looking toward the paddock. As soon as he saw Abdul and Jonas, he whinnied and whinnied. He was so excited that he forgot Carol was on his back.

"Oh my goodness, Biz. That was the strongest and loudest whinny you've ever done with me on your back. I'm impressed. My whole body jiggled like Jell-O."

By the time they reached the paddock fence, Abdul was prancing in place. "Tell us all about it, Biz. How'd you do at the show? We know you did well, but we don't know the details."

Biz cleared his throat. "We did very well. Susan entered us into five classes, and we won every single one. It was an amazing day."

"You won all of them? Blue ribbons?"

"Yes. All blue, but what I loved most was the look in Jill's eyes. She was so proud."

Jonas walked closer. "I bet, but you understand that she was proud of you before you even entered the show ring, right?"

Biz nodded.

"Is it tough being at shows again?" asked Jonas.

Biz chuckled. "I'm completely at home. The only pressure was from deep within myself. I wanted to do well for Jill. It was important to me."

"Was the competition tough?" asked Jonas.

"There were some pretty expensive horses and experienced riders. I didn't recognize any of them except for the ones from Willow Bend, but at the end of every class, I made sure we beat the pants off one rider because she was unpleasant to Jill."

Abdul's ears perked up. "Let me guess. Erinna?"

Biz wondered how Abdul knew. "Yes. Why?"

"Because she didn't have anything nice to say about you or Jill when she came back from the show. I'm not going to tell you what she said because it will hurt your feelings, but I'm glad you beat her ass."

Biz laughed out loud and so did Jonas. "You'll have to excuse Abdul. He's been cussing lately." Jonas chuckled.

Biz looked at Abdul. "Cussing, huh? Why?"

"Because I don't like it when people say lousy things about you or Jill."

Biz stepped closer. "Don't worry about me, Abdul. The people I love don't say those things, and the rest simply don't matter. Listen, I'm not proud of it, but I was so fed up with Erinna that at both shows, each time we beat her, I made sure that I pranced right in front of her with our blue ribbon dangling from my bridle. I know it wasn't the right thing to do, but it sure felt good."

Abdul laughed so hard that he snorted. "Really? That's *awesome*! I wish I saw that."

Biz chuckled. "It *was* awesome. But I hope it didn't create problems for Jill. Erinna's nasty."

Jonas nodded. "She can be very nasty, but I wouldn't worry about Jill. She's as strong as she is sweet. She's a *lot* tougher than you think. And she has a good head on her shoulders."

Biz felt Carol squeeze his sides to let him know it was time to go into the arena for their lesson. "Bye, guys. I'll see you before we go home."

Biz hoped Jonas was right. He loved Jill and didn't want to make her life difficult. She deserved to be happy.

~33~

When show season was over, no one was happier than Carol. She never hid the fact that she found the show scene stressful, but she promised Jill that as long as she wanted to show and they could financially afford it, she'd support her. "But any time you want to quit, just say the word," Carol often said.

Carol was glad she didn't care about showing. She didn't want to be a show mother screaming at her child because she didn't win a ribbon. Like Erinna's mother. Carol wasn't a fan of Erinna, but she also felt bad for her. Her parents put a lot of pressure on her and didn't seem to show her much affection. At shows, some parents were a joy to be around because they loved and supported their children. Others weren't. At one show, Carol heard a trainer yell, "It's a good thing your grandfather wasn't alive to see that performance," and the poor little boy sobbed as he exited the show ring.

At another show, when a young girl made a mistake, her mother marched over to the trainer and loudly demanded to know what he was going to do about it. Carol wondered what anyone could say or do that would make that little girl feel any worse. Carol learned that horse shows were expensive, and some parents expected a return on investment, but Carol wasn't like that. For Carol, shows were supposed to be fun, and if mistakes were made, children learned from them. The horse show was the test following lessons and training. If errors were made, it was between the student and the instructor. And Carol was uncomfortable with the unsportsmanlike conduct of riders who lost, like Erinna.

During Jill's first show season, Carol discovered that her attitude was not the norm among show parents, but her goal wasn't to fit in. She wanted Jill to enjoy herself. She didn't care about showing or ribbons. She cared about Jill and Biz.

***

For the next two years, Carol and Jill continued to love and care for Biz, take lessons, and attend horse shows. Many of the top show horses at Willow Bend, like Günter, competed in the prestigious New England Jumpers' Association shows. Carol thought Jill might eventually do the same, but she sensed that Jill likely preferred the low pressure of pleasure division shows, as well as entry-level three-phase competitions where all the horses competed in dressage, cross country, and show jumping.

When Caleb heard that Jill was doing cross country courses, he gave her a gift certificate to have a customized protective vest made to keep her safe. "Those cross country jumps don't fall apart if you hit them like the ones in the show ring. Get whatever you want. I know it's going to cost a fortune, but you're worth it, sweetheart," he told Jill. To have one made, Carol had to take Jill to the tack shop to have precise measurements taken of her body and pick out custom colors. Then, small pieces of the newest type of shock-absorbing foam were cut to fit and sewn together with tough elasticized fabric, so the vest, which zipped up the front, snuggly hugged her torso to protect her spine, ribs, lower back, and shoulders. Years prior, Jill told Carol that if she was ever lucky enough to have a vest made, it would be hunter green and burgundy because those colors looked great against Biz's copper coat.

Sarah was at the barn often with her son and her little girl and Carol was grateful. Sarah was good company, and when Sarah was around, Sonny was well behaved, which was very important with little children in the barn. Sonny seemed to love the kids and Sarah's eyes lit up when he put his nose next to their heads and took a deep breath, often drawing their delicate hair into his nostrils. It was as if he couldn't get close enough to them. Jill acted like a big sister around the kids, and she enjoyed them so much that she sometimes babysat so Sarah and her husband could go out. Sarah was very generous with compensation, saying that she never worried when she left her kids with Jill because they were in good hands.

During the two years, Carol kept up with everything that happened at Willow Bend. She learned that Melissa went to the barn more often to groom Abdul, but she still didn't ride him because memories of their accident were still too fresh in her mind. Melissa was riding again, but only on Susan's seasoned lesson horses. "I wonder if that makes Abdul sad," Jill said to Carol. Carol felt a connection between Jill and Abdul since the day Jill helped him after the accident. Jill appeared to be drawn to him and he always seemed happy to see her. Whenever Carol and Jill were at Willow Bend together, Abdul's eyes begged Jill to come over and they sparkled when she did. Occasionally, Jill brushed him because he seemed to be asking her to. The poor little guy looked lonely. Jill expressed concern because he didn't look physically fit. Jill said he needed to be worked or he'd end up looking just like Biz when he first arrived.

Jonas continued to pull Noah's wagons at fairs, weddings, and funerals. Noah was so impressed with the running braid on Biz's mane that he asked Jill to do it on Jonas for special occasions. Jill wove beautiful ribbons through the braids, from his ears down to his withers. For funerals, she generally chose grays and blacks. For weddings, it was usually white or cream, along with the colors of the bridal party. For fairs, it depended on the theme. Autumn fairs were cream, orange, rust, and green. Christmas was white, red, and holly green. Carol overheard Noah offering to pay Jill, and she was proud when Jill told him no because he very generously allowed her and her mother to use his arena for lessons free of charge. Though Jonas looked a little bit older due to a few white hairs, sprouting around his nose, it didn't diminish his presence. He still looked distinguished.

Carol also learned that Luis and Sharon had a new trainer named Derrick and they were doing well under his direction. Jill stopped and watched their lessons on the days when she cleaned stalls. Carol happened to be at the barn on a day when Derrick was there, so she stopped and watched too. Derrick seemed confident and extremely knowledgeable, and Carol liked his way of teaching. He didn't correct Sharon. Instead, when he asked her to do something, he watched intently, and asked how it felt. If Sharon wasn't happy with it, he asked what she might do differently to change the outcome. By doing so, he allowed Sharon to figure out the problem and correct herself, becoming an active participant in the training. When she was ready to make the correction, Derrick guided her through every step. He didn't yell and he didn't use a whip. Sharon looked happy. Relaxed. So did Luis. And they successfully moved up to the next level in competition.

During trail rides, Carol ran into Ellen and found out that she and Aiyana no longer did barrel racing. They said goodbye to the western show circuit to enjoy trail rides and have fun.

Opal and Daniella still showed in the in-hand Palomino classes, so she still invested a lot of time into making Opal look beautiful. Opal's light golden coat and cream-colored mane and tail looked fabulous when they arrived at the show grounds. Daniella paraded Opal around as if she was a large gemstone on her finger, but Opal didn't seem to like it. At one show, just before her first class, Opal broke loose from Daniella to roll in a patch of green grass, and when she rolled completely over, she slid into a mud puddle. Grass stains covered her sides and black mud stuck to her coat and slowly dripped off. When Opal shook, mud sprayed all over Daniella's hair and face, as well as her show clothes. Daniella was furious, but Opal seemed pleased with herself when she pranced in place and then took off. It looked like pure rebellion. As bad as the situation was, Carol had a hard time keeping a straight face. So did Jill.

Günter pulled a hamstring on one of the more difficult jumps at a show and had to take time off to heal. Carol noticed that he never looked unhappy, basking in the sun in the paddock.

Biz took home a lot of blue ribbons and, as a result, Susan's reputation as an instructor flourished. She had so many students that she started to offer group lessons to keep up with the demand. She told Carol that several parents called, asking for lessons with Biz and Jill's trainer. Susan loved the additional income, but she looked tired and frequently told Carol how little time she had to ride her horses.

Caleb continued to move at a fast clip at anything he did. He repaired clapboards, fixed gutters, replaced windows, and even painted his house all by himself. He reminded Carol of Jonas. A workhorse. When he wasn't working on his house, he was in the garden, tilling, fertilizing, planting, and weeding. Every year, he planted something new and told Carol he couldn't wait to taste it. Sometimes it was something entirely new, and sometimes it was a new and improved version of something old, like yellow tomatoes that were supposed to be easier on the tummy. Caleb never seemed to age, and that was just fine with Carol because she didn't want Caleb to grow old. She couldn't bear the thought of him dying and she knew Jill couldn't either.

***

The following year, Jill decided not to show anymore. She didn't care about it as much. Her mother was right; even the pleasure division was stressful. And it was expensive. Every year, her tack and clothing had to be show quality, so she always had to buy new things. Show entry fees continued to rise, as did Willow Bend's fees to transport Biz to the show and have her instructor present. And there was so much preparation. She had to clean and polish her tack and make sure her saddle pads were washed. Her show clothes had to be cleaned and her boots polished. Biz had to be shampooed and clipped, and then she had to braid his mane and tail and put checkerboards on his butt. Checkerboards were Biz's trademark. People looked for them, so she couldn't skip that step. Once all of those things were done, Jill had to pack hay and water with electrolytes for Biz, as well as lunch and snacks. She had to inventory Biz's emergency medical kit and make sure it was at the show. And the whole time they were at a show, she worried about Sonny. So did her mother. Jill also stopped showing out of concern for Biz. He was getting older, and she didn't want to stress him out. It wasn't that he couldn't deal with the competition. She was sure he had many more shows left in him, but she felt a need for both of them to enjoy the summer. She just completed her junior year in high school and worked hard to keep her grades up for college applications. She wanted to take some pressure off. Enjoy life. Besides, she remembered how hot it was at horse shows during previous summers and didn't want to put Biz through that anymore. He was nineteen. Almost twenty. Jill thought it was more important to take care of him than show him off.

When word that Biz was no longer competing made its way around the barn, Jill waited for Erinna's reaction. At first, Erinna and her friends looked at Jill and laughed as they whispered amongst themselves. Later, Erinna told Jill she knew it was just a matter of time until Biz was all washed up and a loser again. Jill felt anger rise from her toes. She counted to ten before she turned and walked toward Erinna. The fear in Erinna's eyes made Jill snicker to herself. "Erinna, what happened in your life that made you such a horrible person? You're so mean that I pity you. I truly do."

Erinna's eyes grew wide. "You *pity* me?"

"You have everything, but nothing is ever enough for you. You're the most unhappy person I know. You're empty inside, Erinna. A great big void. So, yes. I pity you and your miserable, pathetic little life."

Jill knew she hit a nerve when Erinna's eyes welled. She felt a tad remorseful when Erinna turned and ran, but not enough to make Jill want to run after her. She was tired of Erinna, and she had a right to stick up for herself.

Biz looked great and he still enjoyed his jaunts down to Willow Bend for lessons. It amazed Jill that the horses still ran to the fence as soon as they heard him whinny. She called them his fan club. She always let him go to the fence to say hi, and every single week, she had to pull him away to get to her lesson on time.

She didn't know if horses had a secret language, but she assumed they did. She didn't know what they talked about, but she could imagine. She could tell that Biz liked Jonas, Abdul, and Aiyana. She often wondered if he still missed his Willow Bend family. She also wondered if he would miss her and her mother if they took a vacation. Her mother talked about a few days by the ocean during the summer since they were not going to any shows. Jill knew Biz would survive, but she didn't think he would thrive without them.

***

Biz still liked horse shows, but he wasn't in love with showing anymore. He wished he could just go and watch because show grounds were still a place where he felt at home. It was where he earned stardom in his youth, and thanks to Jill, it was where he achieved it again later in life. One of his fondest memories was the day the judge called Jill over because she remembered him. It helped him recall how special he was back in the day. He was proud of himself and particularly proud of Jill. He loved her and hoped she knew how much. She gave him his life back. Before he met her, he wasn't living. He simply existed. Each day blended into the next and there was no joy. Jill and her mother gave him the ability to look forward to each day. He went back into the show ring for Jill and was happy to take part in all of the pomp and circumstance. Her love led to his regained self-esteem, but he was content to leave showing behind and just enjoy life. The competitiveness at shows could be intense. People took it seriously. As if their survival depended on a ribbon. He wouldn't miss the drama. He looked forward to spending more time with Jill and her mother and hopefully some extra lessons so he could see his friends more often.

In the barn, he heard Carol and Jill talk about going away on vacation, and then Jill talked to him and Sonny about it while she brushed him. When she told him, he could tell that she was trying to gauge his reaction. He tried to look neutral, but he didn't like the idea because it would be difficult to get through even one day without them. He knew Sarah would come by more often to check on him and Sonny, and Caleb would undoubtedly visit with carrots, but it wouldn't be the same. He wondered who would stay at the house and take care of them.

***

There were very few people Carol trusted enough to take care of Biz. The one she trusted most was Susan, but Carol doubted that she had time to house-sit. After much deliberation, Carol decided to ask Susan anyway. If she said yes, Carol would be able to relax while on vacation. If Susan said no, Carol would ask her to recommend someone. Following her next lesson, Carol asked. "Susan, Jill isn't showing this year, so we have extra time and money. I'd like to take her away on vacation. Someplace with lots of fresh air, salt water, and sunshine. I just need to make sure Biz is in good hands. Can you recommend anyone to take care of the horses?" Carol was overjoyed when Susan said she would stay at the house. When Carol offered to pay her, she said no. "Just let me know when you need me. I take my vacations when show season is over, so I'm around all summer."

Carol checked out hotels and motels on Cape Cod but ended up renting a small cottage on the water for a week. After the cottage was rented, Carol bought books, a lounge chair, and plenty of tanning oil. She was determined to come home as brown as a coffee bean and smelling like salt air. And she wasn't going to cook even one meal. She planned to go out to breakfast and order take-out all week.

As the start of their vacation approached, Carol felt weepy every time she looked at Biz. She yearned for the ocean, but she didn't want to leave him. In the barn, she talked about Cape Cod and told Biz they'd be away for just a short time and back before he knew it. She noticed that he sighed every time she brought it up and she didn't think it was a coincidence. The day they were scheduled to leave, Carol's heart broke when they went out to the barn to say goodbye. Jill saw the expression on his face and cried. "I feel bad, Mom. Look at him. He's so sad. Should we even go?"

Carol was hugging Jill when Susan stopped by to go over the instructions for Biz's and Sonny's care one last time. "What's going on?" she asked.

"He looks sad, Susan. Maybe we should stay home," said Jill.

Susan sighed. "Don't worry. I'll be here to take care of him. He knows me. And I'll be staying right here, so he won't be alone."

Caleb's kitchen door opened and slammed shut as he walked over to the barn. He looked concerned when he saw Jill's red eyes and blotched cheeks. "Isn't this supposed to be a happy occasion?"

Jill let go of her mother and walked over to hug Caleb. He looked at Carol inquisitively. "Biz looks sad, Caleb. Jill's wondering if we should stay home."

Caleb's expression softened. "I was afraid this might happen. It's your first time away from the big guy. Trust me, sweetheart ... Biz will be fine. Susan is staying here, and I'm right next door. I'll come over to check on him several times a day and bring him carrots. He'll have plenty of company. I think we might even be tempted to spoil him."

Jill mustered a small smile.

Caleb tapped his index finger on Jill's nose. "If you leave me a few peppermints, I promise to give him one every day ... Now, you go and have a good time. Biz will be here when you get back and I'm certain he'll be just fine."

Jill seemed reassured, but Carol left reluctantly. They were both in tears as they pulled out of the driveway. Carol watched Biz in her rearview mirror, and Jill turned and watched him through the rear window until he was out of sight. The hardest part was leaving the yard, but the farther they drove, the more their thoughts turned from Biz to Cape Cod. While they were away, they called Susan and Caleb daily to see how Biz and Sonny were doing, and they were assured that both horses were fine. They pined for Biz but managed to have a nice vacation. Carol relaxed in the sun and swam in saltwater. And they enjoyed many wonderful meals out, including fried clams, steamed clams, lobster rolls, corn on the cob, and homemade ice cream. But they still missed Biz terribly.

***

Biz thought it was going to be a tough week while Jill and Carol were on vacation, but he had no idea how hard it was actually going to be. The days were so long that he could hardly stand it. Every night, he went to sleep with a heavy heart and stared out the window at the moon, remembering the evening when Jill stood by his side, gazing out the window at the planets, stars, and constellations. He longed for her. He didn't sleep much so he started each day exhausted and void of ambition. Each morning when the kitchen door opened, for a blissful second, he was hopeful, but disappointment stung when Susan emerged. He didn't dislike Susan. Her only crime, fair or not, was that she wasn't Jill or Carol. All day long, he stood in the paddock, staring at the house, hoping they would come outside. He needed to see their faces and hear their voices. He wondered if they were sad, too. Or if they were having a fabulous time without barn chores. Without him. He felt torn. He wanted them to have a good vacation, but the idea of them having a great time without him was unbearable.

Susan was nothing but smiles each time she went into the barn to feed them or clean stalls, but her happy eyes did nothing to alleviate his grief. He knew she understood how he felt because she seemed troubled by his lack of enthusiasm for everything. She said so. Every morning, she told Biz how many more days until Jill and Carol returned, but the week felt like a year. Sonny even tried to cheer Biz. Every day, he told Biz he was sure Jill and Carol couldn't wait to come home. He stayed close to Biz at all times, likely so he wouldn't feel alone, and he even slid some of his hay over to Biz. But nothing helped. Biz, who was always ravenous, lost his appetite. He assumed that made Susan and Caleb nervous because they were constantly trying to get him to eat apples, carrots, and treats. He refused them all. Around mid-week, they pulled out all the stops with a hot bran mash made with molasses, carrots, apples, raisins, and peppermints. It was a hot summer day, not the typical scenario for a hot mash, but their strategy worked. Peppermints. A secret weapon. He felt his ears stand up and before he knew it, he was nickering. As soon as the mash was in his feed tub, he dove in. It tasted good, especially the peppermints.

"Good boy, Biz. Does it taste good?" asked Susan.

Biz looked at her and she smiled. "It must, because you have bran all over your nose. Enjoy, buddy. I'll be back to check on you later. Thanks for eating, Biz. You were starting to worry me."

Sonny looked over at Biz. "It's good to see you a little bit perky, Biz."

Biz looked down. " I just miss Jill and Carol. I can't wait for them to come home."

Sonny's eyes softened. "Now you know how I felt when Sarah wasn't around. It's awful, isn't it? I'm sorry you're so sad."

Biz looked up at Sonny and tipped his head. "That's a good point. You're right. Now, I know. And yes, it is awful, but you should have handled it better. I haven't tried to hurt anyone, and you shouldn't have either."

Sonny nodded. "I know, and I'm still sorry, Biz."

Biz sighed. "I know you are."

Biz hoped the rest of the week would pass quickly so life could get back to normal. He knew he wouldn't be able to control himself when he heard their car pull into the driveway. He couldn't wait.

At the end of the week, when their car pulled in, Biz ran to the paddock fence and whinnied uncontrollably. Jill ran to him as soon as she shut the car door, but he couldn't stop pacing until both Jill and Carol were by his side. Susan was there and went outside to greet them.

"Are you sure he was all right while we were away, Susan?" asked Carol.

Susan looked at the ground. "Well, I didn't want to ruin your vacation, but he was very sad. It was pathetic. All he did was stand in the paddock and stare at your back door, waiting for you to come out. I can't believe how much this horse loves you guys. He doesn't care about anything else."

"I was afraid Biz would miss us. I missed him like crazy, too," said Jill.

Carol cleared her throat. "In all honesty, I thoroughly enjoyed the first two days of vacation, but after that, I missed Biz more and more every day. I couldn't wait to get home." Carol rubbed Biz's face and he melted. *The three of us are inseparable,* he thought.

***

It was a good year off. Biz liked his relaxing days in the pasture and the many trail rides with Jill or Carol. He especially liked it when they took off the saddle and rode bareback in the small pond near Willow Bend, and then let him graze in the green grass along the shore. Sometimes Sonny and Sarah accompanied them. Sarah gave Jill and Carol permission to ride Sonny, so sometimes Carol rode Biz and Jill rode Sonny. Biz liked those rides the best because they were all together. Jill tried to convince Carol to ride Sonny, but Carol didn't like to ride other horses. "Only Biz," she said.

During that year off, Biz became quite a fixture in the neighborhood. Everybody knew his name and brought him treats, like carrots pulled from the garden, homegrown strawberries, peaches, husks from freshly shucked corn on the cob, and apples. He cherished the times when people brought children to visit. He loved kids, but they were so little compared to him, that he had to pay attention to where they were at all times so they didn't get hurt. Biz loved summer, especially August when Caleb's peaches were ripe. Caleb brought him one every Saturday. He broke it in half, removed the pit, and laughed out loud when Biz ate them because juice always ran down his lips and dripped off his chin. Biz loved Caleb's laugh. It was a big belly laugh. A happy laugh.

Biz's love for peaches was evident when Jill rode him to lessons. When they took the back path, they had to pass by Caleb's peach trees. Biz was often quite determined to have a peach, and sometimes Jill couldn't coax him past the small orchard. The first time Caleb saw it, he went out to help. Jill laughed as she explained that Biz was trying to pick a peach. Biz was relieved when Caleb didn't get upset and reprimand him. Instead, he chuckled and gently led him away from the tree.

"You shouldn't reward him when he's not listening to you, sweetheart, so don't let him have a peach. He can have one later after you get back from your lesson and he's in the barn for the night." Caleb winked.

Biz saw Caleb's wink, so he knew Caleb was amused, but he also knew that Caleb was serious. It bothered Biz that Caleb saw him as disobedient rather than playful and mischievous, but not enough to make him stop trying to grab peaches. After all, he couldn't be the perfect horse *all* the time.

Biz loved being at home with Jill and Carol. Caleb visited him just about every day, and he liked that, too. He didn't leave Tartan Glen except for his lessons and trail rides. Life was good. Sonny seemed happy, too.

Biz still saw his friends at Willow Bend twice a week when he had lessons, and more often when he went on trail rides, but he still wished he could see Jonas and Abdul more. He missed his long talks with Jonas when he lived at Willow Bend because they were always insightful. And he missed being a big brother to Abdul.

~34~

Carol was in the yard, tending to the herb and Montauk daisy garden near the kitchen door when she heard Caleb. "Boy, he's a beauty," he said as he walked over to visit.

Carol's mind went right to Logan. "He is beautiful, isn't he, Caleb." Carol's words weren't a question. They were a statement of fact. "It's such a lovely day that I thought I'd get rid of the weeds in this garden. I can hardly find my herbs and my daisies are barely holding their own."

"Weeding is hard work. You have to be in the right mindset." Caleb said.

"True, but I try to keep up with it, especially in this garden, because Logan planted these daisies for me."

"And he loved doing it. But I think he intended them to be a source of enjoyment, not stress. You're getting to it now. That's all that matters."

Carol nodded because she knew he was right.

Caleb put his hands in his pockets and tipped his head. "I haven't been able to stop looking at Biz all morning. Every time I look out my window and see him, it makes me halt whatever I'm doing. Honest to God, he looked so darn bad when you first brought him home that it tugged at my heart. Now, every time I see him, I think of that saying by Winston Churchill, 'There's something about the outside of a horse that is good for the inside of a man.' He sure does something for me. And I love the way he takes care of Jill. That horse would never do anything to hurt that girl. I grew up with horses and I can tell a lot about their personalities by watching them. This horse is so devoted to you and Jill that it's like he's human. He's got a lot of heart. I truly like the old boy."

Carol stood up. "Since he became part of our family, he's helped me and Jill in ways I can't even describe. He's so special, Caleb."

Caleb looked in Biz's direction, smiled most kindly, and sighed. "This has always been a nice neighborhood. Our houses are far enough apart that we have privacy, but close enough that we can watch over one another. Since Biz arrived, your yard is the place our neighbors visit most. Biz is so handsome that he just draws people in, and his kindness keeps them here."

"Thanks for saying that, Caleb. We love Biz, but we love having you around, too."

Caleb blushed. "And I love hearing you say that."

Carol's heart filled with warmth. When she worked in her office, she sometimes saw neighbors pop over to say hi to Biz and offer him a treat or two, but she never thought of her yard as a neighborhood meeting place. She liked the sound of that.

~35~

Summer ended and it was back to school for Jill, who was starting her senior year of high school, getting ready for college. Every morning before she left for school, she peeked through the barn window to check on Biz and waved goodbye. During school weeks, Carol fed the horses their breakfast and let them out before she went into her office.

It was a chilly September morning. After Jill got on the bus, Carol got dressed, made herself a hot cup of tea, and sat at the kitchen table to read the morning paper before she went out to the barn. About halfway through the paper, she heard a loud noise. She went to the back door to listen and realized that it was coming from inside the barn. She ran outside and went in. Biz was thrashing on his stall floor and Sonny was pacing incessantly in his stall. Colic. She ran to the house and called the vet, then ran to ask Caleb for help.

"This is bad, Carol. He's in a lot of pain," said Caleb as soon as he saw Biz.

"But he'll be fine once the vet gets here, won't he, Caleb? They can fix him, right?"

When Caleb looked at her, Carol knew he didn't want to tell her the truth—some cases can't be cured. Carol changed the subject. "We have to keep him moving," she said, but Biz lay down and refused to get up. They tried everything to get him on his feet but couldn't do it.

"Why can't you just let them stay down?" asked Carol.

"If they are in discomfort, and just lay quietly, you can. If they start rolling and thrashing on the ground, they can twist their intestines and make things worse," said Caleb.

Biz started to thrash again. Carol sobbed and pleaded with him to get up, and then as if a jolt of pain caused him to panic, he got on his feet and they managed to keep him walking until the vet arrived.

Carol was relieved when it was Dr. Norris, not an unfamiliar vet on call. Biz slouched over and pawed at the ground and Dr. Norris winced.

"Oh, Carol. He's in a lot of pain," said Dr. Norris as she examined Biz and asked questions. "Do you know if he has any history of colic?"

"I don't know a lot about his past, but no colic since we've owned him," said Carol.

Dr. Norris gently led him into his stall. "Is this manure from just last night?"

"Yes, I cleaned the stalls after supper," said Carol.

"There's a good amount of manure. Nothing is stopping it from passing out of the large intestine," said Dr. Norris. "Do you do anything to prevent sand colic?"

"Yes, once a week, he gets a supplement to help prevent it," said Carol.

"Can I see the container?"

Carol retrieved the container from the tack area and Dr. Norris read the ingredients. "That's a good one. When horses eat off the ground, they ingest sand and dirt, which can collect in the intestine, weigh it down, and cause a twist. A good preventive supplement absorbs the sand and moves it out in the manure. If he's been getting that supplement every week, sand colic is not likely what we're dealing with."

Dr. Norris put on a plastic glove that went from her fingertips up to her shoulder, to do an internal rectal exam. Carol was amazed at how far Dr. Norris's arm reached inside. It was apparent that the exam was painful for Biz. His breathing changed, his head and neck tipped, and he groaned. Carol wanted to cry. When Dr. Norris finally pulled her arm out, she looked at Carol and shook her head. "I don't feel a blockage, but something is very wrong."

Dr. Norris said that, given the amount of manure in the stall, the problem was likely in the small intestine where she couldn't palpate. She said horses his age with no medical history of colic often have a tumor called a lipoma. The tumor can wrap itself around the intestine and strangle it. "There's nothing more I can do for him here. He needs to go to a hospital where they can further evaluate his condition. If it's a lipoma, he'll need surgery," said Dr. Norris. "He's in a tremendous amount of pain. I'm going to give him a shot of medication to relax him and another for pain. They will last a couple of hours, which should give you enough time to get him on a trailer and bring him up to North Star Equine Emergency Hospital. Go now before the pain medication wears off. Once he's there, they can keep him comfortable while they run tests and you decide what you need to do."

Carol's head was spinning. She never dreamed anything like this would happen to Biz. Surgery? How much would that cost?

Dr. Norris seemed to read her mind. She explained that surgery generally costs between three and five thousand dollars, but it could go as high as ten thousand or more, depending on the age of the horse and whether there were complications. She told her the hospital took credit cards, cash, and checks. "I strongly suggest that you get him there as quickly as possible."

Dr. Norris wrote down directions to the hospital and then called North Star to let them know that Biz was on his way. Dr. Norris asked if they had a horse trailer and truck for the journey. Carol explained that

Willow Bend always transported Biz to shows, so they didn't have either one.

Caleb put his arm around Carol's shoulder. "We'll use my truck, and I'll call Susan to see if we can borrow her trailer. Don't worry. We'll get him there." Caleb immediately went into the house and called Susan and then drove to Willow Bend to get the trailer.

Dr. Norris's hugged Carol tightly. "Are you okay?"

Carol shook her head and started to cry. "No. But he better be. I don't know how we'll ever get by without him. He's part of us. Part of everything we do."

A tear ran down Dr. Norris's cheek. "I know he is. Please keep me posted, Carol. I'm attached to him, too. He's a very special guy."

"Dr. Norris, did I miss something? Is he this sick because I missed symptoms?"

Dr. Norris took Carol's hand. "No. You didn't miss anything and it's not your fault. A lipoma is like a ticking time bomb. It strangles and the intestine can't empty, causing sudden and extreme pain. There's no way to know about a lipoma or prevent colic from one, and I'm just about positive that's what he has."

Carol put her hands over her face. "I'd never be able to forgive myself if I missed something."

Dr. Norris comforted Carol and then started to leave but seemed to think better of it when she looked at Sonny. His eyes were large, his coat glistened with sweat, and he was pacing in his stall. "He's pretty stressed out. I think I should give him a tranquilizer." She reached into her bag, pulled out the medication, filled a syringe to the appropriate level, and went into his stall to administer the dose. Sonny instantly relaxed.

Dr. Norris pulled out of the driveway and Carol felt completely alone. She turned to Biz, hugged him, and sobbed uncontrollably while she waited for Caleb to return with the trailer. She rubbed Biz's face and looked into his eyes, which were dull and void of emotion. "I know you feel awful, but at least you're not in pain anymore, handsome. We have to get you to the hospital so they can make you better."

Carol pulled out her cell phone and called Sarah to let her know what was happening and alert her to the fact that Sonny would be alone. "Sonny was upset, but Dr. Norris gave him a tranquilizer. He'll be fine until you get here. We're leaving as soon as Caleb gets back with the trailer."

Sarah started to cry. "You have to take him to a hospital? I'm so sorry. I'll come to the barn right away and stay at the house until you get back just in case Jill gets home before you."

Carol said she would leave the key to the house under the mat so she could get inside.

When Caleb returned, Susan was with him. The three of them gently loaded Biz into the trailer. As they closed up the trailer door, Sonny screamed for Biz, but Biz didn't answer. He was either in too much pain or too drugged to muster the strength.

"Susan, should I have gotten Jill out of school? Should she be going with us?" asked Carol, weeping.

"There's no time. Besides, we don't know what we're dealing with yet," said Susan.

"Susan, I'm so grateful that you're here, but can you afford to be away from Willow Bend today, especially with such short notice?" asked Carol.

Susan nodded. "Wild horses couldn't keep me away. Before I left with Caleb, I called Noah to tell him what happened, and he encouraged me to follow my heart and be with you. He asked me to tell you that he hopes Biz is okay. As for the barn work, it's all under control. I spoke with my most experienced and trustworthy barn help before I left and wrote the list of chores that needed to be done on the whiteboard. Noah promised to walk through to make sure they were done. And today is my administrative day, so I don't have any students until late afternoon. I'll call them on the way to the hospital to reschedule."

Carol's eyes welled up so much that her vision blurred. She closed her eyes and the tears streamed down her cheeks. "Thank you, Susan." Then she looked at Caleb. "Thank you, Caleb. I don't know what I'd do without either one of you."

Caleb passed Carol his clean handkerchief. "I think we both need to be here for you and Biz. Now, we best get going," he said.

It took just under two hours to get there, and Biz was already uncomfortable. Carol asked Caleb to please go inside to let them know they arrived, while she and Susan guided Biz off the trailer. Carol noted that there was no manure on the trailer floor.

They walked him inside and a veterinarian began the exam. "How old is he?" asked Dr. Adams.

"Nineteen ... almost twenty," Carol said, trying to hold back her tears. She noticed how young Dr. Adams was. She hoped for an older, more seasoned veterinarian with plenty of experience. Someone like Dr. Norris. Dr. Adams appeared to be in her late twenties. She was thin and her long curly dark brown hair was in a ponytail.

"Any manure in the trailer when you arrived?" asked Dr. Adams.

"No," Carol said.

Dr. Adams sighed. "Sometimes they have an obstruction, but they get so nervous in the trailer that they develop loose stools and get rid of it all by themselves. I always hope for that."

Dr. Adams took Biz's temperature, calculated his pulse and respiration rate, drew blood for testing, listened to his heart and lungs, listened to his abdomen, and inspected his gums. Before she began the internal exam, she put on the same type of long plastic glove that Dr. Norris used and reached into his rectum. She said she didn't feel any obstructions either, so she ordered an ultrasound, and then inserted a needle into his abdomen to pull fluid and analyze it for red blood cells, white blood cells, and protein levels. The ultrasound was performed, and then she read the results of the blood and abdominal fluid tests. "I didn't feel any blockages and the ultrasound is inconclusive, but the lab tests indicate that we're dealing with colic. No manure is passing, so there's a blockage, but we can't see it. I strongly recommend surgery."

Carol cried uncontrollably. Caleb and Susan tried to comfort her, but she was barely aware of their presence. Her mind was reeling. "Surgery? Will he survive? Will he be okay afterward? How much will it cost?" asked Carol.

Dr. Adams leaned her back against the wall. "There is no guarantee that he'll survive the surgery because we have no way of knowing what we'll find when we get in there. His quality of life following surgery also depends on what we find. As for the cost, do you have medical insurance for him?"

"Medical insurance? No. I didn't know there was such a thing for horses," Carol said.

Susan and Caleb put their hands on Carol's shoulders.

"Colic surgery will be at least five thousand dollars, but likely more. He's older. At nineteen or twenty, he's not going to bounce back easily, and he'll need post-operative care," said Dr. Adams.

Carol's heart raced, her palms began to sweat, and her mouth went dry. She didn't know what to do. She wasn't prepared for even the thought that Biz could die. And she had no idea that colic surgery could cost so much. Why didn't she know about medical insurance for horses?

Biz started to paw at the ground, so they gave him more pain medication to keep him comfortable. About an hour later, Dr. Hamilton, the hospital owner and lead surgeon, arrived. He looked to be in his fifties with touches of gray in his hair. Carol was relieved because she knew he had a lot of experience. The veterinary assistant read him the results of the lab tests as he began his physical exam. Biz started to paw again so they administered more pain medication. When Dr. Hamilton finished his internal exam, he said he didn't feel an obstruction, but still recommended surgery. He said exactly what Dr. Norris said about lipomas in older horses. "Based on his medical history, the internal exam, and what we know from the lab tests, I believe we're dealing with intestinal strangulation. The amount of manure that was in his stall this morning indicates a problem in the small intestine. The large intestine,

199

which is after the small intestine, was still able to move manure out, so the blockage has to be above it."

Carol groaned as Dr. Hamilton continued. "Realistically, at his age, this kind of colic surgery could be ten thousand dollars with post-operative care. We never know what we'll find until we go in."

Before Dr. Hamilton stepped out of the room, he said Dr. Adams would be back to answer any questions. As soon as he left, Carol looked to Caleb and Susan for guidance. "I don't know what to do," she said as she wrung her hands. "I don't want him to die. I love him."

The questions kept coming. He was almost twenty years old. Would he survive surgery? Would he be able to bounce back? What would his quality of life be? Carol sobbed unapologetically. "I don't think I can afford this. I can't stand it. No one should have to make a decision like this based on finances. It's so unfair. How could I not know about medical insurance for horses?"

Susan put her hand on Carol's shoulder. "Don't do this to yourself, Carol. Most people don't have it."

After a few minutes, Dr. Adams came back and asked if there was anything she could do to help. Carol asked if she could talk with her privately, and they stepped outside.

"I'm assuming I still have to pay the bill even if Biz doesn't survive the surgery."

Dr. Adams nodded.

Carol's voice quivered. "He was given pain medication a half hour ago and he's already pawing the ground. I know he's in a lot of pain, so we need to make the right decision as quickly as possible. At his age, I'm guessing that his odds of surviving the surgery are not good."

Dr. Adams looked at the floor, closed her eyes, and nodded again.

"And if he survives, will his recovery be tough?"

Dr. Adams explained that if he survived the surgery, Biz would need to stay in the hospital for a while so they could keep an eye on him, control his pain, and make sure he didn't develop an infection. When they let him go home, he would have to stay in his stall for at least a month while his incision healed, and his gastrointestinal tract got back to normal. After that, he would have to be in a small paddock to limit his movement for at least a couple more months. They would have to watch for infection, hernia formation, additional colic episodes, which occurred in up to fifty percent of horses, and lameness from laminitis, which was sometimes a complication. She added that some horses have a hard time maintaining weight after surgery. "The older the horse, the longer and harder the recovery. Even young horses have a hard time recovering," said Dr. Adams.

Biz's Journey Home

Carol could not stop the tears flowing down her face. "Dr. Adams, I'm not rich, but we love Biz, and I don't want to give up on him. Please answer me honestly. If this was your horse, what would you do? You have no idea how much he means to me and my daughter. I want to put finances aside and make the decision that's best for him."

Dr. Adams glanced around to make sure they were indeed talking privately, and whispered, "If he was my horse, I'd pump him full of fluids to hydrate him, and drug the heck out of him to keep him comfortable, in hopes that it's a fecal obstruction, not a lipoma. Then I'd repeat a belly tap in a couple of hours to see if his counts have gone up. If they have, then I'm sorry. Based on his symptoms, test results, and his age, I'd euthanize."

Euthanize! The word stuck in her throat. How could she kill Biz? But if she didn't, he would continue to suffer and he was already in excruciating pain. Carol bit her lip and looked deeply into Dr. Adams' eyes. "Okay, we'll try it and hope to God he gets better."

Carol looked at the clock and panicked. It was already early afternoon. Jill would be home from school soon and she had to be there to tell her about Biz herself. She told Dr. Adams she had to leave to meet her daughter as soon as she got off the bus. She asked Dr. Adams to call her as soon as she knew anything, and then she went back to Biz's hospital stall, wrapped her arms around his neck, and sobbed so deeply that she was unable to make a sound. When she finally lifted her head and looked at him, he appeared to have already given up and it broke her heart. "I'm so sorry, Biz. I'm sorry you're sick. I'm sorry you're in pain. My God, I'll never forgive myself if I missed something. Could I have done anything to prevent this? You're our boy, and it's my job to take care of you."

Biz rubbed his head on her shoulder as if to tell her it was not her fault.

"I love you, Biz. I'm sorry, but I have to leave you to get Jill. You're in good hands with Dr. Adams. She'll keep you comfortable. We'll be back soon." She kissed him on the nose and left his stall, barely able to breathe.

Susan, Carol, and Caleb were walking toward the truck to drive home when Carol asked Susan if she could stay with Biz. "I can't bear the thought of him being here with total strangers. Susan, can you stay while Caleb drives me back to get Jill?"

Susan put her arm around Carol's shoulders. "Of course, I can. I'll stay right in the stall with him. Go get Jill. Hurry."

***

Susan felt honored that Carol trusted her enough to leave Biz in her care, but she was concerned that she might feel pressured to put him down if his condition rapidly deteriorated before they got back. Susan realized that Carol never told North Star that she could act on Carol's behalf, but just the idea of it terrified her because it was a no-win situation. If the pain medications became ineffective, Biz would suffer tremendously if she didn't agree with the veterinarian's recommendation. If she did, it would deprive Jill and Carol of the ability to be with Biz when he died. She was left with overwhelming responsibility.

Susan stayed by Biz's side and talked soothingly to him. When he started to sweat from pain, she put cold compresses on his forehead. He seemed to know the sound of her voice because when she spoke, he tried to open his eyes.

In her lifetime of working with horses, Susan was never able to get used to the part where they get sick and die. At that moment, she was walking that path with Biz, and it hurt. Badly. She stood by his side, rested her forehead on his shoulder, and wept as if he was her horse. She loved Biz and everything he stood for. Memories of him, from the day he first arrived at Willow Bend to his last show, filled her head. A phoenix who rose from ashes. She asked herself why a kind horse who loved and protected his owners had to die. Why such a gentle soul? And why was it necessary for Jill's heart to be broken again? It was wrong.

Susan felt helpless, but also grateful that she was able to be with Biz. Be the one familiar face in a sea of veterinarians, veterinary technicians, and assistants, to calm him. She hoped Carol, Caleb, and Jill would get back soon, but she was dreading the moment Jill walked into Biz's hospital stall because she would instantly know what had to be done and be devastated.

***

The ride home was quiet except for the sound of crying. Carol tried to cry quietly, but it was difficult to hold it in. Caleb drove, looking straight ahead like he was trying to hide his red eyes and the tears that gently flowed down his cheeks.

They arrived home only a few minutes before Jill's bus dropped her off. Sonny seemed uncharacteristically calm, so they went directly into the house, and Sarah met them at the door. Carol tried to regain her composure so she could tell Sarah what was happening, but she failed, so Caleb filled her in. Carol was full of fear because her gut told her that Biz would never return home. She asked Caleb and Sarah to stay inside when

Jill came up the driveway so she could talk to her privately. Carol heard the school bus and went outside. As Jill made her way up the driveway, she looked for Biz and then saw her mother standing by the kitchen door. Her body stiffened. She seemed to immediately know something was very wrong.

"What happened? Where's Biz? What's the matter, Mom?" cried Jill as she ran into the barn to look for him. Carol followed her inside and reached out and hugged her tightly.

"I'm sorry, honey. After you left for school, I heard banging in the barn and found him thrashing on the floor."

Where is he? Is he dead? Is he *dead*, Mom?" screamed Jill.

"No, honey. He's not dead. But it doesn't look good. He's up at North Star. Caleb and Susan helped me take him there. I'm sorry. He was in so much pain that there wasn't time to get you out of school. Dr. Norris said to get him there as soon as possible before the pain medication wore off."

Jill looked confused. "But before I left for school, I peeked through the barn window like I always do. He was fine. He was standing there with his ears up, looking at me. How could this happen?" she cried. "We feed him right and he gets plenty of water and exercise. Heck, he's out all day."

Carol explained what Dr. Norris said about lipoma tumors. "If it is a tumor, there was no way for us to prevent it, honey."

Then she told her what Dr. Hamilton said about surgery and what Dr. Adams recommended. She looked deeply into Jill's eyes. "We have to make the decision that's best for Biz. They're watching him, honey. Let's pray for a miracle, but we have to be prepared for the possibility that he might not make it."

"*He might not make it?* But he *has* to make it, Mom. What will we do without him?" Jill sobbed uncontrollably, and then in a deep guttural groan, she said, "Ohhh, Mom, it's like losing Dad all over again."

Jill's words stung. Losing her dad was the hardest thing Jill ever went through and Carol knew this would be just about as hard. Logan passed unexpectedly. So quickly that Carol and Jill were not able to say goodbye. Biz filled a deep void in their lives. He was a continued presence of Logan, so losing Biz would, in some ways, feel like losing her dad twice. She hugged Jill tightly, and when they were both ready, they went into the house together.

Caleb and Sarah took turns hugging Jill. It was just over two hours since they left North Star, so Carol called for an update. She and Jill each had an ear on the receiver.

"It's not good," said Dr. Adams. "I just received the results of the second belly tap. His counts went up. He's in an enormous amount of pain. He's suffering. I'm so sorry, but I have to recommend that you euthanize if you're not going to do surgery."

Jill sobbed. "Can you keep him comfortable long enough for us to get there?"

Dr. Adams responded, "Only if you come right now. The pain medication isn't as effective as we would like. As I said, he's suffering. We will wait for you, but you must hurry."

Carol looked at Jill in a way that asked what she wanted to do. "I don't want him to suffer, Mom. But I *need* to say goodbye. I never got to say that to Dad. I *have* to see Biz."

"We're on our way, Dr. Adams," said Carol as she hung up the phone.

Jill bent over and wailed and for the first time, Caleb cried out loud and grabbed his coat. "Let's go, sweetheart. We have to get you to Biz right now. I'll drive."

Carol grabbed a box of tissues from the bathroom. "God, please don't let him suffer," she whispered as they pulled out of the driveway.

***

The drive to North Star felt like it took forever for Jill, even though Caleb broke speed limits all the way and made it there in under an hour and a half. Her mother called Susan's cell phone as they arrived, and Susan was waiting in the main lobby when they walked in. The receptionist let Dr. Adams know they were there and led Jill directly to Biz's hospital stall. At the sight of him, Jill burst into tears and dropped to her knees. Caleb quickly knelt and held her until she was able to stand. Once on her feet, she hugged Biz's neck and begged him not to leave her. He seemed barely able to hold up his head and his eyes were almost closed, but he somehow managed to rub his chin on the top of her head, as if letting her know that he was aware of her presence. He could hardly stand. Jill didn't know if it was because he was weak or because of all the pain medication. Probably both. He leaned against the wall to keep his balance.

"What am I going to do without you, Biz?" sobbed Jill. "I love you *so* much."

After a few minutes, Dr. Adams walked in to let Jill know it was time.

Jill put her head down and then looked at Dr. Adams. "Are you *absolutely* positive we should do this?" she asked as tears flooded her cheeks.

Dr. Adams' eyes were swimming. "Yes ... I believe so."

"I'm sure you already answered these questions, but I can't let him go until I hear your answers myself. The odds of him surviving aren't good?"

Dr. Adams wrapped her arms around her chest like she was giving herself a much-needed hug. "They're not good."

"And recovery?"

"Very hard. He's almost twenty."

Jill put her head down and wailed, and then out of compassion for Biz, she reluctantly nodded to Dr. Adams, who gently led Biz outside to the soft grass. Jill stayed right beside him. When they stopped, Jill turned his head so she could look deep into his eyes and kiss his nose. "I will stay right here with you, Biz. I promise I won't let you go until God and Dad meet you on the other side. I won't let you be alone. You'll never be alone again. Not ever. Dad will make sure."

As Susan, Caleb, and her mother gathered beside her, Jill saw that tears were flowing down Dr. Adams' face. It touched her because she knew Dr. Adams didn't make her recommendation lightly. She truly believed they were doing the right thing.

Her mother huddled close to Biz and wept openly as she rubbed his neck and kissed him on the cheek. "I love you, Biz. I will miss you *every* day for the rest of my life."

Susan stood at Biz's side and gently stroked his back. She looked broken. Overcome. "In all my years around horses, I've never known a horse like you, Biz, and I'm darn sure I never will again. I love you. And I will miss you so much. God bless."

Caleb was completely choked up when he brushed Biz's cheek. "Goodbye is a very hard word, big fella. I'm sure gonna miss ya," he said in such a raspy voice that it was clear he was barely able to get the words out. He pulled his handkerchief from his pocket just in time to wipe tears from his eyes. "This is just so damn hard, Biz, but it gives me comfort to know that Copper will be there to meet you. Say hi to him for me, okay, big guy?"

Jill wasn't sure who Copper was, but she knew he was important to Caleb, so she grabbed Caleb's hand and squeezed it. When she looked up, Dr. Adams was looking at her in a way that asked if she was ready. With deep sadness, Jill nodded. Her mother and Caleb had their arms around her as Dr. Adams administered the drugs into Biz's catheter. When they entered his bloodstream, his eyes closed completely, his body wobbled, and he fell. The sound of him hitting the ground was more than Jill could bear. All she wanted to do was run to him, but Dr. Adams gently motioned for her to stay put. After a couple of minutes, Dr. Adams listened for a heartbeat. Not hearing one, she said he was gone, and Jill collapsed on top of him. Her mother knelt beside her, gently stroking her back. Caleb and Susan tried to comfort Jill, but it was pointless. She was inconsolable. "I just need to be alone with him," said Jill.

Her mother nodded. "Okay, honey, take as much time as you need."

Susan and Caleb helped her mother get up. As they started to leave, Dr. Adams approached. "I'm so sorry, but I have to ask what you want to do with the body."

"What do you mean?" gasped her mother.

"We have a place where we can bury Biz unless you want to have him cremated or bring him home for burial," said Dr. Adams.

Jill overheard the conversation and, without thinking, emphatically said she wanted to bring Biz home. Caleb immediately told Dr. Adams he would be back in the morning with a trailer.

Caleb knelt beside Jill. "Sweetheart, I have lots of friends who owe me favors. I rarely collect on 'em, but for this, I will. I'll borrow a flatbed trailer and I have a friend with an excavator. We'll give Biz a proper burial at home where he belongs."

Jill looked deeply into Caleb's eyes and thanked him. "You're the best neighbor and the best friend anyone could hope for, Caleb."

Caleb's eyes softened as he looked down at Jill. "Thank you, sweetheart. I'm just happy that I'm able to help."

Dr. Adams looked at them apologetically before she spoke. "One more question. Dr. Hamilton wants to know if you'll allow us to do postmortem surgery. He would like to know exactly what caused Biz to colic. Quite honestly, we would all like to know."

"We want to know, too," her mother said. "But, how much will it cost?"

Dr. Adams put her hand on her mother's shoulder. "It won't cost you anything, but I have to warn you that Biz's abdomen will have a big incision and lots of stitches."

Jill didn't like the idea of Biz being cut open, but she knew the surgery would give them some answers, and possibly some peace of mind if it confirmed that they made the right decision, so she agreed. Dr. Adams sighed with what seemed to be relief and said they would perform the surgery first thing in the morning and his body could be picked up early in the afternoon.

When Jill looked down at Biz, she felt a small measure of comfort because he looked peaceful. His eyes were closed, but not because of pain or drugs. She knelt beside him and traced her finger along his cheekbones, secretly hoping his eyes would open and he would get up. She felt sick inside when he didn't move. Her mother knelt beside her and put her arm around her shoulder. "His suffering is over now, honey. He's at peace."

Jill stayed with Biz when her mother was asked to go to the front desk to settle the bill. During the trip home, Jill lay down with her head on her mother's lap in the back seat. It was dark out, so the ride was quiet and dreary. When they arrived home, Sarah welcomed them with comforting hugs. The house smelled good. While they were gone, Sarah made a fresh salad with homemade dressing and a pan of homemade baked macaroni and cheese with buttered cracker topping. It was still warm in the oven. She didn't realize she was hungry until she smelled the food. She was starving. While Susan brewed a pot of tea, Sarah made a plate for Caleb to take home. When Jill noticed, she said, "Caleb, would you like to stay and eat with us?"

Caleb smiled warmly at Jill. "I would love to, sweetheart, but I'm afraid I'll fall asleep at the dinner table." He rubbed the top of her head with his hand. "I'll see you tomorrow. Try to get some sleep. You're exhausted."

Jill hugged him before he left.

"Call me if you need anything at all," said Caleb. When he took his plate of food, he thanked Sarah.

After Caleb left, Susan and Sarah said goodbye. Before Sarah closed the door, she told them she gave Sonny another tranquilizer to calm him. "I'll be back first thing in the morning to give him another one and feed him. You two should stay out of the barn tomorrow. It will be too painful without Biz. I will take care of Sonny."

Jill was thankful.

***

Jill slept with Carol that night. They both tossed and turned. Carol woke early and tried to slip out of bed, but Jill woke up and clutched her hand. "Mom? Do you think Biz is in heaven with Dad?"

"Yes. I think so, sweetheart."

"I hope so because I don't want Biz to be alone. I feel so empty inside, Mom. Heavy. Just like when Dad died."

Carol understood. She felt the same way. She hugged Jill and rocked her gently. When Carol rocked Jill as a baby, it calmed her just as much as it did Jill, and it still did. As they talked, they heard Caleb start his truck. A few minutes later, he left his driveway. A short time later, Carol heard Sarah's car pull up by the barn. *Thank goodness we don't have to go in the barn today*, thought Carol.

Carol tried to go about her daily routine, but it was pointless because on most days, just about everything she did concerned Biz. She made some toast and tea and managed to call Jill's school to tell them Jill wouldn't be there that day or the rest of the week due to a death in the family. At first, she felt guilty telling them that, but it was true. Biz was family. Their family. Then she called her boss to explain what happened and tell her she needed the rest of the week off to be with Jill. Mid-morning, Caleb pulled back into his driveway. When they peered out the window, they saw a big truck with a long flatbed trailer carrying an excavator and they both started to cry. The sight of it forced Carol to internalize that the prior day's events were not just a bad dream. They were real. Biz was gone. With a heavy heart, they watched Caleb unload the excavator. When he finished, he looked over at the empty paddock, put his head down, and went back into his house. Carol sat silently for quite a few minutes before she went to the kitchen and made hot chocolate and more toast. She needed comfort food and presumed Jill did, too. Together, they nibbled on toast while they sat by the phone and waited to hear the results of the post-mortem surgery. Around ten o'clock, Dr. Adams called, and Carol held the receiver between them so Jill could hear every word.

In a soft and reassuring voice, Dr. Adams said, "I want you to know that Biz would never have survived the surgery. He had a large tumor in the small intestine directly attached to the cecum. Several feet of his intestines were dead. If we tried to remove the tumor along with the dead intestine to attempt a resection, it would never have worked. You made the right decision."

Carol felt her shoulders drop. She thanked Dr. Adams for calling. "At least we know that no matter what we did, the outcome would have been the same. I'm glad we didn't make him suffer through surgery."

Dr. Adams sighed. "Carol, I wish there was more I could have done for you and your daughter. Situations like this are always hard, but it's particularly devastating when a child is involved."

"Dr. Adams, you helped much more than you realize. Thank you for everything, especially your honesty," Carol said.

"You're welcome. Promise that you'll call if you need anything, or you have any questions. Anything at all."

"We will. Thank you," said Carol as she hung up the phone and hugged Jill. Carol knew that Biz's pain was over, but theirs was just beginning.

Carol's heart sank when she saw Caleb heading toward the house. He let her know that he unloaded the excavator and was about to take the lowboy flatbed trailer up to North Star to get Biz. He said his friend, Isaac, would be by later to operate the excavator.

"Would you like us to go with you?" Carol asked.

Caleb looked thoughtfully at the ground, and then lifted his gaze to Carol. "No, I'd rather that you didn't. He isn't going to look the same as you remember him, Carol. And you won't like the way they put him on the trailer. It's just better if you don't see that."

"Okay, Caleb. Before you go, I just got off the phone with Dr. Adams. She said we made the right decision. Biz would not have survived the surgery. It was a large lipoma and several feet of his intestines were already dead."

Caleb bit his lip and started tapping his right foot. "Jiminy cricket, Carol. He looked so darn bad in that stall. It broke my heart. And when Jill saw him, it just about broke me in two ... Well, I guess that if we can't have Biz, we can at least have some peace of mind. Thank goodness for that. Now I'm going to bring him back home where he belongs."

Caleb left the house and walked down the driveway to his truck. His walk was slower than normal, and his body looked heavier.

Caleb pulled out of the driveway and a few minutes later, Susan pulled in. Carol went outside to meet her and was instantly glad she did because Susan looked like a basket case. Her hair was a mess, her eyes were red, and her eyelids were so swollen that her eyes looked like crimson slivers peering out from the darkness. Her knees buckled slightly as she walked over to Carol and hugged her. "Carol, I'm so heartbroken. I didn't sleep all night, and today, I just feel so darn depressed. Grief-stricken. I loved him, Carol. I really loved him."

Carol squeezed Susan in her arms. "I know you did. I saw it in your eyes every time you looked at him. You were proud of him and so happy that you helped Jill."

Susan looked at Carol. "I'm happy that I was able to play a role in getting those two together. Gosh, it was wonderful to see him transform back into such a handsome athlete. He came back to life because of Jill and because of you, Carol. Everyone at the barn is so sad. They want to come by, but they don't know what to say. They know how much you loved him. And you know, this may sound strange, but even the horses seem sad. Like they somehow know."

Carol wondered if horses were able to understand conversations, feel people's emotions, or simply read body language.

***

Jonas was the first to find out. He heard Susan talking to Sharon and his heart sank. All he could do was stare aimlessly out his stall window.
"What's the matter, Jonas? You look sad," said Abdul.
Jonas sighed and leaned against the wall. "You don't want to know."
"Yes, I do. Tell me. Maybe I can help you."
Jonas looked down at Abdul and felt his eyes well with tears.
"You're crying? Jonas, please tell me what's wrong."
Jonas looked at the floor. "It's Biz. He had a bad case of colic."
"Colic?"
"Yes. I'm sorry, Abdul. Biz died yesterday. I just found out."

Abdul gasped. "Ohhh nooo. Nooo. Nooo. Nooo. Not Biz. It can't be. What am I going to do without him, Jonas? He was my best friend. Even after he left Willow Bend, he made sure he came over to talk when he was here for lessons. He always asked how I was and helped me look at things in a way that didn't make me feel so sad."

Jonas exhaled. "I know, little man. He was my best friend too. I'm sure gonna miss him. *Damn! It's just not right. Nothing* about this is fair. He waited his whole life to find the kind of love he had with Jill and her mother. Now it's been taken away. It's wrong. It's gosh darn wrong."

Aiyana walked closer and bowed her head. "My heart feels like it has a big hole in it. He was kind. Gentle. I loved his eyes. They said everything."

Jonas thought of himself as self-sufficient. Strong. He spent more time observing than getting involved, but with Biz, he couldn't help himself because Biz wasn't just an ordinary horse. He was special. Humble. Compassionate. Thoughtful. Trustworthy. News of his death made Jonas keenly aware of how important Biz was to him. They were true friends. Jonas never had a friend like Biz. He doubted he ever would again. He felt lost.

The news traveled around the barn, stall by stall. When the horses went outside, Jonas observed the herd. He thought Luis seemed genuinely sad. But he wondered about Günter, who seemed indifferent.

Luis trotted toward Günter with purpose. "Well, I guess *you're* happy."

"Happy? Why would I be happy?" asked Günter as he stood with his eyes closed, basking in the sun.

Luis stomped his foot. "Because your competition is gone."

"My competition? What are you talking about, Luis? You're aggravating me."

"Don't play dumb."

Günter turned his head slightly toward Luis and looked down at him. "I never play dumb, Luis. It's unbecoming. Now, tell me what you're talking about? What competition is gone?"

"Biz."

Günter squinted. "Biz? What about him?"

Luis looked dumbfounded. "You really don't know?"

"Know what? For Pete's sake, Luis. Spit it out."

"He's dead, Günter."

Günter looked right into Luis' eyes. "Biz is dead?"

"He died yesterday."

Günter looked distraught. "How? What happened?"

Luis put his head down. "Colic."

"Oh my God. I feel so bad," said Günter.

"No, you don't. You never said a kind word about him," snapped Luis.

Günter looked stunned. "It's true that I hated him in competitions. He put a lot of pressure on me because he was *so* good. But I liked *him*." Günter swallowed hard. "I can't deny that I was jealous of him. Jealous of his good looks. His athleticism. And the love he had from his family. I envied him. But secretly, I looked up to him. He had all of that going for him, yet he was humble. He never bragged or looked down on anyone. Even when he was a champion, Biz was always kind."

Jonas was surprised by Günter's honesty and apparently, so was Luis. "I never thought I'd hear you say anything like that about Biz. He *was* kind. And so happy with Jill. You could see it. He didn't care about competing anymore, but he did it for Jill. He was happy just to be part of a family. I can't believe he's gone. I miss him already." Luis shook his head.

"Me too," said Opal. "I feel guilty that I didn't like him in the beginning just because he didn't look handsome. He was always kind. Even when some of us weren't."

Jonas was taken aback by the candidness of the herd, especially Günter and Luis, but he wasn't the least bit surprised that Biz made such an impression.

~36~

Jill heard the excavator start and it gave her a jolt because she knew it was there to bury her best friend. The friend that was always there to greet her. And faithfully listen to all of her worries and secrets as she cleaned the barn and never told a soul. She believed he understood what she said by the way he tipped his head and moved his ears. He owned her heart, just as he did her mother's.

Biz kept them close. One big thing they truly had in common was their love for Biz and that helped keep them united during the years when most kids fought with their parents. Sometimes in bed at night, Jill looked up to heaven and asked her dad if he sent Biz to them. He laid the groundwork by building the barn. Maybe he finished his mission from above. It gave her comfort to believe that he did. Sometimes Jill thought Biz was an angel because, no matter how hard her day was, after she talked to him, things seemed better. Sometimes she cried with him, and when she went back into the house, her heart didn't feel as heavy.

Jill jumped when the man who operated the excavator knocked on the door. "Excuse me. My name is Isaac. I'm a friend of Caleb's. I hate to bother you. I know this is a difficult time, but Caleb didn't tell me where you would like Biz laid to rest."

They hadn't discussed it so Jill called her mother and they quickly agreed that he would be buried just outside the pasture, by the apple tree and the tall oak. "Biz loved to stand there to get out of the afternoon sun. It was his favorite spot," Jill said.

Isaac gently smiled and nodded. When Jill shut the door, she fell into her mother's arms. "We won't ever see him again, Mom. I won't ever be able to look into his beautiful brown eyes again. Why? Why did this have to happen?"

Her mother held her. "I don't know. I've been trying to understand it myself, but I can't."

Jill looked out the window toward the barn and saw that Sarah was still there with Sonny. She wiped her eyes and then she and her mother went outside to tell Sarah what was about to happen. Sarah said she gave Sonny a tranquilizer as soon as she arrived because she knew the sound and vibration of the heavy equipment would upset him.

Jill was worried about Sonny being alone and apparently, her mother shared her concern. "Sarah, you're welcome to keep Sonny here, but I don't know if he'll be able to handle being alone. I think I speak for both of us when I say that we can't bear to put another horse in Biz's stall right now. We'll understand if you decide to move him," said her mother.

Sarah nodded. "Let's get through today and then see how he does. If it's possible, I'd love for him to stay." Sarah's eyes dripped. "Biz was *so* loved. You gave him a wonderful life."

Her mother wrung her hands. "He loved us, too. And he gave *us* a wonderful life. We're grateful that we had the opportunity to have him with us. Our time with him was much shorter than expected, but honestly, an entire lifetime with Biz wouldn't have been enough. He made everything better. He taught me so much. How to be a good horse owner, a better parent, and maybe even a better person."

"A better person?" asked Jill.

Her mother smiled. "He taught me patience. He was incredibly tolerant as I learned the proper way to care for him. He couldn't tell me what he needed. I had to learn from him. His eyes. His body. He taught me to use my instincts and that helped me as a parent." Her mother gently reached out and touched Jill's cheek. "Jill and I have a *great* relationship, but she's stoic like her dad and sometimes she's hard to read. Biz helped me with that, and I can't thank him enough."

Jill didn't realize all of that, but she wasn't completely surprised because he was her therapist too. Her sounding board. Just verbalizing what she felt helped her get things off her chest, and quite often it helped her understand that the situation was much bigger in her head than it was in real life. It felt good to let her feelings out and still feel love and acceptance. It was something everyone should have. Jill wondered if Biz rubbed her mother's shoulder with his nose, too. She hoped so.

Back inside the house, a short time later, Jill heard a truck. She looked out the window and saw Caleb get out of the cab and walk back toward the trailer that carried Biz. His body was covered with a large blue tarp.

"I can't look," cried Jill as she put her hands over her eyes.

Her mother hugged her tightly and rubbed her arms. "It's going to be okay."

Caleb started to walk past the house, but something made him stop suddenly by the living room window and look inside. Jill and her mother were looking back at him. Seemingly full of raw emotion, he put his head down and trudged toward the backyard.

Jill wanted to see Biz before he was buried. She needed to touch his face and say goodbye, but she was afraid. She left the window and sat on the couch with her arms crossed tightly around her chest. She held back a flood of tears until she couldn't any longer. "I want to, but I can't go out there, Mom. I can't."

Her mother sat beside her and put her arm around her shoulders. "You don't have to, honey. You were with him when he passed, and you stayed with him for a long time afterward. If you said all that you needed to, then stay inside. But if there is more you need to say, you can. It's up to you. You believe in heaven, so you know you'll always be able to talk to him."

Jill looked down. "Will he be different ... now that he's been dead for a while?"

Her mother bit her bottom lip, looked toward the ceiling, and then looked back at her. "He'll look the same, but he might not feel quite the same. He won't feel warm, and his body won't be as soft. But if you just sit by his head, it will be the same. I'll go with you if you like."

Jill couldn't answer. Her mother seemed to understand and told Jill she would be in the kitchen if she needed her. She asked if Jill wanted some tea. All Jill could do was shake her head.

"Please let me know if you want to see him. I'll go outside and uncover his head for you. I think it will be easier that way. Okay, honey?"

Jill stared at the floor and nodded.

While her mother was making tea, Jill heard the kitchen door open. Sarah came in from the barn and said she was worried about Sonny. He started pacing nonstop in his stall the moment the flatbed pulled into the yard. While her mother talked with Sarah, Jill quietly opened the front door and slipped outside. She sat on the steps for a few minutes before she mustered enough courage to approach the flatbed. From the outline of his body under the tarp, she could see where Biz's head was. The trailer was low enough to the ground that she was able to climb onto it and kneel beside him. She sobbed and delicately pulled back a corner of the tarp, exposing only his head. When she saw his beautiful face, her torso collapsed over his neck. She cradled her arms around his head and cried deeply. "I'm so sorry, Biz. You were in so much pain. I hope you weren't scared. I stayed right beside you so you wouldn't be alone. You won't ever feel alone again. You had enough of that on this earth. From now on, Dad will stay with you. I *know* he will. But what am I going to do without you, boy? I waited my whole life for you. I need you, Biz. I need you so much. Why did you have to leave me, boy?"

Jill wondered why she had to lose her father and Biz. It felt like too much of a burden to bear. She felt like she was being punished, and she didn't understand why.

***

Carol didn't hear Jill in the living room, so she looked to see if she was okay. When she didn't see her, she quickly walked to the front window and peered outside. Jill was sitting on the trailer, crying, with Biz's head cradled in her arms. Sarah looked out the window, too.

Carol gasped. "Oh, my goodness. I wanted to make sure Biz looked okay before she went out there. I didn't want her to be shocked by anything."

Sarah sighed. "I'm so glad she only uncovered his head. He still looks so handsome. Thank goodness for that. Should we go out?"

"No, I don't think so. I'm sure she has a lot to say to him. She's the one who fell in love with him and brought him into our lives. She talked to Biz about *everything*. He was so good for her. Now she has a big hole in her heart."

Sarah scrunched her face. "She's a brave girl. I don't know if I could have done that at her age. Honestly, I don't think I could do it now."

Carol put her arm around Sarah's shoulder and squeezed. "Saying goodbye is never easy."

Sarah cleared her throat. "I wouldn't know, Carol. I've never lost anyone. Isn't that odd? My parents and my sister are still alive, and so are all of my grandparents, aunts, uncles and cousins. I have no idea how I would handle grief. I can't even imagine losing Sonny."

It was a long time before Jill came back into the house. When she did, her eyes were red and swollen, and she looked defeated. Carol didn't say a word. She just walked over and hugged her. When Jill asked if she could be alone, Carol and Sarah gave her privacy.

While they were at the kitchen table, they heard a racket in the barn, ran outside, and Jill was right behind them. Sonny was screaming, kicking the stall walls, and dripping sweat. His answers from the horses at Willow Bend sounded frazzled.

"The tranquilizer isn't powerful enough," said Sarah as she pulled out her cell phone, called the veterinarian, and left a message with the receptionist. Within a minute or two, Dr. Norris called and said she was on her way.

A half-hour later, Dr. Norris arrived and quickly injected a powerful tranquilizer into a big vein in Sonny's neck. He immediately calmed down. "I'm not surprised. He's all alone in the barn, the heavy equipment is rumbling, and the ground is vibrating beneath his feet."

"I've never heard him screech like that," said Sarah.

Seemingly deep in thought, Dr. Norris gently scraped her bottom lip between her teeth. "Horses have an excellent sense of smell. Sonny can't see Biz, but he knows he's out there. His scent is different. Sonny knows something's wrong. Maybe he's trying to get Biz to answer."

Sarah put her hands over her mouth. "Oh, my gosh. Poor Sonny. What should we do?"

Dr. Norris sighed. "There's nothing we can do except try to keep him calm until Biz is buried." Dr. Norris turned to Carol and Jill. "I'm so sorry about everything you're going through. When North Star called to let me know what happened, my heart broke. He deserved so many more happy years with you."

Carol put her arm around Jill's shoulder. "Thank you, Dr. Norris. Thank you for your kind words as well as everything you did for us and Biz. Life will never be the same. He came into our lives and changed us forever."

Jill walked over and hugged Dr. Norris. "Thank you for always taking the time to teach me when you were here. I appreciate it more than you know."

"My pleasure, Jill."

Sarah cleared her throat. "Should I give Sonny any more tranquilizers today?"

Dr. Norris watched Sonny for a few minutes. "The shot I gave him is potent, but not long-lasting. He'll be groggy for a few hours, but that should be enough time to get him through the worst of it. Once Biz is buried and the heavy equipment is gone, he should settle down. I'm going to leave you some tubes of oral tranquilizer paste because he's going to be antsy for days. It's more potent than what you've been giving him. Administer it just as you do his worming medicine—just squeeze the proper dose, according to his weight, into his mouth. Sarah, we know he doesn't do well alone, so watch him. I know you like it here, but if he doesn't settle in, you will have to move him to a place where he can be around other horses. I don't want to tranquilize him indefinitely. It's not healthy."

Sarah put her head down and nodded.

After Dr. Norris pulled away, Carol wondered how Sonny would get through the days to come. The poor horse was subjected to so much change over the years he was with them. A new barn, new caretakers, a new stablemate, and two little children who took up a huge portion of his owner's time. Carol agreed that long-term use of tranquilizers was not the right path for Sonny, but it would temporarily get him through.

***

Susan had left to go back to Willow Bend. When she came back, she was unhappy when she saw everyone in the barn because she didn't want Carol and Jill in the barn that day. She went inside to find out what was going on.

With tired eyes, Carol looked at Susan. "Sonny keeps screaming."

"That's to be expected," she said as she motioned for Carol and Jill to go back inside the house. "The last thing the two of you need is to be in the barn today. Sarah and I will handle this. Please go back inside the house."

Carol took Jill by the hand and they walked toward the kitchen door. When they were out of sight, Sarah looked at Susan. "Do you think I should tell Sonny what happened to Biz? A couple of my friends told me I should."

Susan shrugged her shoulders. "Some say you should, and others say that horses don't understand us, so what's the point. You know him better than anyone. What do you think?"

Sarah's right leg rested on the ball of her foot, and it was nervously bouncing up and down. "I think I should tell him. If he understands, maybe he'll stop screeching." She walked closer to Sonny's stall, reached in, and gently rubbed his cheek. "Sonny, I'm sorry you're having such a rough time. Yesterday wasn't a good day and today isn't any better. I'm sorry. I know the equipment is loud, but it's here for Biz."

Sonny was heavily medicated, but he looked up at her like he was waiting for more information. After a moment, Sarah reached up and rubbed his forehead. "Sonny, when Biz left yesterday, he went to the hospital because he was sick. So sick that the doctors couldn't fix him. I'm sorry, Sonny, Biz died. The equipment is here because Carol and Jill brought his body home for burial. Caleb and his friend, Isaac, are preparing the grave."

Susan was shocked when Sonny lifted his head, looked directly into Sarah's eyes, and with great force, stamped his front right foot on the stall floor. His nostrils flared and his eyes grew large, and then he bounded to the other side of his stall and looked out the window. He stared in the direction of the heavy equipment and shrieked. The sound was gut-wrenching.

Sarah put her hands over her mouth and cried. "I shouldn't have told him. All it did was make him worse."

Susan put her hands on Sarah's shoulders. "Give him a few minutes to calm down. The tranquilizer is still trying to do its job, but right now, he seems to have enough adrenalin coursing through his body to counteract it. I wouldn't have believed it if I didn't see it, but I think he understood you. If he did, at least he knows what happened to Biz."

Susan advised Sarah to stay out of Sonny's stall so she didn't get hurt. "Panicked horses run back and forth without regard for anyone or anything in their path. Be careful. I've seen too many people get injured because they never thought their horse would hurt them. Trust me, they can without ever meaning to."

Standing outside the stall, Sarah tried to comfort Sonny with treats. He showed no interest, but Susan admired her perseverance. Sarah stayed with Sonny and talked calmly until he settled down enough to be tempted to eat peppermints and then a handful of alfalfa mash. "Sonny, you still have a home with Jill and Carol if you want it. We'll see how you do." Sarah looked at Susan. "Should I give him some tranquilizer paste, Susan?"

Susan shook her head. "No. But you should give him a dose before you leave for the night."

Susan hoped Sonny would be able to calm down, but she was around horses enough to know that he wasn't going to be okay by himself. He needed to be with other horses.

~37~

It took about two hours for the grave to be dug. During the entire time, Caleb stood under the trees, directing to make sure the roots of the apple tree and the big oak were not harmed.

Biz's body would be stiff and difficult to maneuver, so Caleb made sure the hole was long enough and wide enough to properly position his body so he lay flat. When the machinery stopped, Caleb knocked on the door and told Carol he was about to back the flatbed into the pasture so the excavator could lift Biz and place him in his grave. "Please don't look out the window. And please don't come out until I tell you it's okay. Let me get him positioned right. For Jill's sake, I want him to look like he's peacefully sleeping. It's important to me."

Caleb knew his emotions were showing when he saw the look on Carol's face. Her eyes welled with tears and her voice was petal-soft. "Okay, Caleb, let me know when you're ready."

Caleb walked toward the truck and saw Biz's exposed head, so he knew someone visited him to say goodbye. He was sure it was Jill and he hoped she was okay. Out of respect for Biz, he covered his head again before he started the truck and pulled the trailer around the backside of the barn toward the burial site.

Earlier in the day, Caleb asked Isaac to carefully scrape the sod off the gravesite and gently place it to the side. He was pleased that Isaac did exactly that. Next to the sod, the piles of dirt from the excavation were large. And as instructed, Isaac placed the rocks that were too large to lift to one side within the grave and stacked some in a way that allowed Caleb to climb them like steps to get in and out.

Once the flatbed was positioned, Caleb placed thick ropes around Biz so the excavator could lift him off the flatbed and lower him into the grave. The excavator's engine roared as Isaac powered it up to lift Biz. Caleb hoped that Jill and Carol weren't watching. He caught himself nervously glancing toward the house again and again. While Biz was still in the air, Caleb heard Sonny scream and it sent a jolt through his heart.

Once Biz's body was in position, Caleb told Isaac, that until the burial service was over, he only wanted enough earth put back into the grave to cover the backs and sides of Biz's legs, and the incision on his belly because he didn't want Jill or Carol to see it. Isaac did what Caleb asked and then smoothed the earth as best he could.

Caleb's next task was very personal, so he told Isaac to take a coffee break. Using the large rocks Isaac placed to the side for steps, Caleb walked down into the grave and moved gravel and rocks away from Biz, so he lay in what appeared to be a soft bed of sand. Caleb made sure Biz's eyes were properly closed, and then he took out the brush and comb he put in his jacket pocket earlier in the day. With deep affection, he brushed the earth off Biz's coat, combed his forelock and mane, and then gently lifted his tail to the surface, brushed it, and carefully placed it on top of the sand. Caleb wanted Jill to have the best possible memories of this difficult day and making sure Biz seemed at peace was a big part of it. When he finished grooming Biz, Caleb knelt beside him. Even in death, Biz was one of the most handsome horses he ever saw. Before he knew it, his eyes were drowning, and his vision was so blurred that he could hardly see. He stayed by Biz's side until he was able to somewhat regain his composure. When he was ready, he wiped his cheeks, smoothed the dirt as he backed out of the grave to remove his footprints, and then climbed up the rock steps and made his way out.

***

It seemed like it took forever for Caleb and Isaac to prepare the grave, but Carol figured it was because Caleb was being particular. He likely wanted everything to be perfect for Jill. When Caleb finally knocked on the door, Carol and Jill went straight to the barn to get Susan and Sarah so they could all walk to Biz's final resting spot together. With tissues in hand, they stood quietly, looking over Biz. Carol thought Caleb and Isaac did a wonderful job. Sand covered his legs and enough of his belly to hide evidence of his surgery. Biz's eyes were closed. He looked peaceful. It was obvious that Caleb groomed him. There was no dirt on his coat, and it even glistened in the sun. His forelock, mane, and tail were free of tangles, and he looked handsome. Carol was comforted by Caleb's efforts. She looked up at him, smiled through her tears, and said thank you. Caleb managed a slight nod, but the muscles around his jaw bulged and his face looked rigid. From experience, Carol knew Caleb was clenching his teeth, trying to hold back tears. She saw him do it quite often after Logan died.

Carol expected that Jill would have the hardest time, so she decided to start the ceremony herself. She knelt at the edge of the grave, picked up a small handful of soil, and gracefully sprinkled it into the grave. "Goodbye, my friend. I love you more than you know," she said as she reached into her pocket, pulled out a carrot and an apple, and dropped it beside him in the grave. "I thought you would like to have these for your journey home. Rest in peace and God's love. I pray that I will see you again someday. I'm counting on it."

When Carol turned, Jill was on her knees, quietly crying, so she bent down, put her arms around her, and kissed the top of her head. After a moment, Jill moved closer to the edge of the grave. She looked down at Biz and reached into her pocket. With tears streaming down her face, she pulled out two peppermints, silently unwrapped them, and dropped them beside Biz. She opened her mouth, but seemed unable to speak, so Carol went to her side to help her up. They started to walk back to where everyone else stood, and then Jill stopped, walked back toward the grave, dropped to her knees again, and sobbed. "I want you to have peppermints because they were your favorite thing in the whole wide world. I love you, boy. I'll love you forever and miss you every day. I miss you so much already. But you can be with Dad now. Please keep him company. You were his dream, Biz. Take care of him. I know he'll take good care of you, just like he took care of me when he was here." Carol burst into tears as she helped Jill stand up. Around her, all she heard was sniffling. Jill's words seemed to have broken everyone's hearts.

The next person brave enough to step forward was Sarah. She walked to the edge of the grave and sprinkled down some hay cubes. "I don't even know what to say, Biz. I always loved this barn, but when I saw you standing in the paddock, I simply had to meet you. You drew me in. I don't know how you put up with Sonny in the beginning. You were so patient. I will always love you for that. I'll miss you and your soothing presence. I don't know how Sonny will do without you. It's going to be hard for him. I hope you'll help me keep an eye on him and give him a helpful nudge when he needs it."

As Sarah left the edge of the grave, Susan stepped forward and dropped to her knees. Without words, she gazed down at Biz. Susan was a private person, so Carol knew she had lots to say, but wasn't able to with so many eyes watching and ears listening. After a while, she reached into the large pockets of her barn jacket and pulled out handfuls of sweet feed that she must have brought from Willow Bend. "Biz, I know how much you loved fresh corn husks, but I couldn't find any," cried Susan. "Sweet feed has corn in it, so I hope it will do. I will never forget you, Biz. You impressed the heck out of me and you became a legend at Willow Bend. I'm so grateful that I was able to be part of your life. I feel blessed. Truly blessed."

When the women were finished, all was quiet until Caleb knelt and opened his small paper bag. "This is for you, my friend. I'll miss seeing you when I look out my window every morning. And I'll miss feeding you these," said Caleb as he dropped two peaches beside Biz. "I'll especially miss seeing you pick them from my trees on your walks to Willow Bend. You made me smile every single day. But you knew that, didn't cha, boy. It's been an *honor* to know you, Biz. I will always remember how well you took care of your people. And I feel privileged because you always made me feel like I was one of them."

Caleb looked up at Carol and tipped his head as if asking if she was ready to proceed with the burial. When Carol nodded, Caleb gave Isaac the signal to start up the excavator, and then he openly wept.

"He touched all of us. I wonder how many others he helped," whispered Carol as she squeezed Jill's shoulder.

Jill walked over to Caleb and took his hand. "He loved you too, Caleb. I could tell. And I know that you used to sneak over to give him treats after I went to school."

Caleb managed a small smile; the kind a person wears when they've been caught. "And how do you know that if you were in school, young lady?"

Jill smiled. "I know because every Saturday and Sunday morning, he looked toward your house around nine o'clock and stood with his ears up until he heard your door close. Then, he went right over to the fence and waited for you. He knew you were coming before you even opened your door. I guess he had all of us wrapped around his little finger."

Half-laughing and half-crying, Caleb said, "That he did, Jill ... that he did. He was a handsome bugger. I loved to just look at 'im. Ever since your dad died, I kept an eye on you and your mom because I was worried about you. After Biz came, I wasn't as worried. It seemed he was here to take care of you. I loved watching you fuss over him. I never told you because I didn't want to make you feel bad, but he used to stand in the paddock all day, waiting for you to come home from school. He knew the sound of your bus. As soon as he heard it, he left the shade of the big oak and made his way to where he could see you as soon as you turned up the driveway. The love he showed you warmed my heart. God bless him."

Caleb put his arm around Jill and squeezed her. As he turned to make his way over to Isaac, Jill asked Carol if she could stay with Biz. Carol was concerned about Jill being close to the excavator, but Caleb assured her that he would make sure Jill was safe until she was ready to go inside.

"Thank you, Caleb. Thank you so much for *everything*. Before Isaac leaves, please let me know how much we owe him."

Caleb shook his head. "Isaac said he couldn't possibly take anything for this. He already feels bad enough."

Carol looked down. "Well, I appreciate that, but I want to pay him something, Caleb."

"No. He's all set, Carol."

"I understand if he wants to do this for us, but it shouldn't cost him anything. What about reimbursement for fuel? Please, let me give him *something*."

Caleb told Carol he would be right back. A few minutes later, he returned with Isaac. "I appreciate the offer, but no. This is the least I can do for you and my good friend," said Isaac.

"Are you sure?"

Isaac softly smiled. "I'm positive," he said as he turned toward his excavator.

Carol went into the house and sat with Susan and Sarah. She tried to distract herself with the conversation, but her mind was on Biz, Jill, and the distressed horse in the barn. After some time passed, she looked out the window to check on Jill and saw that Isaac was finished and he was driving the excavator onto the flatbed. Shortly after that, Isaac left, but Jill didn't come in, so Carol looked out the window again and saw her standing next to Caleb. He had his arm around her shoulder, probably trying to console her, and then they walked toward the house. Carol swallowed. It was going to be a long, sleepless night. The kitchen door opened, and they walked inside. Jill looked pale. Her eyes were red and swollen and she seemed weak. Carol immediately knew that she needed something to eat, so she put on water for tea and started making Jill's favorite meal—blueberry pancakes with bacon. She loved to eat it for breakfast, lunch, or dinner.

As Carol prepared the pancakes, she asked Caleb, Sarah, and Susan if they were hungry. Susan and Sarah declined. Caleb seemed tempted, but he said no.

Susan looked at Carol and tipped her head. "Do you want me to stick around?"

"I think we're okay, but you're more than welcome to stay if you like," Carol said.

Sarah offered to stay overnight to keep an eye on Sonny, but Carol said she thought he would likely be okay with the oral tranquilizer paste. "We'll keep the baby monitor on. If he sounds stressed, we'll call you."

"You're sure?" asked Sarah.

"I'm sure. You must have a thousand things to do at home."

Sarah looked hesitant. "Okay but promise that if you think he's stressed and needs another dose, you'll call me. I'll come right over."

Carol agreed.

"I'll call you in the morning," said Susan, and then she and Sarah hugged everyone and said goodbye. After they left, Carol made tea just the way Jill liked it—hot and sweet with light cream and brought it to her on the couch where she was wrapped in a fleece blanket. "Pancakes will be ready in a few minutes, honey. Can I get you anything else right now?"

Jill shook her head.

Carol returned to the kitchen to check on Caleb and the bacon. "Thank you so much for all of your help, Caleb. I wouldn't have known who to call. Biz would never have been buried at home if not for you. It just means so much to have him here."

"You're welcome, Carol."

Carol sighed. "Caleb, this feels like a bad dream. It never even entered my mind that Biz would die of anything but old age, right here at home with us. I thought he was finally where he was supposed to be. He was happy. I can't believe he's gone. It's so unfair."

Caleb's eyes welled. "I'm so sorry, Carol." He hugged her and then went into the living room to say goodbye to Jill before he went home. Carol watched Caleb walk home. She was worried about him. He was pale, his pace was slower than normal, and his eyes seemed lifeless.

When the pancakes and bacon were ready, Carol made a plate for Caleb. She knew he was hungry and too tired to make something for himself. As soon as Jill saw the extra plate, she grabbed it and ran next door with containers of soft whipped butter and real Vermont maple syrup. When Jill returned, she ate a tall stack with plenty of bacon. Carol was amazed at how much Jill could eat and never gain a pound. When they finished, Carol did the dishes and curled up on the sofa with Jill until it was time for bed.

At bedtime, Jill asked Carol if she could sleep with her again. Before they brushed their teeth, put on their pajamas, and climbed into bed, Jill got the baby monitor from the living room and placed it on the nightstand. They were so exhausted that they fell sound asleep within minutes, and surprisingly, Sonny didn't make a sound loud enough to wake either of them for the entire night.

***

Caleb lay in bed, thinking about the day. It was a long one. He didn't realize how tired and hungry he was until Carol offered him dinner, but he just wanted to go home. He wasn't going to answer the door until he saw the top of Jill's head through the window. His taste buds danced when he saw the plate. He was starving and that made the smell of bacon seem amazing. Carol always bought Scottish bacon and Caleb loved it. After he ate, he quickly washed his dishes and went to bed. He thought he would go right to sleep, but instead, he tossed and turned. Biz's death took quite a toll on him. And it pained him to see Jill and Carol in turmoil. He liked to fix things, but this couldn't be fixed. All he could do was try to make it better. He spent the last two days attempting to do exactly that and he felt depleted.

Caleb's father once told him that loss was cumulative. He was beginning to understand what that meant. Losing someone you love creates a crack in your heart and each subsequent loss makes the crack deeper. Losing Biz stirred up all the emotions from Logan's death, as well as his beloved wife, Marion's, and even Copper's.

When Caleb saw Biz thrashing in his stall, he felt his knees buckle. He knew what the outcome was going to be the second he laid eyes on him, but he couldn't say a word to Carol. It would have devastated her and at that moment, he understood that Carol needed hope.

If the surgery had any chance for success, Caleb would have gladly paid for it. A lifetime of frugality helped him accumulate quite a nest egg. Money wasn't a concern, but he knew money wasn't going to help Biz, and he was eternally grateful to Dr. Adams for being honest about that. He admired her integrity. Being a veterinarian had its rewards. The hard part was knowing when to give up and put an animal down. As Dr. Adams led Biz outside to the soft grass, Caleb's stomach turned because he knew Biz would soon be gone. After she administered the medication into his catheter, Biz's body folded into itself until it was fully on the ground. It reminded Caleb of a skyscraper. During a controlled demolition, strategically placed charges were detonated, allowing magnificent structures to implode and gracefully fall to the earth. Biz was magnificent. But when he fell, it was the hearts of those who loved him that shattered. Caleb felt like a lightning bolt broke his heart in half and decimated his soul.

Caleb's mind drifted from Biz to Carol and Jill. He hadn't seen that look in their eyes since Logan died. It broke his heart back then, just as much as it did over the past couple of days. He was especially concerned about Jill. He knew her sadness would increase as she understood the permanence of Biz's absence. Grief was like that. It came in waves. For Caleb, the initial loss was hard, but somehow he got through it. Then, just when he thought he was doing better, it came back and bit him in the butt. It perplexed him, but Caleb was always fascinated by the complexity of the human mind.

When Marion died, he saw her laid to rest, but for the longest time after her burial, he waited for her to walk in the door like she'd been away on vacation. It wasn't until she was gone for about three months that it finally sunk in that she was never coming home again. It hit him hard, and he wondered if he would ever be able to crawl out from under the weight of his sorrow. But after reaching out to several people who went through similar losses, he came to understand that grieving is a lengthy process that's different for everyone, and he had to love himself through it. Marion would have wanted him to have a rich and full life, so he carried on. When he met Logan, he was happy because, in his heart, he knew he found the son that he and Marion were never able to have. After Logan died, Caleb persevered because he had to take care of Carol and Jill. It was a silent promise that he made to Logan during his burial. And it was an easy promise to keep because he loved them so much. He wanted to be there for them, and he needed to help make it better.

~38~

The next morning, Jill made herself get out of bed early because she wanted to go out to check on Sonny. Her mother made it known that she wasn't crazy about the idea, but she agreed to it if Jill promised to only make sure he was okay and throw him a flake of hay.

It was difficult for Jill to go into the barn because every morning when Biz heard footsteps, he grunted for his food and paced incessantly until his grain was in his bucket. But that morning, there was no grunting, and Sonny looked lost. He kept looking around, probably in search of Biz. When Sarah arrived, she gave Sonny his tranquilizer, and about an hour later, she put on his halter and let him out. He whinnied as he exited his stall and then cautiously walked around the paddock, smelling the ground. When he got to the big oak, he snorted wildly, let out a scream, and paced frantically.

Jill wanted to go back inside the house but was convinced that Sonny could smell Biz. Smell death. So she stayed put to lend Sarah some moral support. Sonny ran around for over an hour before he quieted enough for Sarah to enter the paddock. She talked to him as she brushed his coat and mane and it seemed to soothe him. Sarah looked at Jill. "I'm sorry you have to deal with this again today. I wish I could have let him visit Biz's grave yesterday, but he was uncontrollable. Do you think it would have been better for him if he could have said goodbye?"

Jill shrugged her shoulders. "Maybe, but someone could have gotten hurt if he spiraled out of control. You did the right thing, Sarah. He was safer in his stall. I think everyone was."

During the rest of the day, Sonny whinnied from time to time and then stood quietly. Every time he whinnied, one of the horses at Willow Bend answered. Each time, Sonny's ears went up and then quickly fell back down. Jill thought he was hoping to hear Biz. She felt sorry for him, but there was nothing she could do to console him. She kept her distance but tried to calm him by talking to him and offering alfalfa cubes over the fence.

***

Caleb left the house early, just as he always did because, no matter how bad things seemed, sticking to a routine helped him. Grief was no exception. He had errands to run because Biz's gravesite wasn't finished, and he aimed to rectify that.

When he returned, he stopped at his house to grab shovels and rakes, and then he drove behind the barn and parked close to Biz's grave. Before he got out of the truck, he bowed his head and prayed that Biz was by Logan's side in heaven and that Marion and Copper were with them. When he emerged from the truck, he put down the tailgate, climbed into the bed, lifted out the shovels and rakes and dropped them to the ground, and then threw out two bales of hay, and bags of topsoil, loam, grass seed, and fertilizer.

With shovels and rakes in hand, he walked over to the grave, knelt for a moment, and then used a shovel to smooth out the small mounds of dirt that the excavator wasn't able to level to his liking. Caleb wasn't a perfectionist, but he had high standards and Biz's grave had to measure up.

After he did all he could with the shovel, Caleb took hold of his heavy steel bow rake. The thick steel teeth grabbed small rocks and pebbles. He pulled them to the side where he could remove them later with a shovel and wheelbarrow. He raked sections and then walked from side to side, checking them from every angle, making sure they were level. If Biz was looking down, Caleb wanted him to see that he was being meticulous and know that he was worth every bit of the fuss.

Caleb reached for the bags of topsoil, heard something near the house, and saw Jill outside by the kitchen door, putting on her boots. She walked toward Caleb, asked what he was doing, and then ran into the barn to get the hose. The two of them worked in tandem with few words spoken and Caleb was amazed at how she followed his every lead. They spread the topsoil evenly, and then gathered the pieces of sod that Caleb asked Isaac to set to the side and put them together like puzzle pieces over the grave. Once in place, they filled in the gaps with loam, raked in some fertilizer, and sprinkled grass seed. Caleb put the hose nozzle on the light mist setting so it would moisten, but not move the seeds, and then he let Jill do the watering. When the ground was suitably wet, they broke apart the bales and loosely spread the hay over the seeds to keep birds from eating them. When they finished, Jill smiled at Caleb and hugged him. "Thank you, Caleb. Biz's grave is beautiful because of you. I can't wait for Mom to see it."

"You're welcome, sweetheart. It looks a little ragged right now, but the grass will grow and fill in the cracks. But we're still not finished. We need something to identify that Biz is buried here and I would like to pay for it. Something really nice. I went over some possibilities in my head. A monument, a bench, or a marker stone that's flush with the grass. Honestly, I think the marker stone is the best option so it's not a trip hazard for people or horses. But we can talk about it. And we need to decide what the marker should say."

"You think of everything, Caleb."

Caleb smiled down at Jill and affectionately tapped his index finger on her nose. She smiled, but Caleb saw in her eyes that, beneath her smile, she was plagued with sadness.

***

A few days after Biz died, Sonny stopped pacing and screaming, but he still seemed stressed. Lonely. All he did was stand in the paddock. Occasionally, he lifted his head and whinnied to the horses at Willow Bend, but when they answered, he didn't react. He didn't seem to care. At the end of the week, during one of Sarah's visits, Carol felt she needed to take Sarah aside. "Sarah, I'm not sure he'll adjust to being alone again. He seems depressed."

Sarah scrunched her lips and placed her hand on Carol's arm. "He does seem depressed, but isn't that to be expected? Carol, I understand your concern, but I'd like to give it a little more time. This is only his first week without Biz. I don't want to jump the gun and move him if I don't have to. I'll come by and spend more time with him and see if it helps him adjust."

Sarah convinced Carol to wait a week before making a decision, but by the end of that week, Sonny started chewing the pine boards in his stall and kicking the walls. Then his frantic pacing and screeching started again. His whinnies became shrill, and he was constantly soaked with sweat. He wasn't adjusting. He was worse. Way worse. Carol noticed that he was losing weight and asked Susan to stop by.

"He's going to run himself ragged," Susan said when she saw him.

"What should I do?" asked Carol. "Sarah wants to give it more time, but I don't think it's going to work."

Susan sighed. "He's not going to adjust. We have to get him with other horses. Biz was his herd. Now Biz is gone and he's taking it pretty hard."

Carol felt guilty. "I hate to make him leave, but I can't bring another horse here to keep him company. Not yet. I'm just not ready to put another horse in Biz's stall. Neither is Jill. I feel awful, but I just can't."

Susan put her hand on Carol's shoulder. "Nobody's saying that you should. How you feel is understandable. We have to find him a new home. Are you sure you're ready to have a barn with no horses?"

Carol's head spun. No more horses? No more horse sounds? Or smells?

Susan smiled at Carol in a way that let her know she was reading her mind. "Think about it. I have a stall available at Willow Bend that I can offer to Sarah for a tad more than she's already paying you."

Carol was relieved. Sonny would be in good hands with Susan. For the rest of the day, Carol pondered about what life would be like without horses. She wasn't sure she was ready for that, but Sonny kicked the walls all night. She and Jill were up the whole time, constantly checking to make sure he wasn't thrashing from colic. Caleb walked over to check on him too.

When morning arrived, Carol made arrangements for Susan and Sarah to talk. Sarah said she wasn't thrilled about moving Sonny but made peace with the fact that it had to be done. Carol was comfortable with the move because Jill was still working at Willow Bend, so she could keep an eye on him. The decision was made to move him early the next morning before breakfast. Carol and Jill followed along as Sarah walked him there and he screeched the whole way.

***

Jonas overheard Susan tell barn workers to get a stall ready for Sonny, so when the screeching sounded like it was getting closer, he figured Sonny was on his way. Based on what Biz shared with him, Jonas feared he'd have a tough time transitioning. Jonas hoped Sonny would be able to settle down and enjoy Willow Bend, where he'd be surrounded by horses. He couldn't imagine why Sonny wouldn't.

"Good Lord, what is all that screaming?" snarled Luis as he ate breakfast.

"I think its Biz's stablemate," said Günter.

"*Why* is he making such a *ruckus*? Is a peaceful meal too much to ask for?"

"They're walking him down here. I heard Susan tell Sharon that he's coming here to live because he can't stand being alone," said Günter.

"Well, that screaming better stop once he gets here or I'll *snap*," Luis said.

"Why does *everything* have to be about you?" asked Aiyana.

"Ohhh, so I'm awful because I don't like to start my morning with *shrieking*? Good Lord. The boy's got to get a grip," Luis said.

Opal rolled her eyes.

Jonas whinnied to Sonny, hoping it might calm him. Abdul did the same. It might have helped Sonny, but apparently, it annoyed the heck out of Luis because when they looked up, he was glaring at them. "Please, don't encourage the little twit."

Jonas figured that Sonny was going to be needy. He wondered if Sonny would emotionally latch onto just one of the horses or be happy being around lots of them. Jonas worried that he might latch on to him. And screech every time he was out of sight. Just like he did with Biz. If he did, Jonas was going to have to figure out how to help Sonny from a distance. He had no desire to become Sonny's security blanket.

Jonas was happy to help Biz when he first arrived at Willow Bend, but that was different. Biz was broken inside, but stoic on the outside. If he was needy, he never showed it. Jonas was the one who initiated their conversations, not Biz. They grew to like one another, and over time, their friendship grew. Jonas was going to need breathing room, so Sonny was going to have to accept the company of many horses, not just him.

There was only one empty stall at Willow Bend, and it was Biz's old one. After Biz left, Susan used it for storage, and since there were no subsequent horses, it would still smell like Biz. Jonas wasn't sure if it would comfort Sonny or stress him out.

Susan was at the main door of the barn, waiting for Sonny and Sarah to arrive. Jonas noticed that Jill and her mother walked down with them, likely to assist if Sonny acted up. Sonny screamed when he entered the barn, but then he immediately stopped. Jonas assumed it was because he saw *all* the horses. His head bobbed from left to right as he passed by each stall. When they arrived at their destination, Jonas wasn't surprised when Jill's jaw dropped.

Susan must have seen her expression because she put her hand on Jill's shoulder. "It's the only stall we have. Maybe it will comfort him. Time will tell."

Jill inhaled and slowly exhaled. "I hope so. I didn't expect it, but I should have. I knew the barn was full."

Sarah didn't seem to understand and looked at Carol inquisitively.

"It's Biz's old stall," Carol said.

Sarah raised her eyebrows and looked at Jill.

Jonas wished he could hug Jill. When Biz was at Willow Bend, she stopped by his stall all the time. After Biz left and was enjoying life at Tartan Glen, Jill sometimes stood in front of that stall and smiled. Jonas figured it was a sacred place for her. The place where she first met Biz. Where her mother met him too. Susan opened the stall door and Sonny entered. Inside, waiting for him was a bucket of water, a warm alfalfa mash, and a flake of hay.

Sarah seemed pleased. "I appreciate that you let Sonny come here."

"Happy to help. He should be fine back here with Jonas and Abdul. Hopefully, Biz's scent will be familiar and comforting. I'll put him out with the other horses when they're all done with breakfast. Based on his history, I think it's better to do that than keep him inside when they all go out. I separate new horses when they first arrive to keep everyone safe, so

Sonny will be in a private paddock. But he'll be surrounded by the other horses and eventually, he'll be turned out with a buddy."

Sarah nodded.

Jonas watched Sonny eat his mash and check out his new surroundings. Sonny walked the perimeter of the stall, sniffing the walls and floor, and then he whinnied loudly. When he looked up, he locked eyes with Jonas.

"What's wrong, son?" asked Jonas.

"I smell Biz," said Sonny.

"Yes. It's because that was Biz's stall before Jill took him home. Does it comfort you?" asked Jonas.

Sonny inhaled. "It makes me miss him."

"Try to focus on good memories. It helps. So we're going to be neighbors."

Sonny walked closer. "Yes. My name is Sonny."

"I'm Jonas. Biz and I were good friends."

Sonny looked at the floor. "Biz is gone now. He got sick. They put him in a trailer and took him away. He didn't come back until the day they buried him, and then I was all alone."

Picturing Sonny all alone made Jonas feel ill. "I'm sorry, my friend."

Sonny looked visibly upset. "Everyone's so sad without him."

Abdul walked to the side of his stall closest to Sonny. "I miss Biz too. I'm Abdul. Biz was my very best friend. I was sad when he left here to go home with Jill. He was all I had for a long time. I guess he was all you had at Jill's house too."

Sonny looked confused. "How was Biz all you had in a barn with oodles of horses?"

Jonas waited to hear Abdul's explanation.

Abdul continued. "Before Jill, Biz didn't have anyone. Right after Biz got here, my owner and I had an accident. She got hurt and didn't come to see me for months. Biz understood how I felt and was the only one I could talk to about it."

Sonny looked down. "Biz didn't talk to me too much especially when I first got there."

"That's because there were times when he wasn't happy with you," said Jonas.

"Why?" Sonny asked, appearing hurt.

"He didn't like the way you nipped at him, and he was angry when you charged at Jill and her mother. He told me how he pinned you against the barn wall. Good gracious, he must have been upset. I never saw that boy get mad at anything or anyone," Jonas said. "He didn't have a mean bone in his body."

Sonny snorted. "He was *really* mad at me. I did those things because I was angry."

"Angry at Biz?" asked Jonas.

"No. At my owner. She had a baby and was never around. I was all alone. And I was jealous of the love and attention Biz got. But he put me in my place. I never tried it again. I was afraid to."

Jonas chuckled. "I bet you were."

After breakfast, Susan put Sonny outside in a small paddock by himself. He whinnied and paced and then finally stopped and looked around. Jonas assumed that seeing all of the horses soothed him.

Luis walked over to the fence near Jonas. "So has the little twit calmed down yet?"

Jonas sighed. "Can you *please* give him a break? He's been through a lot, Luis. Have some compassion."

Luis stared down his nose at Jonas. "Is he *calm* now?"

"Yes, Luis. He seems to be okay."

Luis turned and glared at Sonny. "Well, he better be, because I need tranquility, not chaos created by a neurotic little twerp who can't get it together. When I have tranquility, I'll find compassion."

At a loss for words, Jonas shook his head.

***

Abdul liked Sonny. They had something in common, so starting their day together in the sunny corner of their paddocks felt right. "Do you like your paddock?"

"It's okay, but I wish I was with other horses," Sonny said.

"Susan *never* puts a new horse out with other horses. She needs to see how you behave first."

"What does that mean?

"She's watching to see how you act around other horses. Don't kick or try to nip and you should be okay. If you do those things, you'll be alone."

Sonny put his head down and munched on hay. "Does your owner come to see you now, Abdul?"

Abdul turned. "No. Not really. She keeps making excuses for why she can't ride, but I know she's afraid. But she does come to brush me now. For a long time, she didn't even do that."

Sonny looked into Abdul's eyes. "That's too bad. I remember how it felt when Sarah didn't have time for me."

Abdul swallowed. "Well, at least you got to live with Jill. I like her. The day I had my accident, she was nice, and it helped me."

"She was nice to me too," said Sonny. "I'll miss her."

"You don't have to miss her," beamed Abdul. "She works here. I'm sure she'll come by to check on you." Abdul could tell that his comment made Sonny feel better.

"I think I'm going to like it here," said Sonny. "Jill's here. You're here. Everyone has been friendly. I hope we can be friends, Abdul."

Abdul nodded. He hoped they could be friends, too.

***

After Sonny left, Jill couldn't go into their empty barn. It was too painful. From the back porch, she often stared at the paddock. Sometimes she thought she caught a glimpse of Biz out of the corner of her eye. And a couple of times, she even thought she heard him grunt for his supper. Was it her imagination? Was Biz trying to let her know that he was still around? That he was okay? She wondered if her mother was experiencing the same things.

Jill didn't think she would ever get another horse. It would be too hard to find a horse that could fill Biz's shoes. Would it be fair to expect another horse to even try? She and her mother would have to get used to an empty barn again. Just thinking about it made her want to cry.

Jill continued riding lessons at Willow Bend, but her mother stopped riding, saying that if she couldn't ride Biz, it just wouldn't be the same. Jill tried to talk her into riding Jayden, but she said no. Jill didn't push because her mother never wanted to ride any horse but Biz, but Jill was worried about her. She seemed lost. There was no spark in her eyes. And she seemed withdrawn. Absent. Her mother's grief seemed deeper than her own and that troubled Jill. Did her mother love Biz more than she did? Jill didn't know how that was possible. Jill wondered if she was coping better than her mother because she still had horses in her life. Riding Jayden helped. In some ways, Jayden reminded her of Biz. They didn't look anything alike, but they both had long strides and a comfortable canter.

Her mother was a neatnik, so Jill knew she went into the barn to tidy up. She wondered how much she cried in there. Losing Biz left a gaping wound in her mother's heart and lately, her mother's smiles seemed unnatural. Forced. Jill wanted her to smile the way she did when Biz was alive.

Weeks after Biz was laid to rest, her mother asked Caleb to remove the manure from the property. With his tractor, Caleb scooped it up, delivered it to his yard, and tilled it into his gardens. As the manure disappeared, so did the smell of horses. The smell of Biz. It made Jill sad, and though her mother always encouraged her to talk about her feelings, when Jill brought it up, she quickly switched the subject. Jill was concerned that if her mother didn't let her emotions out, she would become even more distant.

One night after supper, her mother silently stared at the barn from the kitchen window as she washed dishes. Jill knew that stare because she did the same thing from her bedroom window, where she had a perfect view of the barn and paddock. Jill walked over to the sink. "Mom, are you okay?"

Her mother mustered a smile. "Yes, of course, honey. Why do you ask?"

"Because I'm worried about you."

Her mother turned and kissed the top of the head. "I'm fine, honey. Honest."

"No, you're not, Mom. It's like you're not here anymore. I feel like I'm losing you."

Her mother looked like she'd been stabbed in the heart and immediately reached for Jill. "I'm so sorry, honey. I'm still here. I promise. But my heart is so broken. I can't stop thinking about Biz. And ever since he died, I can't stop thinking about your father. I feel like I'm grieving him all over again. When I met Biz, I felt like a piece of your father came back to us. Now it's gone. And it hurts something awful." Her mother sobbed unapologetically.

"I know, Mom. I feel the same way. I miss Biz, and I can't stop thinking about Dad either. I'm so sad. Please don't shut me out. I don't feel like I even have you anymore."

Her mother grabbed her hands and looked into her eyes. "*Nothing* on this earth is more important than you. I'm so sorry. I never meant to shut you out. I didn't tell you how much I was suffering because I didn't want you to worry about me. I was trying to protect you. I was trying to be strong for you."

Jill looked up at her mother and smiled through her teary eyes. "You are strong, Mom. Being honest about how you feel won't add to my pain. It'll help me understand. Besides, you're not supposed to be the one who's hard to read in this family. Didn't you tell Sarah that *I* was the stoic one?"

Her mother chuckled and held her tight as tears poured down her cheeks and dripped on top of Jill's head. Jill stood quietly, trying to find the right words. "Mom, just before we buried Biz, you told me I would always be able to talk to him. What did you mean? How can I always talk to Biz if he's not here?"

Her mother gently took her hand, and together, they walked to the living room and sat facing each other on the couch. "Honey, some people believe that when you die, you go away forever. I *never* believed that. I believe that when people die, it's their body that dies, but their spirit remains. And I believe spirits stay close to the ones they love."

Jill thought for a minute. "Like guardian angels?"

"Yes. Like guardian angels. And if we're really lucky, we get some kind of a sign that they're around."

"A sign?"

"Yes. It can be anything. Even a simple phrase. If a person said something all the time when they were alive, you might suddenly hear others say the same thing."

Jill felt herself come to life. In her head, she heard her father's voice and the words he used to say to her—*Jill! Look! Can you see him out there? He sure is a beauty!* Jill was excited. They were about to discuss the very thing she tried to find the courage to talk about since she started to see her father in the barn and smelled his aftershave.

Her mother continued. "Please don't think I'm strange, but sometimes, just for an instant, I see your father. I've seen him in the barn, and once I saw him in the field by the apple tree, in the shade of the big oak. That was his favorite place to sit and think. He said it would give a horse nice shade from the hot summer sun. I don't think it's a coincidence that it was Biz's favorite spot."

Jill felt warmth in her heart as she listened. *My dad is still around me*, Jill thought, as happy tears filled her eyes. Goosebumps covered her arms and she waited eagerly for anything more her mother had to say.

Her mother's gaze shifted to the window. "I've sometimes felt a gentle breeze, and then smelled your father's aftershave. Every time that happened, I was alone, so it wasn't someone else wearing the same scent. Occasionally, Dad's beloved barred owls somehow found me when I was on a trail ride, and even flew along the path just ahead of me. Once, a big one perched on a low-hanging branch and look deeply into my eyes as I passed by. It was so close that I felt like I could have reached up and touched its talons. And I've even smelled horses and peppermints in the house since Biz passed away. In my mind, I've gone over this dozens of times and it feels like they are all signs that Dad and Biz are still with us. It seems unbelievable and wonderful because it means that when loved ones die, they don't go far, and we're never really alone."

Jill started to cry because she knew exactly what her mother was talking about. "Oh my gosh, Mom. Sometimes I see Dad too. And sometimes *I* smell his aftershave. It makes me feel good, but it also breaks my heart, because sometimes, I just *need* him. I miss talking to him. I miss his smile. I miss the way he brushed the top of my head with his hand. The way he pinched my cheek. The way he tapped his finger on the tip of my nose. How he grinned when he heard his barred owls. And sometimes I need to cry with him. About losing him and not being able to say goodbye. About how my life changed since he's been gone. And about Biz. It might sound weird, but I feel like Dad brought Biz to me."

Jill looked down at the sofa because she knew it sounded insane. She was relieved when her mother lifted her chin with her hand, looked in her eyes, and said, "It's not weird at all. I knew that the day I met Biz. A tall chestnut with a long white blaze and two white socks. The horse your father envisioned. Your father's presence was undeniable as Biz stood in his stall and looked right into my soul."

Tears streamed down Jill's cheeks. "Mom, if I talk to Dad and Biz, do you think they can hear me?"

"I believe they can."

Jill told her mother about how she sometimes caught a glimpse of her father in the barn. She recounted the times she smelled Old Spice, and she told her mother about the many times she heard her father's words, in her dreams and from others. And how owls often hooted precisely when she was thinking about him, as if he was letting her know that he was with her. They sat on the sofa and talked for hours before they called it a night. Before they retired for the evening, they promised that in the future, they would share every sign. Jill brushed her teeth and climbed into bed. As she pulled up the blankets, she let out a sigh. She felt better. She was relieved that her mother finally opened up. It was comforting to know that her mother was experiencing the same things, but even more comforting was knowing that her father and Biz were with her.

***

A couple of weeks later, Jill promised she'd spend an entire day helping Susan straighten out the areas of the barn that weren't regularly cleaned, like the grain room and the hayloft, where cobwebs and dust got out of control.

It was almost dusk when she finished, so she took a short break and then turned on the floodlights and started bringing the horses in from their paddocks. The first horse was Sonny. He looked excited to see her, yet he seemed relaxed. What a difference in him since he was stabled at Willow Bend. Once Sonny was safely in his stall, Jill went back outside to get Abdul. As she approached the paddock, a large bird flew overhead and the shadow it cast when it flew under the floodlights was impressive. It landed on the lowest branch of the tall sugar maple tree just outside the barn. The floodlight caught its eyes as it turned its head and Jill felt her heart burst. A beautiful barred owl seemed to be looking directly into her eyes. Jill was mesmerized until Abdul's whinnies reminded her of her task. She attached the lead line to Abdul's halter and glanced back, but the majestic bird of prey was gone. As she closed the paddock gate, she heard its distinct call and felt love envelop her.

Abdul pranced and nudged her with his nose all the way to the barn. Jill was laughing out loud by the time they reached the entrance, but Abdul lost the bounce in his step when they went inside. Jill understood why when she saw Melissa, who said she was there to groom Abdul and thanked Jill for bringing him in. Abdul seemed less than enthused when Jill handed Melissa the lead rope.

"You two seemed to be having a good time together," said Melissa.

"He's like a happy puppy. He has so much energy."

"Yes. He's got plenty of that," said Melissa. Then the expression on her face changed. "Jill, would you ever want to ride him?"

"Ride Abdul? I don't know. I never really thought about it."

Melissa tipped her head and looked up at Jill. "Well, think about it, okay?"

Jill felt uneasy. "Why?"

Melissa visibly swallowed. "Because I can't get back on him. I'm afraid. He has too much oomph. I don't know what to do with him anymore, but somebody has to do *something*. He's wasting away. I don't want him to look like Biz when he first came here. You worked wonders with Biz. Maybe you can do the same with Abdul. Will you try?"

Jill didn't know what to say. She looked at Abdul and he was looking right back at her with upright ears.

Melissa continued. "Jill, when I came to groom him today, I felt jealous. You were having more fun than I've had with him in ages. I know the problem is me. I can't overcome my fear. You're not afraid of him. He's comfortable with you and he likes you—*everyone* sees it."

Jill had mixed feelings. Part of her felt happy to have a horse to work with again, but that happiness also made her feel guilty. Disloyal. Like she was replacing Biz. And though it was true that Abdul needed exercise and she wanted to help, she knew it would give Melissa an excuse not to ride her horse and avoid working through her fear. Jill promised to think about it, for Abdul's sake, but she wasn't sure she was doing the right thing and planned to discuss it with her mother over dinner that night.

During dinner, Jill got everything off her chest and her mother reached across the table and held her hands. "Honey, I don't know if we'll ever get over losing Biz, but I guess we have to try. Maybe Abdul is the first step."

Jill knew they would never get over Biz, but she agreed that they had to try. Biz would want them to. And in her heart, she knew Biz would want her to help his little buddy, Abdul.

* * *

As she tucked herself in that night, Carol felt torn. She wanted Jill to be happy and she wanted Abdul to be well, but she was having a hard time moving on without Biz and Logan. She started to fall asleep when her bedroom door flew open.

"Mom, I forgot to tell you about the owl." Jill told her everything. "It flew right over me and then sat on the lowest branch of the tree and looked right into my eyes. It was *so* cool."

The smile on Jill's face said everything. "And how did it make you feel?"

Jill sat on the bed. "Warm inside."

"And?"

"Like Dad was there. Watching over me."

"Do you think it's a coincidence that it flew over you when you were with Abdul?"

Jill looked down at her hands. "You think it was a sign?"

"You're the one who experienced it. What do you think?"

Jill smiled. "As soon as I saw it, I knew it was Dad."

"Without any thought, you knew?"

"Yes. I felt it. I felt *him* close by."

"Maybe he thinks you should help Abdul."

Jill stared off with a tranquil smile. "Maybe."

"Helping Abdul might help you too ... help you heal."

Jill's eyes were glossy pools. "I think I need to go to bed now. I have lots to think about.

"Sweet dreams, honey. If you need to talk, I'm always here."

Jill left the room and Carol lay in bed with thoughts of Logan swirling in her head. Her heart told her, without reservation, that the owl was a sign, but her logical mind questioned it. Was it just wishful thinking? Was she giving her daughter false hope? Was there life after death? Nobody had proof. It was all just theory. If it was just one incident, she might be more willing to pass it off as a coincidence, but there were too many. Dreams. Silhouettes. Glimpses. Old Spice. Logan's words. Barred owls. And a new and compelling experience with the kind of owl that Logan cherished, seemingly offering guidance.

Since the day she saw Biz, Carol knew Logan brought him. The image of the horse he envisioned, waiting in the paddock for Jill to come home from school. And now Abdul. Was it a coincidence that it was Jill who rescued Abdul from his panic following his accident? That she was the one standing inside the barn, at the very door he ran to? Carol didn't think so.

After a less than restful night, when the alarm went off, Carol decided not to stay in bed and overthink things, so she got right up, washed, and dressed, and went downstairs to make tea. She was surprised to find Jill already at the kitchen table, eating breakfast.

"You look tired, Mom."

"I tossed and turned."

Jill nodded. "Me too."

Carol kissed the top of her head, and then drank her tea on the living room sofa while she mindlessly glanced through a magazine. Then, just as she did every morning, she looked out the kitchen window at the barn as she washed her mug. She was about to go into her office when, inside the open loft door, she saw something moving. It was big. She showed Jill and then grabbed her jacket. Jill followed her out the door. The barn was quiet as they entered, then up in the rafters, Carol saw it and gasped. Without making an audible sound, a barred owl gracefully swooped down. As it passed by to fly out the open barn doors, the owl glanced sideways and looked deeply into Carol's eyes. They followed it outside and watched it fly around the house and barn, and then settle on a branch in the tall pine, where it hooted loudly and repeatedly. So much so, that Caleb came outside. "What the heck is going on out here?" asked Caleb

Carol and Jill pointed, and as Caleb descended his steps, the owl left its branch. Soaring high in the sky, the owl circled the house and barn again, and then it circled Caleb's house before it swooped in front of all of them, flew directly over the Montauk daisies, and landed in Logan's beloved birch tree, where it rested for a few minutes before soaring high into the air again. Carol couldn't believe it flew so low and close to the house. And the expression on Jill's face when the owl landed in her father's tree brought tears to Carol's eyes.

Jill shuffled over to the garden, picked a daisy, and then made her way back to Carol and Caleb. She gently handed the lovely fall bloom to Carol, who started to cry. Uncontrollably.

"He's with us, Mom. Dad is really with us," said Jill with eyes like water globes.

Caleb seemed mesmerized. As a single tear dripped from his right eye and streamed down his cheek, Carol reached for his hand and squeezed it. Then Carol hugged Jill and remembered the questions her logical mind presented to her just a few hours before. False hope? Wishful thinking? Coincidence? Not a chance. She would never doubt again.

About the Author

Jean grew up in Andover, Massachusetts, across the street from the Shawsheen River, near a dairy farm with an ice cream stand, a palomino barn, and a horse boarding facility. The neighborhood was her definition of Heaven, so when her family moved across town, her heart remained there. Unable to afford a horse of her own, every week she saved her allowance until she had enough to rent a horse at a stable and gallop through the woods. It wasn't until the age of 36 that she brought her first horse home. He became one of her greatest teachers and changed her life. All of her animals - horses, dogs, cats, and even the sheep that kept the horse company - taught her something. She believes they all can if you're willing to listen.

Jean's writing career began as a freelance newspaper columnist. She went on to become a reporter, assistant editor, and then Editor-in-Chief of The Haverhill Gazette in Massachusetts. As the first woman editor of the paper since its inception in 1821, Jean earned first- and second-place awards for editorial writing from New England Newspaper & Press Association.

Her first novel, *Biz's Journey Home,* is a tribute to her first horse. She resides in Merrimac, Massachusetts with her husband, Greg. Her proudest accomplishments are her children, Jillian and Jason, and she's a devoted grandmother to Amelia.

ALL THINGS THAT MATTER PRESS

FOR MORE INFORMATION ON TITLES AVAILABLE FROM
ALL THINGS THAT MATTER PRESS, GO TO
http://allthingsthatmatterpress.com
or contact us at
allthingsthatmatterpress@gmail.com

Made in the USA
Middletown, DE
14 September 2023